Language and and Culture

Written by Luo Changpei
Translated by Peng Guoyuan

CHICAGO ACADEMIC PRESS

Language and Culture
Author: Luo Changpei
Translator: Peng Guoyuan
Language: English
Word Count (for space of all pages): 298 thousand words
Number of pages: 298
Publisher: Chicago Academic Press, April 18, 2025
ISBN 978-1-965890-20-2

Publishing   Chicago Academic Press
             5923 N Artesian Ave
             Chicago IL 60659
E-mail   contact@chicagoacademicpress.com
Website   http://chicagoacademicpress.com/

Book Size   6 x 9 inches, 298 pages
First Edition April 18, 2025

Introduction to the Translator

PENG Guoyuan, with a Master's degree in translation from Nanjing University, is currently teaching at Guangxi Normal University in Guilin, and serving as a council member of the Translators Association of Guangxi. With two decades of dedication to translation practice, teaching and studies, she has offered a range of translation courses for both undergraduate and graduate students, published multiple academic papers and three translated books (with the fourth forthcoming), as well as leading and participating in numerous research projects.

Translator's Preface

This book is hailed as the " seminal work " of Chinese cultural linguistics. Through meticulous empirical research, this pioneering work embodies interdisciplinary rigor, demonstrating with substantial evidence that language is both a product and a carrier of culture, reflecting a symbiotic and interactive relationship between language and culture. Since its initial publication in 1950, this book has undergone multiple editions, maintaining its status as a milestone in the field of linguistics and attesting to its enduring academic vitality. Regrettably, this Chinese academic classic has not been translated and published internationally, which motivated the translator to undertake this endeavor.

Embarking on this translation journey with deep reverence, the translator has approached the task with painstaking effort. The book's extensive references to Chinese classics and historical materials, a testament to the author's erudition and scholarly rigor, posed significant challenges to the translation. Furthermore, the abundance of proper nouns, compounded by linguistic and cultural differences, further heightened the difficulty of achieving precise equivalence. Although the translation strives for perfection, flaws are inevitable. Nevertheless, this translation aspires to honor the author's intellectual legacy. It is hoped that this translation will convey the scholarly brilliance of this great Chinese linguist and introduce this seminal work to the international academic community.

Preface

The first draft of the first seven chapters of this book was completed on the night of January 28, 1949, which was the eve of the lunar New Year, the year of Wuzi. At that time, Beijing had already been peacefully liberated, but the People's Liberation Army had not yet entered the city. When I laid down my pen after finishing the last word, I never imagined that on the anniversary of Beijing's liberation, the full manuscript would be printed and soon meet the academic world!

In the summer of 1943, at a lecture series on literature and history hosted by the Southwest United University in Kunming, I had publicly delivered a lecture on the topic of "Language and Culture," and my student Ma Hanlin had recorded the outline of the lecture. The structure of this book was thus established at that time.

In 1945, while living on the West Coast of North America in Claremont, I spent weekends squeezing some time to add supplementary materials to this work. However, I was constantly distracted by other matters and had no chance to finalize it. After the 50th anniversary celebrations of Peking University in 1948, with little to do in the besieged city, and only a minor effort toward the safety concerns of my colleagues in the Shatan District, I concentrated my energy on writing this book. The sounds of artillery and the whistling bullets did not affect my psychological state of being "more inner peace amidst noisier outside world." I recall that the Defense of the Great Wall had inspired my Phonetics of the Northwestern Dialects in the Tang and Five Dynasties, and the fire at the Lugou Bridge sparked my Linchuan Phonology. Although my mental state then was quite different from that at the end of the previous year, my attitude of loyalty to what I had studied remained unchanged. After the liberation, my thoughts began to shift, and I abandoned the old notion of "pursuing scholarship for its own sake." After considerable time spent contemplating and learning, it wasn't until the first seven chapters were almost ready for printing that I finished the eighth chapter, the "Conclusion."

The content, purpose, and viewpoints of this book have already been explained in the "Introduction" and the "Conclusion," so there is no need to repeat them here. Although the material was gathered from various sources, the overall arrangement and structure were my first attempt at such an undertaking. Needless to say, both in form and substance, there are many shortcomings, and I hope readers will offer constructive criticism to help improve it further.

First, let me express my sincere gratitude to Mr. Wu Yuzhang, Mr. Lu Zhiwei, Mr. Xiang Jueming, and Mr. Ji Xianlin! They thoroughly reviewed the manuscript and provided many valuable criticisms and corrections. Mr. Wu and Mr. Lu, to encourage the author, both offered inscriptions and wrote prefaces for this book. Others who directly or indirectly contributed to the completion of this work, besides those already acknowledged in the book, include Mr. Wang Liqi, Mr. Wu Xiaoling, Mr. Zhou Dingyi, Mr. Yu Min, Mr. Yin Huanxian, Mr. Zhang Qingchang, Mr. Chen Shilin, Mr. Yu Shichang, Mr. Yang Zhijiu, and Mr. Qi Shengqiao! They each contributed significantly in areas such as supplementing materials, reviewing content, and proofreading the manuscript. The transcription of the entire manuscript was completed with the assistance of my colleagues, Xu Jianzhong and Zhang Liren.

The publication of this book owes much to the help of Mr. Zeng Zhaolun from the Peking University Publishing Committee, Mr. Li Xuzu from the Publishing Department, and the various staff members. Thanks to their encouragement and cooperation, the book is now able to meet readers ahead of schedule. In expressing my gratitude, I also realize the insignificance of individual power and the greatness of collective effort!

January 31, 1950, the anniversary of the liberation of Beijing
Written by Luo Changpei
at the Laboratory of Phonology and Musical Rhythm,
Institute of Humanities, Peking University

Contents

Chapter 1 Introduction

The late American linguistics professor Edward Sapir once said, "There is something behind language. And language cannot exist without culture. Culture is the total of socially inherited habits and beliefs, which determine the organization of our lives."[1] L.R. Palmer also stated, "The history of language and the history of culture are parallel, and they can assist and inspire each other."[2] Furthermore, the anthropologist E.B. Tylor defined culture as "a complex whole which includes knowledge, belief, art, morals, law, custom, and any other capabilities and habits acquired by a man as a member of society."[3] From these statements, we can infer the close relationship between language and culture and the breadth of their scope.

This compilation attempts to discuss the relationship between language and culture from the perspective of word meaning, with a heavier emphasis on semantics and less involvement in phonetics and grammar. I plan to cover six aspects: firstly, tracing cultural relics through the etymology and evolution of words; secondly, examining the cultural level of a nation through the psychology of word creation; thirdly, observing cultural contact through loanwords; fourthly, analyzing ethnic migration patterns through geographic names; fifthly, exploring ethnic origins and religious beliefs through surnames and aliases; and sixthly, investigating marriage systems through kinship

---

[1] Edward Sapir, *Language*, p.221.
[2] L.R. Palmer, *An Introduction to Modern Linguistics*, p.151 (hereinafter referred to as Modern Linguistics).
[3] E.B. Tylor, *On a Method of Investigating the Development of Institutions*, J.A.I. XVIII, 1889, pp.245-272.

terminology. These are all crucial issues in sociology and anthropology. If my attempt can make any contribution, it may serve as a bridge between linguistics and anthropology research. This is not uncommon abroad, as evidenced by Sapir's shift from linguistics to anthropology in his later years [4] and Bronislaw Malinowski's transition from anthropology to linguistics [5]. Given my academic background, I dare not compare myself to these renowned scholars. Moreover, this approach is a novel direction in China, and there may inevitably be omissions in temporarily gathered materials. Upon the publication of this compilation, I sincerely hope that experts in both linguistics and anthropology will provide rigorous feedback, potentially leading to the refinement of my research findings in the future.

---

[4] For instance, E. Sapir, *Time Perspective in Aboriginal American Culture: A Study in Method*, Memoir 90, No.13, Anthropological Series, Canada Department of Mines, Ottawa, 1916 (hereinafter referred to as Time Perspective).
[5] For instance, B. Malinowski, *Coral Gardens and Their Magic*, London, 1935; and his *Supplement to C.K. Ogden* and I.A. Richards, *The Meaning of Meaning*.

Chapter 2 Etymology and Evolution of Words as Traces of Cultural Relics

In various languages, many words carry meanings today that differ significantly from their original etymology. Without understanding their historical and cultural background, it is nearly impossible to trace the connection between the current and original meanings. However, by uncovering their history, not only can we observe fascinating semantic shifts, but we can also gain a glimpse into the stages of cultural development. For instance, the English word "pen" originates from the Latin word *penna*, meaning "feather." Initially, it was strictly used to refer to "quill pens" made from bird feathers. Even though the material of pens has changed over time, the term remained in use, so a word that once denoted "feather" now represents a writing instrument with a metal nib. Conversely, analyzing the connection between the modern word "pen" and feathers reveals insights into the writing tools of ancient times.[6] Similarly, the English word "wall", along with equivalent terms in other Indo-European languages, often has a fundamental meaning related to "wicker-work" or "wattle". The German word *Wand* derives from the verb *winden*, which means "to wind" or "to interweave." The Anglo-

---

[6] Take the Chinese character "笔" (pen) as another example. The traditional form of this character is "筆", which is composed of "竹" (bamboo) and "聿". In the small seal script, it was written as "𥬇". The *Shuowen Jiezi* explains that "聿" means "the tool for writing." Modern scholar Luo Zhenyu said that "it resembles the shape of holding a pen in hand." The way it was written in the small seal script was similar to the appearance of a pen. During the Qin and Han dynasties, most of the pen holders were made of bamboo, so the radical "竹" (bamboo) was added on top. Compared with the West, the relationship between the form of the Chinese character "筆" and the shape of the pen is somewhat simpler.

Saxon phrase *windan manigne smicernewah* translates to English as "to weave many a fine wall," which, in modern terms, means "to weave many fine walls." But how can walls be "woven"? Archaeological findings at prehistoric sites reveal impressions of wickerwork on burned clay blocks. This refers to a building method known as *wattle and daub*, where a framework of woven twigs or reeds is plastered with clay. Such findings suggest that walls in ancient Europe were similar to modern rural fences in China, bamboo walls in Sichuan, or the traditional rammed-earth structures of ancient times, rather than being made of steel and concrete.[7] Another example is the English word "window", which translates literally as "wind-eye." In many languages, compound words for "window" often include the term "eye." For instance, the Gothic[8] *auga-dauro* translates as "eye-door," the Anglo-Saxon *eglyrel* as "eye-hole," and the Sanskrit

---

[7] Regarding the " wattle and daub" style of architecture, the Willow Palisade in the early Qing Dynasty can serve as evidence. From the reigns of Shunzhi to Kangxi, a willow fence was built in sections starting from Fengcheng in the southeastern part of Liaoning, extending northeastward, then northwestward to Kaiyuan, and finally turning towards Shanhaiguan, which roughly followed the present eastern, northern, and western boundaries of Liaoning Province. It was called the Old Palisade. Another willow fence was built from Kaiyuan northward to Jilin City, which was called the New Palisade. To the east of the Old Willow Palisade was the hunting ground, under the jurisdiction of the Ministry of War of Shengjing, while to the west was the Mongolian pasture, under the jurisdiction of the General of Fengtian. The New Palisade was under the jurisdiction of the General of Jilin. There were gates set up along the palisades. Building the willow palisades was less labor-intensive and more convenient than building brick walls. Its purpose was to divide the spheres of influence internally and serve as a partition. Since it was not for defending against enemies, it didn't need to be that solid. In addition, in many places in the north, in order to cultivate melon and vegetable seedlings early, people often used woven fences to block the northwest wind. Some were made of sorghum stalks, and those with better conditions would weave willow branches, which could be used for many years. For the fences made of willow branches, mud was smeared on them to enhance the wind-blocking effect.

[8] The Gothic language, also known as the Gotische Sprache. The Goths were an ancient ethnic group in Europe, belonging to the eastern branch of the Germanic people. After entering Romania, they were gradually assimilated by the Romance language family and lost their own language.

grvaksa means "ox-eye." Similarly, the Russian word *okno* shares a root with the Latin *oculus*, meaning "a little eye." To explain these terms for "window," we must reflect on the architectural practices of ancient times.

As discussed earlier, the earliest houses were either constructed using woven wickerwork or built with wood. Under these two architectural systems, large square windows were not feasible. Even today, the Luoluo[9] people living in the suburbs of Kunming refers to the windows as $\left[\ \text{şu}^{\neg}\ \text{gu}_{\sqrt{}}\ \text{na}_{\sqrt{}}\ \right]$, meaning "window eye". Another example is the English word "fee", which evolved from Old English *feoh*. Its meanings included "live-stock, cattle, property, money." Among the Germanic cognates, only the Gothic *faihu* ['fehu] retained the meaning of "property," while others, such as German *Vieh* [fi:] or Swedish *fä* [fe:], are limited to meanings like "a number of livestock" or "a number of cattle." Similarly, in other Indo-European languages, the cognates reflect this trend, such as Sanskrit *paçu* or Latin *pecu*. However, Latin expanded the root to include *pecūnia* ("money") and *pecūlium* ("savings" or "property"). These examples strongly suggest that livestock once served as a medium of exchange in ancient times. In the same way, the historical background can clarify the relationships among a group of German words like *Lade*, *Laden*, and *einladen*, which carry complex meanings. The verb *laden*

---

[9] Luoluo was the old name for the Yi ethnic group. Historically, it was also called "罗罗", "罗落", "卢录", "落落", etc. "罗罗" was mentioned in *Yunnan Zhi Lue* by Li Jing in the Yuan Dynasty: "Luoluo, that is, the Wuman people." There were distinctions between the Black Luoluo (Heiyi) and the White Luoluo (White Yi). In the Yuan Dynasty, the Luoluosi Xuanwei Department was established in what is now the Liangshan area of Sichuan.

means "to load," and its phonetic similarity to Anglo-Saxon *hladan* and Slavic *klada* (meaning "to lay" or "to put") helps explain its origin. The noun *Lade* originally meant "drawer," which is closely related to Old Norse *hlaða* ("storehouse") and English *lath*. Both terms share the root meaning of "a storage place." However, *Laden*, meaning "shop" or " window-shutter/Fensterladen," requires further historical exploration to understand. Originally, *Lade* referred to "wooden slats" (compared with English *lath*), which were commonly used as window shutters before glass was introduced. Additionally, street vendors often displayed goods on wooden boards propped up by two wooden frames in marketplaces, calling this setup a *Lade*. This primitive structure eventually evolved into the modern concept of a "shop." By studying cultural history further, we can also understand the connection between *einladen* ("to invite") and *Vorladung* ("a summons"). Meringer once noted a widely practiced custom in which courts delivered a wooden board as a summons for individuals to appear. In some parts of Bohemia[10], this custom of delivering a "Gebotbret" still persists. The *Gebotbret* is a wooden board with a handle, onto which a notice is pasted or nailed. Thus, *Laden* is a verb derived from the noun laþ (meaning "to board a person"), and its usage happens to be just like that of "blackball"[11] in British and

---

[10] Bohemia, a historical geographic name. In the Germanic language, it refers to the Czech Republic. In a broad sense, it refers to the whole of the Czech Republic, and in a narrow sense, it refers to the Czech Republic except for Moravia.

[11] In British and American customs, a black ball is used when casting a veto vote. Originally a noun, it has gradually evolved into a verb. For example, "to blackball a candidate."

American English and "to ostracize"[12] in Greek. The modern meanings of *einladen* ("to invite") and *Vorladung* ("a summons") developed from the practice of delivering wooden boards to summon individuals to court.

In addition, there are two words we use daily but whose origins are rarely considered: *dollar* and *money*. The word *dollar* ultimately comes from the German *Taler*, which is short for *Joachimstaler*, derived from *Joachimstal* ("Joachim's Dale"), a valley in Bohemia. In the 16th century, silver coins were minted in this valley, and over time, the name became synonymous with silver coins, eventually giving rise to the word "dollar." As for *money*, its etymology traces back to ancient Rome. The Roman mint was located in the temple of *Jūnō Monēta*, where *monēta* originally meant "warner" and had no inherent connection to currency. Since coins were produced in this temple, the Romans began using *Monēta* to mean both "mint" and "coin" (or "money"). The English word *mint* was directly borrowed from Latin through Old English, while *money* came indirectly via Old French during the Middle Ages.[13]

The word "style" has many meanings in modern English, with several popular ones: (1) the genre or mode of expressing thoughts in language; (2) distinctive or characteristic mode of presentation,

---

[12] In the customs of ancient Athens in Greece, whoever was detested by the people, regardless of whether they were guilty or not, if the public voted affirmatively, would be exiled abroad for ten or five years. Since the votes were recorded on oyster shells, it was named "ostracism". From this word, when it is turned into a verb, it contains the meanings of "banish" or "reject". For example, "He is ostracized by polite circle."

[13] For all the Indo-European language examples cited above, please refer to L. R. Palmer, *Modern Linguistics*, pp. 152-156; Leonard Bloomfield, *Language*, pp. 428-429. [*Language*, translated by Yuan Jiahua et al., The Commercial Press, 1980]

construction, or execution in any art, employment, or product, especially in any of the fine arts; (3) mode or manner in accord with a standard, especially in social relations, demeanor, etc.; (4) fashionable elegance. However, if we trace its origin, the word differs significantly from these meanings. It comes from the Latin word *stilus*. In Roman times, people wrote on wax tablets, not with pencils or pens, but with a tool made of iron, hard wood, or bone. This tool had a pointed end for writing and a flat end for erasing—used to smooth the wax surface for reuse. This instrument was called a *stilus* or *stylus*. Initially, *stilus* referred specifically to the writing instrument. Over time, its meaning expanded to include the content written with it, the style or manner of writing, and the characteristic mode of expression. When the word entered French, it became *style*, pronounced as [sti:l], retaining these meanings. Upon entering English, the pronunciation shifted to [stail]. The meanings of "refined demeanor" and "fashionable elegance" were later developments in both English and French. Interestingly, the original sense of the word is still preserved in *Webster's Dictionary*, where the first definition of *style* is "an instrument used by the ancients in writing on wax tablets." Meanwhile, the Latin-derived word *stylus* was also directly borrowed into English, retaining its original sense. Today, as *stylus* has become more common in English, the earliest meaning of *style* has gradually faded.

The word *needle* can also be traced back to very ancient origins. However, it originally did not refer to the finely crafted steel instruments we associate with the word today. Initially, it applied only to a prototype made of bone, and gradually it came to be associated with those made of steel. Nowadays, anything pointed, such as sharp crystals, rocky peaks, obelisks, etc., can also be called a *needle*. This reflects its original meaning of a sharp tool. From the concept of "needle," we can also draw a connection to the word *spinster*. In its modern sense, this word refers exclusively to an unmarried older woman. However, based on its structure, at one time it clearly had the meaning of "one who spins." Over time, through associations with specific individuals, it gradually acquired its present specialized meaning. The transition from its original meaning to the current one, with the original meaning completely lost, must have taken a long period. From this purely cultural fact, we can reasonably speculate that the technique of spinning has existed since ancient times and was in the hands of women. While this fact can be directly supported by history, we can also make judgments based purely on linguistic evidence. The age of the word *spinster* can also be determined by its use of the relatively rare agentive suffix *-ster*. This suffix is found in only a few other words, such as *huckster* ("peddler") and *songster* ("singer"), and in fixed surnames like *Baxster* (derived from the *baker*, "one who bakes bread") and *Webster* (from the *weaver*, "one who weaves"). Therefore, the suffix *-ster* is certainly older than more common suffixes like *-er* or *-ist*.[14]

We can also find examples of cultural traces in Native American languages. For instance, in the Athabaskan [15] languages of the

---

[14] E. Sapir, *Time Perspective*, pp. 59-60.

[15] The Athabascan people, who call themselves "the Dene people", are a branch of the North American Indians, distributed in Alaska in the United States, western Canada, and the western

Mackenzie Valley, the term corresponding to "glove" is *la-djic* in Chipewyan[16], *lla-dji* in Hare[17], and *nle-djic* in Loucheux, which means "hand-bag." However, in the Navajo [18] language, *la-djic* specifically refers to mittens, which only separate the thumb. Since these thumbed mittens are an ancient element of Athabaskan material culture, we can infer that in this culture, the term "glove" originally referred exclusively to mittens, not to the modern gloves with separate fingers.[19]

Another example from Athabaskan languages is the non-descriptive noun stem $t\text{'}\dagger e\dagger$, which in Chasta Costa[20] and Navajo means "matches." From other considerations, this cannot be the original meaning of the word. Comparing it with other Athabaskan dialects (such as Chipewyan), the original meaning of $t\text{'}\dagger e\dagger$ was "fire-drill." When matches replaced the ancient method of fire-making using fire drills, the meaning shifted from "fire-drill" to its modern sense of "matches."[21] This small example provides significant insights into the socioeconomic changes in Athabaskan societies.

---

region of the contiguous United States. The Athabascan language belongs to the Na-Dene language family.

[16] The Chipewyan people, a branch of the Athabascan people, live around Great Slave Lake in western Canada.

[17] The Hare people, a branch of the Athabascan people, are distributed in western Canada.

[18] The Navajo people, also translated as the Navaho people, who call themselves "the Dene people", are a branch of the Athabascan people, distributed in Arizona, New Mexico, and Utah in the United States.

[19] E. Sapir, *Time Perspective*, p. 58.

[20] The Chestatee people, a branch of the Athabascan people, had only 153 people left in the 19th century and were resettled in the Siletz Reservation in Oregon, the United States.

[21] E. Sapir, *Time Perspective*, p. 58.

When discussing the relationship between ancient Chinese language and culture, one cannot ignore the significance of characters. For example, characters related to currency, such as 财 (wealth), 货 (goods), 贡 (tribute), 赈 (relief), 赠 (gift), 贷 (loan), 赊 (credit), 买(買) (buy), 卖(賣) (sell), 贿 (bribe), and 赂 (offer), all belong to the 贝 (shell) radical. But why would a simple shell be used to represent money? Xu Shen's *Shuowen Jiezi* explains, "In ancient times, people traded using shells and valued turtles as treasures. By the Zhou Dynasty, coins emerged, and by the Qin Dynasty, shells were replaced by currency." This shows that in ancient China, shells were once used as a medium of exchange. Although shells were abandoned as currency after the Qin Dynasty, this ancient monetary system left its imprint on the structure of characters. Even as late as the Ming Dynasty, Yunnan still used a form of "haibei," a remnant of shell currency. Similarly, modern Chinese paper is made from bamboo and wood pulp, but why does the character for paper (纸) include the silk radical (系) instead of a bamboo or wood-related radical? The *Shuowen* only defines it as "a sheet for fluff," without referencing its

modern usage. According to Duan Yucai's interpretation, the term 箔

refers to "bleaching the floss mat," and 潎 refers to "beating the floss in water." The *Book of Later Han* notes: "(Cai) Lun devised a method using tree bark, hemp, rags, and fishing nets to produce paper, presenting it to the court in the first year of Yuanxing, after which it was widely adopted and called 'Marquis Cai's paper.'" According to the process of papermaking, it originated from bleaching silk floss. Initially, silk floss was used to make it, and it was formed by padding. Now, bamboo, wood, and bark are used to make paper, and sometimes dense bamboo curtains are used for padding as well. The *Tongsu Wen (Popular Literature)* says, "A sheet of fluff is called paper." and *Shiming (Explanation of Names)* says, "Paper, like a grindstone, is smooth." This indicates that before Cai Lun's invention, paper was made from silk fluff in China.

Other examples of characters tied to historical practices include 砮, which the *Shuowen* defines as "stone used to make arrowheads," reflecting the use of bows and arrows during the Stone Age. The character 安 is explained in the *Shuowen* as "peaceful, with a woman under a roof," implying that keeping women confined to the home symbolized tranquility, revealing ancient Chinese attitudes towards women. Similarly, the brutal punishment of being drawn and quartered (车裂) was a cruel practice in ancient China. While modern humanitarian values view it as barbaric, the structure of the character 斩 (to behead) reflects this history. The *Shuowen* explains, "斩 derives from 'cart' (车) and 'axe' (斤), referring to the punishment of being drawn and quartered." Duan Yucai elaborates: "The 'cart' indicates the original method, while the axe represents the later tool used for executions, but the character retains the cart radical." This suggests that such punishments were not unique to figures like Shang Yang but were widely practiced. While many examples can be explained through the *Shuowen*, some characters defy such interpretations. For instance, the character 家 (home) is described in the *Shuowen* as "to dwell, radicaled with 宀 and its pronunciation is derived (in a simplified form) from that of 豭 (boar)." Xu Shen's attempt to interpret it as a phonetic-semantic compound seems overly convoluted. Duan Yucai proposed that the original meaning of 家 was "the rear of a pig," later extended metaphorically to mean "the rear of a person," much like 牢, which initially referred to the rear of a cow but later came to mean a prison. Duan's interpretation is more plausible, but I hypothesize that early Chinese dwellings may have housed people on the upper level and pigs below. Such structures still exist in rural Yunnan today.[22] This offers a compelling linguistic and sociological insight, echoing the ancient maxim "Seek what has been lost in the countryside."[23]

---

[22] Yang Shuda wrote a short article in April 1935 titled "Explanation of 圂". The article said: "In the sixth volume of the *Shuowen Jiezi*, under the radical '口' (mouth), it is stated that '圂, means toilet, composed of the radical '口', with the image of a pig in the '口', it is a pictographic-ideographic character.' According to this, the reason why a pig in the '口' can represent a toilet is that in the *Discourses of Jin*, it is said that 'King Wen was found when someone urinated in the pigsty.' We can know that in ancient times, the pigsty was originally used for both toilet and manure purposes. So Wei Zhao said that 'the pigsty is the toilet', which is correct. Even today in rural areas of Changsha, the toilet and manure are still in the pigsty, which is a remnant of the ancient system." (From the Enlarged Edition of *Jiweiju Xiaoxue Jinshi Luncong [Essays on Philology, Epigraphy and Archaeology]*, Zhonghua Book Company, 1983). I lived in Pingshan County, Hebei Province for a year in 1948. There, toilets were built on flat ground. There was a big pit connected under the latrine pit, and pigs were raised in the pit. When I visited the place again in 1999 and asked about the situation of raising pigs in the toilet, the answer was: "It's still the same now." This can corroborate what Yang Shuda and others discussed.

[23] Linguistics and sociology are closely related. All aspects of social life will be reflected in language. For example, when a person stops breathing and loses their life, it means death, but different people's deaths have different names. The *Book of Rites: Qu Li* described the situation in ancient times: "When the Son of Heaven (Emperor) died, it was called '崩' (a shortened form of 'the collapse of the mountain and the mausoleum'), when a feudal lord died, it was called '薨', when a high official died, it was called '卒', when a scholar died, it was

called '不禄', and when a commoner died, it was called '死'. As the hierarchical relationship between officials and the people changed, there were new regulations. The *New Book of Tang: Treatise on Officials* stated that: "For funerals, those above the third rank were called '薨', those above the fifth rank were called '卒', and from the sixth rank down to commoners were called '死'. Even in modern times, there are certain conventions. The term '逝世' can only be used for people of a certain rank. Ordinary people's deaths cannot be described with '逝世'. Here is an example related to the use of characters. The writing form of '原来' is rarely found in documents before the Ming Dynasty, because it was previously written as '元来'. Starting from the Ming Dynasty, '原来' basically replaced '元来'. During the Ming and Qing dynasties, some people explained that since the Yuan Dynasty was the regime overthrown by the Ming Dynasty, people avoided using the character '元 (Yuan)'. Li Xu (1505 - 1593) in the first volume of *Jie'an Laoren Manbi (Random Notes by Jie'an Old Man)* said: "My ancestors were divided in Guanzhong. When writing '吴 (in 1367, the name of Zhu Yuanzhang's initial regime) 原年', '洪武原年', they didn't use the character '元'. I think that in the early days of the country, people hated the name of the previous dynasty and avoided it, so the common people followed this practice." Wang Yingkui (1683 - 1759/60) also had a similar statement in the third volume of *Liunan Suibi (Random Notes from the South of the Willows)*: "After Emperor Taizu of the Ming Dynasty ascended the throne, to avoid the name of the previous dynasty, he changed '元年' to '原年.'" It seems that Wang Yingkui adopted Li Xu's statement, and he also said later that "this is what was passed down among the common people." Shen Defu (1578 - 1642) also had a similar record in *Wanli Yehuo Bian Bubu (Supplement to the Unofficial Records of the Wanli Reign)*. This explanation has some merit and has been widely spread. However, Tan Qian (1594 - 1657) disagreed with this explanation. In *Zaolin Zazu (Miscellaneous Records of Zaolin)*, he said that "this is to avoid the imperial taboo", that is, to avoid the personal name taboo of Zhu Yuanzhang. He also gave examples such as "六科原士." Tan Qian's explanation may be more in line with the actual situation, because his explanation is consistent with the convention of avoiding the imperial name taboo throughout history.

14

Chapter 3 Word-Formation Psychology as a Reflection of Ethnic Cultural Level

From the common words or slang in many languages, we can often glimpse the psychological process behind word formation and the cultural level of the people who speak them. Setting aside a few languages of more culturally advanced groups, let us look at some examples of the languages of ethnic minorities along the southwestern border of China. 1. Near Kunming, in Yunnan, the Luoluo people call a wife " $\bar{}$ $\gamma\gamma$ $\rceil$so $\downarrow$ mo $\downarrow$ " [24] (translated as "needle-threading mother").[25] 2. The Trung[26] people of the Gaoligong Mountains refer to marriage as " $\cdot$ p $\lq$ o $\rceil$ ma $\rceil$ uan $\rceil$ " (literally "buying a woman").[27] These terms reveal the views of the Yi ethnic group[28] society towards wives and remnants of marriage by purchase. The Trung also use the term [$\cdot$ dʑio $\rceil$] for hemp cloth, clothing, and

---

[24] All the examples of the Luoluo language in the suburbs of Kunming in this chapter are quoted from Gao Huanian's *A Study of the Heiyi Language in the Suburbs of Kunming*, a master's thesis of the Institute of Humanities, Peking University, 1943. The same applies below. ("Heiyi" is another name for the Yi ethnic group. In the Yi language, "Nuohe" means black. In the old days, those referred to as "Heiyi" were mostly from the slave-owner class among the Yi people.)

[25] Ibid.

[26] The "Trung" was the name for the Delong ethnic group in ancient books. It was recorded as "Qiao" in *The Unified Gazetteer of the Yuan Dynasty*, and as "Qiu People" in *Illustrated Records of Tributary Peoples in the Qing Dynasty* and *Yunnan Tongzhi (General Annals of Yunnan)* compiled during the reign of Emperor Yongzheng.

[27] All the examples of the Trung language in this chapter are quoted from the author's *A Preliminary Study of the Gongshan Trung Language*, the third mimeographed paper of the Institute of Humanities, Peking University, 1943. The same applies below.

[28] The Yi ethnic group was the former name for the Bouyei ethnic group, which can be found in *Zhenning County Annals* of the Republic of China period. However, "Yi" was often used to generally refer to ethnic minorities. It seems to be the latter case here.

bedding because these three items are essentially unified in their lives: hemp cloth serves as material, clothing during the day, and bedding at night. Since their material life doesn't differentiate between the three, their language lacks distinct words for them. Similarly, in the Sani[29] language of Lunan[30] in Yunnan, functional descriptions form words:

A belt is called " dʐu ˧n " (literally "waist tie"), A hat is " o˥q'u˥. " (literally "head cover"), A ring is " le˩ tʂ̩ ˥pʐ̩ ˥. " (literally "finger closure").[31] In Fugong, the Lisu people call side dishes for rice " dza ˥ts' ʐ̩ ˩. " (literally "rice lure"), which resembles the Cantonese character ⁺餸' . Their types of liquor include "wine" [dʐ̩ ˩p'ɯ ˩], "rice wine" [dza ˥p'u ˥dʐ̩ ˩], "sorghum wine" [m ɯ̄˥dʐ̩ ˩], "water wine" [ts'y ˩dʐ̩ ˩], and "fire wine" [li ˩tɕi ˥], which is enough to prove that they are a tribe that enjoys drinking alcohol.[32] Investigating less tangible words, such as those representing actions or states, can be more challenging but also intriguing once their

---

[29] "Sani" is the self-appellation of the Yi people distributed in Mile, Shilin, Yiliang, Luoping, Luxi and other places in Yunnan.
[30] "Lunan" refers to what is now the Shilin Yi Autonomous County.
[31] All the examples of the Sani language in this chapter are quoted from Ma Xueliang's *Grammar of the Lunan Sani Lolo Language*, a master's thesis of the Institute of Humanities, Peking University, 1941. The same applies below.
[32] All the examples of the Lisu language in Fugong in this chapter are quoted from the author's *A Preliminary Study of the Fugong Lisu Language*, a manuscript in 1944. The same applies below.

psychological roots are understood. For example, the Luoluo people in the outskirts of Kunming refer to anger as "blood rolling" [sๅ ˧n' ã ˅], bullying as "look foolish" [ɲi ˧ŋɚ ˥], heartbreak as "heart cold" [ɲi ˅dʐɑ ˅] (similar to the literal Mandarin term "cold heart (have a chill in one's heart)"), and sadness as "crossing poverty" [ko ˅ ʂu ˥]. The structure of these words is somewhat related to the psychology of these actions or states. In early human societies, phenomena in nature that went beyond their knowledge often led to many mystical interpretations. For example, the Lisu in Fugong call a rainbow "yellow horse drinking water" [ɑ ˥mo ˩ ji ˩ ʂฺ ˥], the Sani in Lunan call a solar eclipse "the sun being eaten by a tiger" [lo ˩ ts z˥ ma ˧ la ˥l I ˧ dzɑ ˩], and a lunar eclipse "the moon being eaten by a dog" [ɬo ˧ ba ˧ ma ˧ ts'z ˩ l I ˧ dzɑ ˩]. Liu Xi's *Shiming (Explaining Names): Shitian (Explaining the Heaven)* states: "Rainbow, it is seen when the sun sets in the west and rises in the east, as it drinks the water vapor from the East." This is similar to the Lisu legend. In some places, a solar eclipse is also referred to as "the sky dog eating the sun's head," which is a remnant of early human society. As for the Luoluo in the outskirts of Kunming calling ice "lock frost bar" [ɲɛ ˧ dʐ̩ 'u ˩bɑ ˩] (literally "frost bar lock"), it is

17

similar to the Sani in Lunan calling thunder "sky sound"
$[\text{m̩} \downarrow \text{ tsɑ } \urcorner]$, both of which are new terms created due to a lack of understanding of natural phenomena.

In these languages, the concept of direction is not very clear. They often use the sun's rising and setting as a standard. For the east, the Luoluo people near Kunming call it "sunrise land" $[\text{dʑi} \downarrow \text{ du } \vee \text{ mi } \dashv]$, while the Lisu people in Fugong call it "sunrise cave" $[\text{mɪ}{\dashv}\text{m } \urcorner \dashv \text{du } \urcorner\text{k'u } \vee]$. For the west, the Luoluo call it "sunset land" $[\text{dʑi} \downarrow \text{ dɤ } \vee \text{ mi } \dashv]$, and the Lisu in Fugong call it "sunset cave" $[\text{m ɪ}{\dashv}\text{ m ɪ}\dashv \text{ gɯ } \nearrow \text{k'u } \vee]$. The Chinese character for "east" originates from the idea of "the sun in the tree," while "west" is represented by the shape of a "bird nesting in a tree," and the original meaning of the English word "orient" is also "sunrise." All of these concepts share a common origin. However, the local language in Wuming[33] calls the east "inside" $[\text{ʔdaɯ } \dashv]$, and the west "outside" $[\text{ʔøk } \urcorner]$,[34] while the Lisu in Fugong calls the north "water head" $[\text{ji } \urcorner \text{ nɛ } \urcorner]$ and the south "water tail" $[\text{ji } \urcorner \text{ m}$

---

[33] "local language in Wuming" here refers to a dialect of the Zhuang language. In the 1950s, the Wuming dialect was regarded as the representative dialect of the Zhuang language.
[34] According to Li Fanggui.

18

ɯ ↓] , which seems to be based on geographical features, such as elevation.

When these tribes encounter new and unfamiliar things, they often associate them with existing concepts. For example, the Lisu in Fugong calls the word "letter" a "gift-giving word" [t'o ↓ɣɯ ↓ lɛ ʌ ʂɿ ˥]. The Luoluo people in the outskirts of Kunming call a temple "Buddha room" [bɯ ˥ xɚ ↓] and steel "hard iron" [çɛ ˧ xɔ ↓⊦]. The Trung people in Gongshan call a car "wheel house" [ku ˧ lu ˧ tçiəm ˥]. The Sani people in Lunan call a bicycle an "iron horse" [xɯ ˧ m̩. ˥]. As for the newest transportation and military technology—the airplane—, their views are even more varied: the Trung people in Gongshan call it "flying house" [biəl ˧ tçim ˥], the Lisu in Fugong also call it "flying house" [dʑy ʌ x ˧˥], and the Chashan[35] people of Pienma's[36] call

---

[35] "Chashan" is the name used by the Han people to refer to some of the Jingpo people who call themselves Laqi. They are also known as Lang'e, Langsu, Shantou, etc.

[36] "Pianma" is the name of a village and also a historical regional name. It is located on the west side of the Gaoligong Mountain in Lushui County, Yunnan Province, close to the China-Myanmar border. During the Yuan Dynasty, it belonged to Yunlongdian Military and Civilian Prefecture. In the Ming Dynasty, it belonged to Chashan Tusi (Chieftain) of Yongchang Prefecture. In the Qing Dynasty, it was under the jurisdiction of Denggeng Tusi in Baoshan County. From 1910 to 1927, the British army continuously invaded this area and set up military and administrative institutions. Later, although the British army admitted that this area belonged to China, they did not withdraw their troops. On some maps published in China in the 1930s and 1940s, the "Pianma area" was marked as an undetermined border area. In 1960, the *Sino-Myanmar Boundary Treaty* stipulated that Pianma and the adjacent Gulang,

it "wind boat" $[\text{lik} \downarrow \text{saŋ} \dashv \text{p} \, ' \, \text{ɔ} \downarrow]$.[37] The Sani people in

Lunan call it "iron eagle" $[\text{xɯ} \dashv \text{tɬe} \,\, \urcorner]$, while the Baiyi[38] people

in western Yunnan call it "sky train" $[\text{lɑ} \,\, \urcorner \text{t} \, ' \, \text{ɑ} \, \textit{ʎmi} \,\, \urcorner]$.[39] These

descriptive terms reveal their method of analogizing the unknown

with the known, creating seemingly plausible yet actually inaccurate

descriptive forms.

In the Nootka[40] language of the Native Americans in North

America, there is a term $\text{łutch} \, \text{a}^{\circ} \text{-}$, which shares a remarkable

similarity with the previously mentioned example of Trung's

$[\text{p} \, ' \, \text{o} \, \urcorner \text{ma} \, \urcorner \text{uan} \, \urcorner]$. In their society, the word $\text{łutch} \, \text{a}^{\circ} \text{-}$

encompasses both ceremonial and economic procedures related to

marriage, equivalent to our concept of wedding rituals. Strictly

speaking, this term should apply only to the transfer of property from

the groom and his supporters to the bride's family as the price for

obtaining her. Its original meaning was simply "buying a woman."

Gangfang and other places should be returned to China, and the handover procedures were completed the following year. It now belongs to Gugang Township, Lushui County.

[37] The examples of the Chashan dialect are quoted from the author's *A Study of the Three Ethnic Languages on the Yunnan-Myanmar Border*, a manuscript in 1944.

[38] "Baiyi" was the general name for the Dai ethnic group from the Qing Dynasty to the Republic of China period. The "Western Yunnan Baiyi" refers to the Dai ethnic group in the area of what is now Dehong Autonomous Prefecture in Yunnan. In the Ming Dynasty, the Lu Chuan Ping-Mian Military and Civilian Pacification Commissioner's Office was once set up here.

[39] This example was relayed by Zhang Yintang. Also, Xiang Jueming said: "The missionaries of the China Inland Mission felt difficulties when translating the word 'sea' into the Miao language when they translated the Bible." This can also serve as a supplementary example.

[40] "Nootka" is a branch of the North American Indians. In 1906, there were 2,159 people, mainly distributed in the west of Vancouver, Canada.

However, the Nootka people now use it to include all the singing, dancing, and speeches that precede the "purchase" and dowry exchange, much of which is not directly related to the transaction itself. For instance, they have an entire set of songs called *lutcha'yak*, meaning "songs for buying a woman." The connection of these songs to marriage is purely customary. Moreover, the bride's family immediately redistributes the gifts received to their fellow villagers, and notably, they soon return a special dowry and gifts of equal or even greater value than the "bride price" they received. This practice often reduces "buying a woman" marriages to a mere formality. Nevertheless, the cultural value of the term *lutcha* clearly lies in its original meaning of a purely economic marriage transaction. As the accompanying rituals increase, the economic significance diminishes under the current marriage system.[41]

The Nootka language also contains interesting suffixes that indicate marriage-related procedures. For example, ⌐ʼO°ʼiɫ⌐ means "to ask for something as a gift in a girl's puberty potlatch"; −t̓o°ɫa means "to give a potlatch for someone"; −ʼinɫ means "to give a feast of some kind of food in a potlatch." The term "potlatch" refers to a custom of certain Pacific Coast Native American groups where gifts are distributed among members of one's tribe or neighboring tribes, accompanied by feasting. These suffixes indicate that in

---

[41] E. Sapir, *Time perspective*, pp. 61-62.

Nootka society, the potlatch ceremony has long been connected to certain cultural concepts.[42]

As mentioned earlier, the Lisu language has as many as five terms for alcoholic beverages, proving that they are a tribe fond of drinking. A similar case can be found in English, where there are numerous terms related to cattle farming, such as *cow* (female cow), *ox* (male cow), *bull* (male cow), *steer* (castrated bull), *heifer* (young cow), *calf* (young cattle), *cattle* (livestock), *beef* (cow meat), *veal* (calf meat), *butter, cheese, whey, curd, cream, to churn* (to make butter), *to skim* (to remove cream from milk), etc. These terms are widely used and clearly differentiated. [43] In contrast, despite the flourishing orange-growing industry in the western United States, the vocabulary unique to this industry is relatively sparse and less specific. From such linguistic evidence, we can deduce the relative historical significance of cattle farming and orange cultivation in American culture.[44] In ancient China, the vocabulary related to cattle and sheep was also particularly rich. For example, in the *Shuowen Jiezi*, the "牛" (cattle) section includes terms for the age of cattle, such as 牸 (two-year-old cattle), 㸬 (three-year-old cattle), and 牭 (four-year-old cattle); terms for gender, such as 牡 (male cattle) and 牝 (female cattle); terms for physical characteristics and diseases, such as 犅 (a special kind of

---

[42] E. Sapir, *Time perspective*, p. 66.
[43] Words are closely related to people's living and production forms and thus develop. According to Wuti Qing Wenjian (*The Five Languages Clear Script Mirror*), there are more than 130 Manchu words related to the forms of rivers, more than 60 words related to the forms of ice and snow, and more than 70 words related to fish.
[44] E. Sapir, *Time perspective*, p. 66.

cattle), "特" (the male of a certain kind of cattle), "犗" (castrated bull), "㹃" (cattle with mixed black and white hair), "犖" (cattle with mottled colors), "牉" (cattle with mottled colors like stars), "牷" (a complete and intact cattle), "犧" (cattle used for sacrifices in ancestral temples), "牻" (cattle with mixed white and black hair), "犅" (cattle with a white spine), "㹇" (cattle with yellowish-white color), "犉" (yellow cattle with black lips), "㹀"(white cattle), "犝" (cattle with a long spine), "牷" (cattle of a single color), "㹀" (livestock of a single color), "牼" (the bone under the knee of cattle), "衿" (a disease of the tongue of cattle); regarding the actions and characteristics of cattle, there are "牧" (cattle walking slowly), "犨" (the sound of cattle breathing), "牟" (the sound of cattle mooing), "牵" (pulling forward), "犕" (driving cattle and riding horses), "㸩" (plowing), "辈" (plowing on both sides), "牴" (butting), "犟"(cattle kicking), "㹷" (cattle being gentle and cautious), "犟" (cattle being stubborn and not following when being pulled), "犉" (sheep and cattle having no offspring); regarding raising cattle, there are "犓" (feeding cattle with grass stems), "牿" (the pen for horses and cattle), "牢" (the pen for raising horses and cattle at leisure). In the "羊" (sheep) section,

23

regarding the age of sheep, there are "羔" (lamb), "𦎝" (young lamb), "羜" (lamb born in May), "𦏲"(lamb born in June), "𦍍" (sheep that has not reached one year old); regarding the gender of sheep, there are "羝" (male sheep), "羒" (female sheep), "牂" (female sheep), "羭" (the male of summer sheep is called 羭), "羖" (the male of summer sheep is called 羖); regarding the shape and color of sheep, there are "羠" (castrated sheep), "羳" (sheep with a yellow belly); regarding the actions and characteristics of sheep, there are "芈" (the sound of sheep bleating), "羏"(the appearance or behavior of sheep mutually crowded together), "羵" (the state of sheep crowded together), "'羴'"(a group of sheep are in the situation of mutually crowded together), "羴" (the smell of sheep). Words derived from the character "羊" include "羣" (a group), "美" (sweet, beautiful), "羨" (advancing towards goodness), "羌" (shepherds of the Western Rong[45] people). Most of these words have become obsolete in modern Chinese due to social and economic changes, but their presence in ancient lexicons like *Shuowen Jiezi* preserves a record of a pastoral lifestyle in ancient Chinese society. The demise of these words results entirely from shifts in social and economic systems.

---

[45] "Western Rong" was the general name for the ethnic groups in the northwest in ancient times. Originally distributed in the upper reaches of the Yellow River, the northwest of Gansu Province and the southeast of Qinghai Province, they gradually moved eastward. Later, they were also called the Qiang ethnic group.

In ancient China's feudal society, the founding emperors of each dynasty were often regarded as "true lords," "mandate-receiving sons of heaven," or "true dragon emperors." Similarly, in Taoism, a successful practitioner is referred to as a "true person". Comparable examples can be found in other early societies. For instance, the Tsim Shian people[46] of North America called their chiefs səm'ɔ°g id (singular) or ¡səmgigad (plural). Analyzing these terms reveals that səm— means "very" or "true," while gad is "man" in singular form and gigad is the plural "men." This is yet another example of the psychological patterns behind word formation shared across different cultures.[47]

---

[46] The "Tsim Shian People" live in Alaska in the United States and British Columbia in Canada. The Tsim Shian language belongs to the Penutian language family.
[47] E. Sapir, *Time perspective*, p. 63.

Chapter 4 Loanwords as Evidence of Cultural Contact

The essence of language can certainly reflect the cultural hues of history. However, when it encounters and interacts with foreign cultures, it also absorbs new elements, blending them with its existing components. The so-called "loanwords" are the foreign elements incorporated into a language. These loanwords can illustrate the linguistic impact of cultural interactions, and conversely, the fusion of languages can provide insights into cultural exchanges. Sapir remarked, "Language, like culture, is rarely self-sufficient. The needs of communication bring speakers of one language into direct or indirect contact with speakers of neighboring languages or those of culturally dominant languages. Communication can be either friendly or hostile. It can arise from mundane connections like business or trade, or it may encompass borrowed or shared intellectual nourishment such as art, science, or religion. It is difficult to point out a completely isolated language or dialect, especially among primitive peoples. Neighboring groups of people come into contact, and such interactions, regardless of their extent or nature, generally lead to some degree of linguistic influence."[48]

China, throughout its history, has interacted with many nations. Regions such as India, Iran, Persia, Malaya, Siam, Burma, Tibet, Annam, the Xiongnu, Turks, Mongols, Manchurians, Koreans, Japanese, and, in modern times, those from Europe and the Americas have had relationships with the Han Chinese. Each cultural wave has

---

[48] E. Sapir, *Language*, p. 205.

left some loanwords in the Chinese language, while Chinese has also lent some terms to other languages. By carefully studying these mutual loanwords, one can uncover interesting explanations regarding cultural history. The scope of mutual loanwords can roughly estimate the breadth and depth of cultural interactions between China and other nations. Let us consider a few examples:

1. The Lion Anyone who has visited a zoo or watched films like *Tarzan* would not find lions unfamiliar. However, if one were to ask, "Are lions native to China? If not, when were they introduced?" these are not questions that the average person could answer. The character for "lion" (狮) was also written as "师." According to the annotation to the *Book of the Later Han: Biography of Ban Biao* by Li Xian: "师 refers to 师子 (lion)." The *Biography of Ban Chao* records: "Initially, the Yuezhi assisted the Han in defeating Jushi. In 88 A.D., they presented treasures, including lions, and sought a Han princess in marriage. Ban Chao refused and sent their envoys back, inciting their resentment." The *Annals of Emperor Shun* states: "In the second year of Yangjia (133 A.D.), the state of Shule presented lions and oxen." Li Xian notes: "The *Records of the Eastern View* states: 'The king of Shule sent an envoy named Wen Shi to the capital of Han.' Lions resemble tigers, are golden in color, and have a mane, and a tuft of hair at the end of the tail the size of a peck. Oxen with raised humps on their shoulders are named after this feature, akin to today's zebu."[49]

---

[49] In the entry on the country of Alexan dria Prophthasia in the "Biography of the Western Regions" in the *Book of Han*, it is recorded that "There are Tao Ba, lions, and rhinoceroses". Meng Kang commented, "Lions look like tigers. They are bright yellow with manes on their

However, the *Luoyang Qielan Ji (Record of Buddhist Monasteries in Luoyang)* (Vol. 3, *Yongqiao*) mentions: "Lions were gifts from the King of Persia." Therefore, according to the records, lions were said to have originated from three sources: the Yuezhi (Indo-Scythians), Shule (Kashgar), and Persia. Based on phonetic transcriptions, Thomas Watters suggested that the Chinese word for lion, *ši* (狮), originated from the Persian *sēr*.[50] Berthold Laufer, however, was not entirely satisfied with this theory, arguing that in 88 A.D., when the first lion was presented to China by the Yuezhi, the so-called "Persian language" did not yet exist. He proposed that the term entered China through the Yuezhi as an East Iranian language term, where the original phoneme was *šē* or *ši* (Tokharian A: *si šāk*), consistent with the Chinese 师(*si*), which lacked a final consonant.[51] French sinologists including Edouard Chavannes[52], Paul Pelliot[53], and Henri Gauthiot[54] also noted the phonetic resemblance. Pelliot argued against adopting the etymology linking the Persian *sēr* to *xšaθrya* and

---

cheeks, and the tip of their tails is as big as a peck". Yan Shigu noted, "Lions are what is called 'Suanni' in the 'Er Ya'... The manes on the cheeks are also called 'Er' and pronounced as 'ér'. What is recorded here pertains to the situation in the Western Regions at that time and is close in era to the events recorded in the *Book of Later Han: Biography of Ban Chao*.

[50] Thomas Watters, *Essays on the Chinese Language* (hereinafter referred to as Chinese Language), Shanghai, 1889, p. 350.

[51] Berthold Laufer, *The Si-hia Language, T'oung Pao* (hereinafter referred to as T. P.) s. II, XVII (1916), p. 81; and also his *The Language of the Yüe-chi or Indo-Scythians*, Chicago, 1917, p. 4; *Chinese Pottery of the Han Dynasty*, pp. 236 - 245.

[52] Edouard Chavannes, Les Pays Occident d'après le Heou Han Chou, *T. P. s.* II , VIII (1907), p. 177, note 5, "符拔, 狮子"; *Trois Généraux Chinois de la Dynastie des Han Orientaux, T. P. s.* II, VII (1906), p. 232.

[53] Paul Pelliot, *T. P. s.* II, XXI (1922), p. 434, note 3, (*Review to G. A. S. Williams' A Manual of Chinese Metaphors*, p. 128).

[54] cf Horn, *Mémoir de Societé de Linguistique*, XIX (1915), p. 132.

attributed the word to Sogdian (* šryw, or * šary ə , meaning "lion"). Although some scholars do not agree that the term originates from Persian, there is little dispute about its Iranian linguistic roots. Bernhard Karlgren also cited Professor G. Morgenstierne, affirming that the Chinese *si* (师/狮) was a phonetic equivalent of the Iranian šary at the time.[55]

2. Shibi *Shibi* (师比) refers to a type of metallic belt hook. It appears in historical texts with variations such as 犀比(Xibi), 犀纰 (Xipi), 私毗(Sipi), 胥纰(Xupi), and 鲜卑(Xianbei). The *Chu Ci (Songs of Chu): Zhao Hun (Summons of the Soul)* states: "Xibi made in the state of Jin, waste the hours of the day." In the *Da Zhao*: "Small waists and slender necks, like the *Xianbei*." Ruan Yuan's *Ji Gu Zhai Zhong Ding Yi Qi Kuan Zhi (Ji Gu Zhai's Inscriptions on Ancient Bronzes such as Bells, Tripods and Sacrificial Vessels)* (Vol. 10, *Bingwu Shenhook*) comments: "The head is shaped like a beast's face, similar to the form of a *Shibi. The Records of the Grand Historian* notes that Emperor Wen of Han presented the Xiongnu with 'golden belt hooks,' which were written as 犀毗(Xipi) in the *Book of Han*. Zhang Yan commented: 'The *Xianbei* refers to hooked belts, also the name of an auspicious beast. They were favored by the Eastern Hu people.' The *Strategies of the Warring States* records: 'King Wuling of Zhao bestowed golden belts and *shibi* to Zhou Shao.' Yan Du stated,

[55] Bernhard Karlgern, Word Families in Chinese, *Bulletin of the Museum of Far Eastern Antiquities* (hereinafter referred to as B. M. F. E. A) No. 5 (1934), p. 30, Stockholm

'*Shibi* is a leather belt hook used by the Hu people.' Ban Gu, in his *Letter to Dou Xian*, noted: 'He once again granted me (Ban Gu) a gold headband adorned with *Xibi*.' Similarly, the *Dong Guan Han Ji (Eastern View of the Han)* records that 'Deng Zun, after defeating the Xiongnu, was awarded a golden belt with *xianbei* patterns.' Hence, 师比(Shibi), 胥纰(Xupi), 犀毗(Xipi), 鲜卑(Xianbei), and 犀比(Xibi) are phonetic variants written with different charaters referring to the same object." Based on phonetic variations, this term was most likely a loanword rather than an indigenous Chinese term. So where did shibi originate?

The interpretations of this question vary considerably: many archaeologists and sinologists believe that the term "shibi" was borrowed by the Han people from the nomadic tribes of western and northwestern China.[56] Wang Guowei merely referred to it as a "Hu name."[57] Paul Pelliot and Shiratori Kurakichi thought it was derived from the Xiongnu word *serbi*. Shiratori also associated it with the modern Manchu word *sabi*, meaning "auspicious omen" or "happy omen."[58] Peter Boodberg, while not specifying his views on the origin of the word, compared *serbi* with the Mongolian word *serbe*.[59] According to Kovalevskij's *Mongolian-Russian Dictionary*, *serbe*

---

[56] A catalogue is listed in Egami Namio and Mizuno Kotoku's *Inner Mongolia and the Region of the Great Wall*, pp. 103 - 110 (Tokyo and Kyoto, 1935).
[57] *Hu Fu Kao* in Volume 22 of *Guan Tang Ji Lin*, p. 2.
[58] P. Pelliot, *L'Edition Collective des oeuvres de Wang Kuowei*, T. P. XXVI (1929), p. 141; Shiratori Kurokichi, *Memoirs of the Research Dept. of the Tokyo Bunko* No. 4, 5 (Tokyo, 1929), p. 5.
[59] Peter Boodberg, *Two Notes on the History of the Chinese Frontier*, Harvard Journal of Asiatic Studies (hereinafter referred to as H. J. A. S.) I, 1936, p. 306, n. 79.

means "small hook" or "notch," and *serbe-ge* refers to "notch, small hook, gill, crest, or agraffe."[60] In summary, regardless of whether the Xiongnu spoke Mongolic, Tungusic[61], or Turkic languages, based on these hypotheses, the word *Shibi* is unlikely to have Indo-European origins. However, Otto Maenchen-Helfen recently proposed that both *Shibi* and *Guoluo* were derived from Indo-European languages. He argued that since the term *Xianbei* ("Small waists and slender necks, like the *Xianbei*") appeared in the *Da Zhao* and predated 230 BC— when the Chinese were still unaware of the Xiongnu—it is unlikely that Chu people borrowed words like *Xianbei*, *Shibi*, or related terms for belt hooks from them. Based on this, he reconstructed the terms as follows:

1.*Shibi* as *serbi*. The term "belt hook" can be compared to Indo-European words related to "hook" or "sickle," such as Old Church Slavonic srъpъ, Lithuanian *sirpe*, Greek σρπη, Latin *sarpi*o and *sarpo*, and Old Irish *serr*.

2.*Guoluo* as *kwâklâk*. The term "belt" can also be compared with Indo-European words, such as Proto-Indo-European *IE.* kuekɪlo – ^ ^ , Greek κμκλοσ ("circle"), Sanskrit *cakrá*, Old Persian caxrō ; and Tocharian *kukäl* ("wheel"). There is no semantic difficulty in comparing these terms to "belt."[62]

---

[60] Kovalevskij, *Dictionaire Mongol-Russe-Francsais*, II. p. 1373.

[61] Donghu (Tungus), nowadays is commonly translated as "Tungus". It will be referred to as "Tungus" later in the text.

[62] Otto Maenchen-Heilfen, *Are Chinese Hsi-pi and Kuolo IE Loanwords?* Language, XXI, 4 (1945), pp. 256 - 260.

I will refrain from critiquing Maenchen-Helfen's reconstruction. However, I find his disassociation of the terms from Xiongnu linguistic origins based solely on the word *Xianbei* in the *Da Zhao* to be unconvincing. In my view, the discovery of the term *Xianbei* may instead resolve the long-debated question of the dating of the *Da Zhao*. [63] Thus, I still lean toward Pelliot and others' hypothesis regarding *shibi* as *serbi*.

3. *Biliuli* In the *Shuowen Jiezi*, under the character "珋" in the 玉 (jade) section, it states: "璧珋 (*Biliu*) is a stone that shines" (corrected by Duan Yucai). Duan Yucai annotated: "璧珋 (*Biliu*) refers to 璧流离(*biliuli*) (a kind of precious stone)." According to the *Geography Treatise*, 'people trade in pearls and biliuli by the sea.' The *Biography of the Western Regions* states, 'The State of Guobin produces *biliuli*.' The term biliuli is a foreign name, just as *xunganqi* is foreign term. The murals in the Wu Liang Ancestral Hall of the Han Dynasty mention *biliuli*, stating, 'When a ruler does not conceal his faults, positive outcomes will follow.' The *Wu Guo Shan Bei (Wu Kingdom Mountain Stele),* recording auspicious omens, also mentions

---

[63] You Guo'en said in *Pre-Qin Literature*: "The author of *Da Zhao* is neither Jing Chai nor Qu Yuan. It was probably written by someone between the Qin and Han dynasties who imitated *Zhao Hun*. There doesn't necessarily have to be the person being summoned in reality... Looking at it, there is no preface at the beginning of the piece and no 'luan' (a structural part in ancient Chinese literature) at the end. It only imitates a middle section of *Zhao Hun*. The literary expressions are far inferior, and the traces of imitation are quite obvious. There is no doubt that it was written later." You Guo'en also took the paragraph about "Xian Xi Gan Ji" which mentioned Chu three times and the word "qing" in "Qing Se Zhi Mei, Mei Mu Mian Zhi" as evidence that it was a term after the Qin Dynasty. (Pages 157 - 159) [The Commercial Press, 1933]

biliuli. Buddhist texts refer to *feiliuli,* where *fei* sounds similar to *bi*. According to the *Biography of the Western Regions*, Meng Kang noted that 'biliuli is blue, like jade.' In modern editions of the *Annotations to the Book of Han*, the character *bi* is omitted, leading readers to mistake *bi* and *liuli* as two separate items. Today, people abbreviate it to 流离 (*liuli*), changing the character to 瑠璃; ancient texts abbreviated it to 璧珋. The pronunciation of "珋" is the same as that of "流" and "瑠." In Yang Xiong's *Yulie Fu (Rhapsody on Hunting)*, he wrote: 'Strike the *liuli*, make it emit light at night' indicating that the abbreviation to *liuli* was ancient." Regarding the origins of the term *biliuli* before the Han Dynasty, Duan Yucai's explanation is comprehensive, though he only identified it as a foreign term without investigating its linguistic origin in depth. Based on phonetic correspondence, the term can be divided into two categories: the older translation *biliuli* or *feiliuli* and the newer *pitouli* or *bitouli*. The former originates from the Prakrit term *veluriya*, while the latter derives from the Sanskrit term *vaidurya*.[64] The original meaning was "blue gem," but it later became a general term for colored glass. It shares the same origin as Greek βιρυλλοσ, Latin *beryllos*, Persian and Arabic *billaur*, and English *beryl*. From the numerous historical

---

[64] Thomas Watters, *Chinese Language*, p. 433; Fujita Toyohachi, translated by He Jianmin, *A Collection of Studies on Ancient Communications in the South China Sea*, page 115 [The Commercial Press, 1936]; Feng Chengjun, *Annotations on Zhu Fan Zhi*, pages 132 and 133 [The Commercial Press, 1940]; Ji Xianlin, *On the Transliteration of Sanskrit*, 1949, pages 29 and 30.

references cited by Duan Yucai, it is evident that *biliuli* as both an object and a term was introduced to China during the Han Dynasty from India via Central Asia.

4. Grapes (葡萄) According to the *Records of the Grand Historian: Ranked Biography of Dayuan*, Emperor Wu of Han introduced grapes and alfalfa to China from the Dayuan region, indicating that these two items were brought back by Zhang Qian. Grapes were referred to as "蒲陶" in the *Records of the Grand Historian* and *Book of Han*, "蒲萄" in the *Book of Later Han*, and "蒲桃" in the *Records of the Three Kingdoms* and *History of the Northern Dynasties*. Western Sinologists such as W. Tomaschek [65], T. Kingsmill[66], and F. Hirth[67] hypothesize that the term derives from the Greek word βότρυσ ("a bunch of grapes"). Similarly, Terrien de Lacouperie agreed with this theory. However, Laufer argues that grapes had long been cultivated in the northern part of the Iranian Plateau, predating the Greeks. The Greeks adopted grapes and wine from Western Asia. He suggests that the Greek βότρυσ likely originated as a loanword from Semitic languages. Fergana argues that the people of Dayuan would not have used a Greek word for a plant they had cultivated locally for a long time. He proposed that the term

---

[65] Sogdiana, *Sitzungsher. Wiener Akad.*, 1877, p. 133.
[66] *The Intercourse of China with Central and Western Asia in the 2nd Century B.C.*, Journal of the Royal Asiatic Society (hereinafter referred to as J. R. A. S.), China Branch XIV (1879), pp. 5, 190.
[67] *Fremde Einflüsse in der Chin. Kunst*, p. 25; and Journal of American Oriental Society (hereinafter referred to as J. A. O. S.) XXXVII (1917), p. 146.

"grape" corresponds to the Iranian *budāwa* or *buðawa*, derived from the root *buda* and the suffix *-wa* or *-awa*. According to Laufer, *buda* might relate to the New Persian *bāda* (wine) and Old Persian βατιάκη (a wine vessel), equivalent to Middle Persian *bātak* and New Persian *badye*.[68] Recent research by Yang Zhijiu suggests that the term "grape" might derive from the *Book of Han: Biography of the Western Regions*' reference to the "Putiao" (扑挑) kingdom in Wuyishanli. The characters 扑挑 likely correspond to "朴桃" in the *Book of Han Biography of the Western Regions*, which matches the Bactrian city Bactria according to Saussure.[69] Since the area was known for its abundant grape production, the fruit came to be named after this region.[70][71]

5. Alfalfa In the *Book of Han*, alfalfa is written as *Musu* (目宿). Guo Pu wrote it as *Muxu* (牧蓿), and Luo Yuan as *Musu* (木粟).

---

[68] Berthold Laufer, *Sino-Iranica*, pp. 225 - 226; cf. Horn, *Neupersische Etymologie*, No. 155.
[69] Edouard Chavannes, *T. P. s.* II, VI, (1905), p. 514.
[70] Yang Zhijiu, *An Exploration into the Etymology of "Putao"*, the full text was published in the 6th issue of Qingdao's *Zhongxing Weekly*, pages 11 - 14, 1947.
[71] As for "putao" (grapes), on November 15, 1956, the Polish Sinologist Janusz Chmielewski gave a lecture titled "On the Problem of Loanwords in Ancient Chinese Taking the Word 'putao' as an Example" at an academic seminar held by the Department of Chinese Language and Literature at Peking University. The translation of the lecture was published in the first issue of the "Journal of Peking University" in 1957. He cited a wide range of materials but did not mention Mr. Luo Changpei's book (presumably he hadn't seen it). His conclusion was the same as Mr. Luo's. As mentioned earlier, the capital city of the Bactrian Kingdom was Bactria. In relevant texts, it was referred to as "Balh" in the *Nestorian Stele*, as "Boluó" in the *History of the Northern Dynasties*, as "Fuwahē" in the *Records of the Western Regions*, as "Bānchéng" in YeLü Chucai's *Record of a Journey to the West*, as "Bānlèhé", "Bālihēi" in the *History of Yuan Dynasty*, and as "Bǎlihēi" in the *History of Ming*, all of which should refer to the same place. According to the *Record of a Journey to the West*, in this area "there are many putao (grapes) and pears and other fruits", and the wine made from grapes "tastes like the Nine Brews of Zhongshan". The old Zhongshan region produced fine wines, and the brewing sites have been discovered in present-day Dingzhou, Hebei Province.

Laufer discovered that ancient Tibetan used *bugsug* as a phonetic equivalent for this term[72], reconstructing its original Iranian form as *buksuk, buxsux,* or *buxsuk.*[73] W. Tomaschek attempted to compare this word to Gīlakī (a kind of Caspian dialect)[74] term *būso* ("alfalfa").[75] If it can be demonstrated that *būso* derives from a root similar to *buxsux*, this would be a satisfactory explanation. Early East Iranian peoples that first interacted with the Chinese lacked written records, and their languages have since disappeared. Nevertheless, thanks to Chinese records, the term for *Medicago sativa* used by the people of Dayuan, *buksuk* or *buxsux*, has been preserved—a testament to Zhang Qian's achievements.

6. Betel Nut (Binlang) In the *Book of Han*, Sima Xiangru's *Shanglin Fu (Rhapsody of Shanglin)* mentions "Renpin Binglü (仁频并闾)," with Yan Shigu noting, "Renpin (仁频) refers to Binlang; pin (频) sometimes written as bin (宾)." Song Dynasty scholar Yao Kuan cited the *Xianyaolu (Records of Immortal Medicines)* in his *Xixi Conghua (Collected Talks of Xixi)*, stating, "Binlang is also called Renpin." This term likely corresponds to the Malay word *pinang*. In Javanese, *pinang* is referred to as *jambi*, which might also be a phonetic transcription of "Renpin."[76]

---

[72] B. Laufer, *Loanwords in Tibetan*, T. P. s. II, XVII (1916), p. 500, No. 206.

[73] B. Laufer, *Sino-Iranica*, p. 212.

[74] The Gilaki language belongs to the Iranian branch of the Indo-European language family. Its speakers are distributed along the southeastern coast of the Caspian Sea and in the nearby mountainous areas, with a population of about two million.

[75] Pamir-Dialekte, *Sitzungsber. Wiener Akad*, 1880, p. 792.

[76] T. Watters, *Chinese Language*, p. 343; and also refer to Fujita Toyohachi, *A Collection of Studies on Ancient Communications in the South China Sea*, the part of "The Maritime Trade

7. Zhezhi Dance In Duan Anjie's *Music and Dance Records*, the Zhezhi Dance is listed as one of the courtly music and dances. Tang Dynasty author Shen Yazhi noted in his Preface to the *Zhezhi Wu Fu (Rhapsody of Zhezhi Dance)*: "Among the local music and dances now performed in court, only those of the Hu tribe remain, and the Zhezhi Dance is even more prevalent."[77] Yan Shu also identified it as a Hu dance.[78] In Liu Yuxi's poem *Watching the Zhezhi Dance*, it goes like this: "How magnificent and splendid are the Hu-style costumes! The dancers gracefully ascend the beautiful steps." It only generally describes the attire as Hu dress but does not specify its origin.[79] According to Xiang Da, "The dance likely originated from the Shi kingdom (modern Tashkent). In the *Book of Wei*, Shi is rendered as 'zheshe'; in Xuanzang's *Records of the Western Regions*, it is 'Zheshi'; in Du Huan's *Jing Xing Ji (Travel Records)*, it is 'Zhezhi.' The *Book of Tang: Records of the Western Regions* mentions that Shi was also called 'Zhezhi,' 'Zhezhe,' or 'Zheshi,' located north of Dayuan. The *Comprehensive Examination of Literature: Barbarian Studies*: Turkic Studies mentions 'Zhejie,' which also refers to the Shi kingdom. All these terms, including 'Zheshe,' 'Zheshi,' 'Zhezhi,' 'Zhezhe,' and

Offices and Regulations in the Song Dynasty", page 241; Feng Chengjun, *Annotations on Zhu Fan Zhi*, pages 117 - 118.

[77] *The Collected Works of Shen Xiaxian*, in the *Si Bu Cong Kan* edition, page 8.

[78] In the manuscript copy of *Yan Yuanxian Lei Yao* collected by the National Library of China, Volume 29, in the entry of "Miscellaneous Song Titles", it is recorded: "Wu Tian Zhe Zhi Heng Chui", with the original annotation: "According to 'Gu Jin Yue Fu Lu', it is Hu music."

[79] Volume 5 of *The Collected Works of Liu Mengde*

'Zhezhi,' are translations of the Persian word Chaj."[80] Xiang Da's hypothesis is thus firmly supported by phonetic and textual evidence.

8. The Term "Zhan" (standing or station) The original meaning of the character *zhan* was "standing for a long time," as recorded in the *Guangyun*, and it originally contrasted with the character *zuo* (sit). However, the modern usage of *zhan* in terms such as "postal station" or "train station" derives from the Mongolian word ꞏꞏJam . This word shares the same root as the Turkish or Russian *yam*. The *History of Yuan Dynasty* refers to *zhanchi* as the phonetic transcription of ꞏJamǒi , meaning "station manager."[81]

9. Mynah Birds The mynah bird (bāgē) is an alternative name for the quyu bird. According to the *Fuxuan Miscellaneous Records*, "The Southern Tang Emperor Li Houzhu avoided the character 'yù' (as it was part of his name) and renamed the quyù bird as bāgē." The *Erya Yi (Exegesis on Erya)* also mentions: "The quyù flies in flocks and is called the 'bābā' bird." The term bābā' is a phonetic transcription of the Arabic *babghā* or *bābbāghā*. In Arabic, parrots are referred to as babghā. Since both quyù and parrots are songbirds capable of mimicking human speech, the names could be used interchangeably.

---

[80] Xiang Da, *Chang'an of the Tang Dynasty and Western Region Civilizations*, pages 94 - 95 [1933, 1957].

[81] Feng Chengjun, *Translation and Compilation of Researches on the History and Geography of the Western Regions and the South China Sea* - Paul Pelliot, *The Mongolian Language in the History of Goryeo*, page 78, which is the summary of reading Shiratori Kurokichi's *The Explanation of the Mongolian Language Seen in the History of Goryeo* (published in "Toyo Gakuho", Volume 18, pp. 72 - 80, Tokyo, 1929).

10. Myrrh (moyao) Myrrh was first included as a medicinal substance during the compilation of the *Kaibao Bencao (Materia Medica during the Kaibao Period)* in the sixth year of Kaibao (973 A.D.). Ma Zhong noted: "Myrrh (moyao) originates in Persia, where it comes in irregularly sized chunks that are black and resemble benzoin." The term is a phonetic transcription of the Arabic *murr*, meaning "bitter." In Chinese, it is written as either 没药 (mòyào) or 末药 (mòyào), both pronounced similarly to *murr*. Li Shizhen mistakenly claimed, "Both 没 (*mò*) and 末 (*mò*) are Sanskrit terms," a misunderstanding due to lack of knowledge about the true origin.

11. Fenugreek Fenugreek (húlúbā) was first recorded as a medicinal substance in the *Jiayou Supplemented Bencao* during the Jiayou era of the Song Dynasty (1057 A.D.) and was also known as "bitter beans." Liu Yuxi described it: "It originates in Guangzhou and Qianzhou, sprouts in spring, and bears seeds in summer, which grow into fine pods harvested in autumn. People today often use those from Lingnan. Some say it is the seed of a foreign radish, but this is uncertain." Su Song's *Illustrated Bencao* states: "Fenugreek now comes from Guangzhou, and some say it is cultivated on the southern islands, where it is considered the seed of the local radish. Before the Tang Dynasty, it was not in use, and it was not recorded in earlier *Bencao*, suggesting it was a more recent import." The term húlúbā is a phonetic transcription of the Arabic *hulbah*, likely introduced to China around the 9th century.

12. Emerald   The green beryl gemstone, also known as "emerald," is referred to as zǔmǔlǜ (祖母绿, literally "grandmother green") in Chinese. The *Zhenwan Kao (Treatise on Rare Antiques)* also calls it zǔmǔlù, while the *Chuogeng Lu (Records after Stopping Farming)* records it as zhùmùlà and the *Qingmicang (Secret Treasures of the Qing Dynasty)* as zhùshuǐlǜ (助水绿), with the character "water" likely a miswriting of "wood." These latter three terms are all phonetic transcriptions of the Arabic *zumurrud*.[82]

The examples above include words with both early origins and widespread usage, making them noteworthy. Other examples include dànbāgū (tobacco) and yéxīmíng (jasmine), borrowed from Persian *tambaco* and *jasmin*, and āfúróng (opium), from the Arabic *afyun*. This list is far from exhaustive; only some common examples are highlighted here.

Since the relaxation of maritime prohibitions, exchanges between China and modern Western nations have increased, and so has linguistic interaction. It is impossible to enumerate all cases, but for clarity, modern Chinese loanwords can be divided into four categories:

1. Phonetic Substitution

This method involves transcribing the sounds of foreign words or combining their sounds with Chinese meanings to form new terms. Subcategories include:

(1) Pure Transliteration

---

[82] I would like to express my special thanks to Professor Ma Jian for his guidance on the Arabic transliterations in these four examples!

40

For example: Cantonese terms like 燕梳 (yīnsō) for "insurance," 士担 (sítdām) for "stamp," 夜冷 (yēhlíhng) for "yelling," 嘜 (māak) for "trademark," 孖𧶧 (māhngjī) for "merchant," 花臣 (fāhsān) for "fashion," 磨打 (mótā) for "motor," 打臣 (dāsān) for "dozen," 骨 or 刮 (gwāt/gwāai) for "quarter," 則 or 赤 (chīuk/chēk) for "check," and 先 (sīn) for "cent," are also English borrowings. In Shanghainese, terms such as 引擎 (yīnchīn) for "machine," 沙发 (shāfā, sofa) for "soft chair," 水汀 (shuǐtīng, steam) for "heating pipe," 扑落 (pūlò, plug) for "electric plug," and 刚白度 (gāngbǎidòu, compradore) for "foreign trade broker" were also adopted from English. Widely known terms like 咖啡 (kāfēi, coffee), 可可 (kěkě, cocoa), 雪茄 (xuějiā, cigar), 朱古力 (zhūgǔlì, chocolate), and 德谟克拉西 (démókèlāxī, democracy) belong to this category.

(2) Phonetic-Meaning Intergrations

Although some loanwords are transliterations, the characters chosen often have some relation to the meaning of the objects they represent. For example, in Jilin, the machine used for farming is called 马神 (машина), in Harbin, they call bread 裂粑 (хлеб), and a stove is called 壁里砌 (печь), which are all influenced by Russian. Additionally, in Cantonese, the term for consul is 江臣 (gōngsān), for telephone is 德律风 (dākleuihfūng), and some people translate a popular American soft drink as 可口可乐 (Coca-Cola) or translate

Esperanto as 爱斯不难读 (Esperanto). These are all examples of this category.

(3) Phonetic-Meaning Combinations

This category of loanwords consists partly of the original transliterations, with an additional part carrying the local meaning. For example, in Cantonese, 恤衫 (seutsāam, shirt) refers to a shirt, and 则纸 (jākjí, check) is used for a check, and in Mandarin, terms like 冰激凌 (bīngjīlíng, ice cream), 卡车 (kǎchē, truck), 卡片 (kǎpiàn, card), 白塔油 (báitǎyóu, butter), and 佛兰绒 (fúlánróng, flannel) all belong to this category. The name of the medicine 金鸡纳霜 (quinine) doesn't exactly match the English term, but we should note that the first part of the word, 鸡纳 (quina), corresponds to the Spanish word *quinquina*, while 霜 (frost) describes the appearance of the white powdery substance.

(4) Misinterpreted Phonetic Transcriptions

For example, the term "爱美的" (aimede) was originally a phonetic translation of the English word "amateur," meaning a non-professional enthusiast. However, some people, misinterpreting the word based on its literal meaning, mistakenly understood "爱美的戏剧家" (amateur dramatist) as referring to someone who pursues female roles in a lewd manner, which unfairly misrepresents this group of "ticket friends" (enthusiasts of opera or drama).

2. New Phonetic-Compound Characters

42

When foreign words are borrowed into China, Chinese scholars often try to sinicize them. They apply the traditional method of "assigning the '鳥' (bird) radical to bird-related characters and the '魚' (fish) radical to aquatic-related characters" to force the foreign terms into phonetic characters. To those unfamiliar with their origin, these characters often appear completely devoid of foreign influence. This method has a long history. For example, the character 琉 (liu), which has the radical "玉" and the phonetic component "丣", is found in Xu Shen's *Shuowen Jiezi*; few people know that it is an abbreviation of the Sanskrit word *veluriya* (refer to the earlier section on *biliuli*). Similarly, the character 袈裟 (jiāshā) with the radical "衣" and the phonetic component "加" or with the radical "衣" and the phonetic component "沙", found in Ge Hong's *Ziyuan (Dictionary of Characters)*, is rarely recognized as a translation of the Sanskrit term *kāsaya*. Furthermore, plants like *cumin* (莳萝) from Middle Persian *zira*, and *jasmin* (茉莉) from Sanskrit *malli*, are terms that the average Chinese reader would likely not recognize as having been imported from foreign lands. Since the introduction of scientific terms, there has been an explosion of such borrowings, including chemical names like 铝 (aluminum), 钙 (calcium), 氨 (ammonia), and 氦 (helium). As for the Cantonese term for a water pump (压水机), which is called "泵" (bèng), it seems to be a newly coined character based on a conceptual understanding rather than a phonetic compound.

3. Loan-Translation Words

When foreign concepts previously unfamiliar to Chinese culture were introduced, translators, unable to match them with existing ideas, often directly translated the foreign terms word-for-word. This process is known as loan translation. Such words are often abstract nouns. After Buddhism was introduced to China, Buddhist scriptures contained many examples of loan-translated terms, such as 我执 (*ātma-grāha*, "self-attachment"), 法性 (*dhanmakara*, "dharma-nature"), 有情 (sattva, "sentient being"), 因缘 (hetupratyaya, "causes and conditions"), 大方便 (*mahopāya*, "great skillful means"), and 法平等 (*dharmasamatā*, "dharma equality"). Modern borrowings also include many philosophical terms, such as Thomas H. Green's *self-realization* translated as 自我实现 and Friedrich W. Nietzsche's *Übermensch* translated as 超人 ("superman"). These are also considered loan-translation words.

4. Descriptive Forms

When certain foreign things cannot be matched with equivalent native terms, a new word is often coined to describe them. Alternatively, terms for local objects that bear some resemblance are appended with words like "胡" (hú), "洋" (yáng), "番" (fān), or "西" (xī), which are used as descriptive markers. This method of borrowing characters has existed for a long time. In ancient China, when all Western ethnic groups were grouped as "胡人" (hú rén, "Barbarians"), words like 胡葱 (Kashgar's onion), 胡椒 (Indian pepper), 胡麻 (flax and sesame from abroad), 胡瓜 (cucumber), and 胡萝卜 (carrot) came

44

into use. A bit later, the general term "胡" was further modified into place names or national names, as seen in 安息香 (ān xī xiāng, the fragrant substance from Arsak or Parthia)[83] or 波斯枣 (Persian date). In modern borrowing of words, some descriptive terms include a country name, such as 荷兰水 (Dutch soda water), 荷兰薯 (Dutch potato), 荷兰豆 (Dutch peas). Some use the character "西" (xī), such as 西米 (sago)[84] and 西红柿 (tomato). Others use "番" (fān), like 番茄 (tomato) and 番枧 (soap). Some use "洋" (yáng), such as 洋火 (match) or 洋取灯儿 (match), 洋烟卷儿 (cigarettes). There are also cases where no geographic prefix is added, and the term is created purely based on the nature of the object, such as in Guangzhou where they call 煤油 (petroleum) "火水" (fire water) and 洋火 (match) "火柴" (fire stick). All of these are examples of what is known as descriptive words.[85]

The examples above highlight some categories of foreign borrowings in Chinese. A comprehensive study would require a detailed analysis and could result in a substantial volume. However, such work is challenging because it demands not only linguistic training but also a deep understanding of the history of Sino-foreign

---

[83] Thomas Watters, *Chinese Language*, pp. 328 - 331.

[84] "Sago" is also written as "Sha Gu" or "Xi Gu" in China. It is pronounced as "saku" in Annam, "sagu" in India, and "sagu" in Malay. Grawford (*Des Diet. Indian Isl.*) thought that this word was not originally from the Malay language at all but evolved from the vernacular language of the Molucca Islands. See the previously cited book by Thomas Watters, pp. 342 - 343.

[85] For the four categories into which modern loanwords are divided, see Luo Changpei's manuscript *Chinese Loanwords from Indic*, pp. 3 and 4.

interactions. Without this, errors are inevitable. For example, in *A New Study of Ancient Chinese Society*, Li Xuanbo stated: "The Latin term *focus* refers to sacred fire. The ancient Chinese pronunciation of 火 (fire) was close to 'Buddha' (佛) and similar to the French *feu*. This pronunciation is still preserved in Cantonese and Shaanxi dialect. The shift in emphasis from *focus* to 火 resembles the transition from Latin *focus* to French *feu*, with the loss of the final syllable." This claim can be refuted without delving into the complex theory of "absence of labiodental phonemes in ancient Chinese." Simply noting that the 火 sound falls into the [x] category, not the [f] category , undermines the argument. Comparative linguistics is not so simple; presenting isolated phonetic similarities without systematic explanation is futile. Moreover, forcing connections between Latin and Chinese phonetics results in errors akin to early missionaries' mistaken attempts to link Chinese and Hebrew.

When two cultures interact, the higher culture generally influences the lower one more significantly. However, in terms of linguistic borrowing, Chinese exhibits a net import rather than export of terms. This phenomenon certainly cannot be solely judged on the basis of cultural hierarchy. It stems from several factors:

1.Historical Isolation: During periods of closed-door policies, China viewed itself as the "Heaven Kingdom" (tianchao), considering itself superior to surrounding regions. Foreign philosophies, religions, arts, and cultures were seldom adopted, limiting linguistic exchanges to trade goods or official titles.

2.Lack of Language Study: Traditionally, China paid little attention to studying foreign languages. When interaction required interpretation, it relied on a few interpreters, with little awareness of words spreading abroad.

3.Modern Practices: After the relaxation of maritime restrictions, Westerners translated numerous Chinese classics into their languages. However, outside of proper nouns or untranslatable terms, they rarely adopted the "phonetic substitution" approach. Loan-translated and descriptive terms were often overlooked by the general public.

4.Dialect Diversity: The dialects of Chinese are too diversified, so words borrowed from one dialect might be incomprehensible to speakers of another, which obscured its Chinese origin.

Given these reasons, it is not surprising that there are more imported words than exported words in the Chinese language.

Studies on Chinese loanwords in foreign languages include contributions from: Gustav Schlegel (on Malay),[86] Li Fanggui (on Thai),[87] Ko Taw Seim (on Burmese)[88], and She Kunsan (in English).[89] However, systematic research would require collaborative efforts from multiple specialists. Here are some simple examples:

Some Chinese words borrowed into foreign languages were later retranslated back into Chinese by translators who failed to restore the

---

[86] Gustav Schlegel, *Chinese Loanwords in the Malay Language*, T. P. I (1890), pp. 391 - 405.
[87] Li Fanggui's *The Native Language of Longzhou*, Nanjing, 1940, pp. 20 - 36, *Some Old Chinese Loanwords in the Tai Language*, *H. J. A. S.* VIII, p. 344 (March, 1945), pp. 332 - 342.
[88] Ko Taw Seim, *Chinese Words in the Burmese Language*, India Antiquiry, XXXV (1906), pp. 211 - 212.
[89] She Kunshan, *Chinese Characters in English*, in the 1st issue of *Wen Xun*, pages 5 - 17, published by the Wentong Bookstore in Guiyang.

original meanings due to ignorance of the origins, resulting in unrelated characters being used. In this way, through successive mistranslations, even "the Tang people could not recognize these as Tang words!" For example, in *The Secret History of Yuan Dynasty*, the term "太子" (Crown Prince) in the phrase "捏坤太子" was rendered as "大石" in *Shengwu Qinzhenglu (Campaigns of Genghis Khan,* Wang Guowei's edition, p. 35), "大司" in the *History of Yuan Dynasty* (Chapter 17, *Genealogical Table*) and *Records after Stopping Farming*, and "泰实" in *Mongolian Sources* (vol. 3). In fact, 泰实 is just the Mongolian transliteration of the Chinese term "太师" (Grand Tutor) as "taiši."[90] Similarly, the term "桑昆" (sänggün or saänggum) in *The Secret History of Yuan Dynasty* is commonly believed to be a transliteration of "将军" (general), but Berthold Laufer suspected it to be a transliteration of "相公" (a respectful term for a husband).[91] Moreover, Naketongshi believed that the Mongolian "兀真" (or "乌勤," ujin) was the equivalent of the Chinese "夫人" (wife), and "领昆" (linkum) was the equivalent of "令公" (a respectful term for a high-ranking official).[92] Following this pattern, the Manchu term "福晋" (fujin), though meaning "公主" (princess) in Chinese, is phonetically

[90] Paul Pelliot, *Annotations on Turkestan during the Mongol Invasion*, seen in Feng Chengjun's translation *Translation and Compilation of Researches on the History and Geography of the Western Regions and the South China Sea*, Volume Three, page 40.
[91] Ibid., page 42.
[92] Li Sichun, *Study on the History of Yuan Dynasty* [Zhonghua Bookstore, 1927]. Chapter Three, pages 126 - 127 quotes from Nakatsuka Michiyo's *The True Record of Genghis Khan*, page 33 and the preface of that book, page 59.

closer to "夫人" (wife).[93] The English word "typhoon," first used by F. Mendes Pinto in 1560, has a debated etymology. Some Western sinologists claim it comes from the Greek "typhon," while others suggest it derives from the Arabic "tufan." Some believe it is a transliteration of the Cantonese "大风" (strong wind), while others argue that it comes from the Taiwan word "台风."[94] Among these opinions, I personally lean toward the third one. However, the term "台风" appears in the *Fujian Tongzhi (General Chronicles of Fujian)* (Vol. 56, *Tufeng Zhi (Records of Local Customs)*) in 1684 and was used in Wang Yuyang's *Xiangzu Biji (Fragrance Ancestor's Notes)*, indicating it had appeared in Chinese texts as early as the 17th century, though it was not included in the *Kangxi Dictionary* (1716).

Sapir said: "When borrowing foreign words, their phonetics are often modified. Certain foreign sounds and accent features may not fit the phonetic habits of the native language. Therefore, these foreign phonetic features are changed to make them as compatible as possible with the native language's phonetic system. This often leads to compromises in pronunciation. For example, the word *camouflage*, which was recently introduced into English, in its current common pronunciation does not align with the typical phonetic habits of either English or French. The aspirated 'k' at the beginning, the vague vowel in the second syllable, the sound quality of 'l', and especially the strong stress on the first syllable, are all results of unconscious assimilation

---

[93] Thomas Watters, *Chinese Language*, pp. 356 - 366.
[94] Henry Yule and A. C. Bumell, Hobson—Jobson, *New edition*, edited by William Crooke, pp. 947 - 950; G. Schlegel, *Etymology of the Word Taifun*, T. P. VII (1396), pp. 581 - 585.

to English pronunciation habits. As a result, the English pronunciation of *camouflage* is clearly different from the French pronunciation. On the other hand, the long and stressed vowel in the third syllable and the 'zh' sound (like the 'z' in *azure*) at the end position are obviously 'un-English', similar to how, in Middle English, the use of 'j' and 'v' at the beginning of words initially felt inconsistent with English norms, but this sense of unfamiliarity has long since worn off."[95] Bronkfield also said: "The people who borrow words or later use them often prefer to avoid the dual muscle adjustment required for foreign pronunciation, instead using their local pronunciations to replace the foreign ones. For example, in an English sentence, when encountering the French word *rouge*, they would replace the French uvular r with the English [r], and the French non-diphthongized tight [u] with the English [uw]. This phonetic substitution can vary in degree between different speakers and different situations; those who have not learned French pronunciation are sure to do this. Historians regard this phenomenon as a form of adaptation, where foreign words are modified to fit the basic phonetic habits of the native language."[96] From the remarks of these two famous linguists, we can understand that loanwords bring significant changes to the original language. Now, let's take an example of a commonly recognized loanword in Chinese, though we cannot yet confirm the original Chinese characters:

---

[95] Edward Sapir, *Language*, pp. 210 - 211.
[96] Leonard Bloomfield, *Language*, pp. 455 - 456.

In 7th-century Turkic inscriptions, there is a word *Tabghač*, which was used by the Central Asians to refer to China. This name persisted in certain regions until the early Yuan Dynasty. In 1221, when Qiu Chuji was traveling west, he heard the term *Taohua Shi (Tabghač) in Yili*.[97] This name also appears in Eastern Roman and Islamic writings, but some versions are written as *Tamghaj, Tomghaj, Toughaj*, and others as *Taugaš, Tubgač*. Its origin was not initially clear, and the reason for calling it *Taohua Shi* remains unknown. Scholars like F. Hirth and B. Laufer believed these words were renditions of "Tangjia" (Tang family),[98] while Kuwabara Jitsuzo further explained it as "Tangjiazi" (Tang family members).[99] Berthold thought the name *Taohua Shi* appeared in 7th-century works by *Theophylact Simocatta* and noted that he recorded events and names from the late 6th century, which were not actually related to the Tang Dynasty.[100] He investigated the origin of the name *Taohua Shi*, suggesting it might refer to Tuoba (拓跋). Although the phonetic correspondence is not exact, it is a plausible hypothesis. Historically,

---

[97] *The Travel Record of Changchun Zhenren*, Volume One: "On the 27th day of the ninth month, we arrived at the city of Alima... The local people called fruits 'Alima' because there were many fruits there, and thus named the city after it... The local people only fetched water with bottles and carried them back. When they saw the water-drawing utensils in the Central Plains, they happily said: 'The people of Taohuashi are really ingenious after all.' 'Taohuashi' refers to the Han people." In the *Collection of Integrated Books*, page 12.

[98] F. Hirth, *Nachwörte zur Inschrift des Tonjukuk*, p. 35.

[99] The views of Kuwabara Jitsuzo can be seen in his book *The Deeds of Pu Shougeng, a Western Region Man Who Was in Charge of the Maritime Trade Office at the End of the Song Dynasty*, pages 135 - 143 (Chen Yujing's translation *A Study of Pu Shougeng*, pages 103 - 109; Feng You's translation *The History of Maritime Communications between China and Arabia*, pages 132 - 143), and also in Volume 7, Issue 4 of *Shilin*, pages 45 - 50. Refer to Xiang Da's *Chang'an of the Tang Dynasty and Western Region Civilizations*, page 25, note 1.

[100] Refer to Edouard Chavannes' *Documents sur les Touki ue Occidentaux* (pp. 230 - 246). Yule had already stated in 1866 that due to the mismatch in the era, it was impossible to identify Tabghač as the Tang Dynasty (in *Cathay and the Way Thither*, I, L III).

the Northern Wei Dynasty occupied northern China and was well-known by its surname "土 Tu" in Central Asia, leading the people of Central Asia to refer to China as Tuoba. Similarly, when the Liao Dynasty later occupied the territory of the Northern Wei Dynasty, its ethnic name "Khitan" was used by Central Asians to refer to China.[101] However, these three hypotheses, when strictly analyzed phonetically, cannot be considered precise. Though "Tangjiazi" could be read as *Tamgghaj* or *Tomghaj* through assimilation, and the northwest dialect could loosely interpret the word "Tang" as *Tau* or *Tou*, the forms *Tubgač* and *Tapkač* still don't fit well into this analysis. Ultimately, the original pronunciation of the Chinese word was so distorted in the borrowing that, even after many experts have speculated on it, the exact source remains unclear—this is certainly unfortunate!

However, the challenges of explaining foreign loanwords from Chinese are not limited to this. In my opinion, there are two other difficulties related to time and space:

Anyone who has a basic understanding of the history of Chinese language change should realize that Chinese phonetics have evolved from the Zhou and Qin dynasties to the present. If we measure loanwords from different periods by modern Chinese standards, it becomes difficult to make sense of them. For example, the character

---

[101] P. Pelliot, *L'orgine du Nom de "Chine"*, T. P. s. II. XIII (1912), pp. 727 - 742; Feng Chengjun's *Translation and Compilation of Researches on the History and Geography of the Western Regions and the South China Sea*, Paul Pelliot's *The Origin of the Name "China"*, pages 45 - 46. In Russian, China is called Китай [k'i-t'ai], which is the transliteration of "Khitan".

"石" (stone) was pronounced as ᶻïäk in Middle Chinese, but sï in modern Chinese. In Tibetan loanwords, "滑石" (talc) is pronounced *hasig*, while "玉石" (jade) is pronounced *yü-si* and "钟乳石" (stalactite) as *grun-ru-si*.[102] The -k ending in the first example is preserved, but entirely absent in the latter two, showing that these three words were borrowed at different times. If we rely solely on modern pronunciation, we cannot confirm that *sig* and *si* originally referred to the same word, and we would miss the valuable evidence of phonetic change. The times when Tibetan loanwords were borrowed are well-documented. For example, the character "笔" (brush) was borrowed into Tibetan as *pir*. The *Tang Hui Yao (Institutional History of Tang)* records that Tibetan king Sron-btsan Sgam-po asked Emperor Gaozong of Tang (650-683 A.D.) to send paper-making craftsmen.[103] This indicates that the writing brush had entered Tibet by the 7th century. The -*t* ending in ancient Chinese was commonly represented by -*r* in Central Asian languages, so *pir* is a precise phonetic match for the ancient Chinese *piĕt*. Similar examples can be found in loanwords like "萝卜" (radish) as *lá-bug* or *la-p'ug*, and "缺子" (gap) as *a-jab-tse*, which preserve the Middle Chinese -*k* or -*p* endings. These loanwords were certainly borrowed earlier than

---

[102] B. Laufer, *Loanwords in Tibetan*, T. P. s. II, XVII (1916), pp. 509, 521.
[103] *Tang Hui Yao*, Volume 97, page 3b. In the version by Wen Renquan, Volume 146a, 3a.

words like 粟米 (su-mi, corn) and 鸭子 (yā-tse, duck), as the -k and -p endings are missing in the latter two words.[104]

The divergence of Chinese loanwords in different dialects is similar to the differences found in ancient and modern pronunciations. China initially traded with the Malays mostly through Xiamen or other Min Nan (Southern Fujian) regions. Therefore, not only did many Malay words seep into Min Nan dialect, but also Malay loanwords from Chinese were limited to this dialect, making it difficult for people from other regions to recognize that they originated from Chinese. For example, in Malay, *angkin* comes from "红裙" (red skirt), *bami* comes from "白面" (white flour), *bak* or *bek* comes from "墨" (ink), *tjit* comes from "拭" (wipe), *niya* comes from "领" (collar), and *tehkowan* and *tehko* come from "茶罐" (tea canister) and "茶鼓" (tea drum). Anyone who speaks Xiamen dialect would recognize these Chinese characters and pronounce them very similarly to:

$$[\text{aŋ} \text{kun}] \quad , \quad [\text{baʔ m}] \quad , \quad [\text{bak}] \quad , \quad [\text{biɔk}] \quad ,$$

$$[\text{tɕʻ it}] \quad , \quad [\text{n ĩā}] \quad , \quad [\text{te kuan}] \quad , \quad [\text{te kɔ}] \quad , \text{etc.;}$$

conversely, hearing these Malay sounds would make them associate them with these Chinese characters.[105] However, if a person from a different dialect area who has never heard Xiamen or any other Min Nan dialect were to encounter these words, they would find it

---

[104] For examples of Tibetan loanwords, refer to Laufer's previous citation, *T. P. s.* II, XVII (1916), pp. 503, 508, 518, 522.
[105] Refer to Gustav Schlegel, *Chinese Loanwords in the Malay Language*, *T. P. I* (1890), pp. 394, 400, 402, 403; Luo Changpei, *The Phonetic System of Xiamen*, Beijing, 1930.

impossible to match them to any corresponding Chinese characters. This phenomenon can also be seen in loanwords borrowed from foreign languages. For example, the Sanskrit word *Bodhidharma*, which has traditionally been translated in Chinese Zen Buddhist texts as 菩提达摩 or simply 达摩 (Dharma), is written as 陈茂 (Chen Mao) in Xiamen dialect.[106] This not only sinicizes the name of the Zen patriarch, but also, when pronounced in Xiamen, *Chen Mao* $[$ tã ⟋ mɔ ˥$]$ sounds very similar to *Dharma* $[$ tat ˧ mo ⟍$]$. Similarly, the founder of Islam, Mohammed, is usually translated as 穆罕默德, but Zhao Rushi in *Zhufan Zhi* wrote it as 麻霞勿 (Ma Xia Wu).[107] When pronounced in Mandarin, the latter translation sounds very different from Mohammed, making it difficult to see the connection. But if a person from Guangdong were to pronounce 麻霞勿 $[$ ma ⌐ ha ⌐ mɐt √$]$, it would be a much more accurate phonetic match, possibly even closer than 穆罕默德.

In the past century, China had the most contact with the UK and the United States, so the linguistic exchange has been the greatest. Regarding English loanwords in Chinese, I briefly mentioned them earlier, but here I would like to give a few examples of words borrowed from Chinese into English. Since China's foreign trade

---

[106] Thomas Watters, *Chiness Language*, pp. 393 - 394.
[107] Friedrich Hirth and W. W. Rochhill, *Chau Ju-kua, His Work on the Chinese and Arab Trade in the 12th and 13th Centuries, entitled Chu-fan-Chih*, St. Petersberg, 1912, pp. 116 - 120.

largely revolved around silk, porcelain, and tea, let us first discuss these three items.

The current English word *silk* originally appeared in Middle English as *silk* or *selk*. It evolved from the Anglo-Saxon words *seole* or *seoloc* and is related to Old Norse *silki*, Swedish and Danish *silke*, Lithuanian *szilkai*, Russian *shelk'*, Latin *sericum*, *sericus*, Greek *sēres*, and *sērikos*. In English, words like *seres*, *seric*, *sericeous*, *serge*, and *sericulture* are all derived from it. [108] The modern Chinese pronunciation of 丝 (silk), $s\gamma$, and its Middle Chinese pronunciation $si\colon$, although not closely aligned with these Indo-European words, can be traced back to the ancient Chinese pronunciation $^*s\,i\partial g$, which shares several phonetic elements with them. Therefore, these words in Indo-European languages regarding "silk" were undoubtedly borrowed from the ancient Chinese $^*s\,i\partial g$. Historically, silk production was first invented in China and became one of the earliest aspects of Chinese material culture spread throughout the world. Our methods of sericulture and silk weaving reached Japan by the 3rd century. Initially, Japan sent several Koreans to China to learn the process, and when they returned, they brought four Chinese women who taught various weaving techniques to the imperial palace. Later, a temple was built in Settsu Province to honor these women.

---

[108] Refer to *The Oxford Dictionary*, IX, si, p. 46; Walter W. Skeat, *A Concise Etymological Dictionary of the English Language*, p. 485; *Webster's New International Dictionery of the English Language*, 2nd. Ed., pp. 2285b - 2337b.

According to legend, in the 5th century, a Chinese princess sewed silkworm eggs and mulberry seeds into her hat, and then passed to India through Hoten and the Pamir Mountains. By the time the Mediterranean people learned how to cultivate silkworms, it was already the 6th century. Emperor Justinian of Rome sent two Persian monks to China to learn the secrets of sericulture and weaving. Around 550 A.D., these two monks hid silkworm eggs in a bamboo stick and brought them to Constantinople, where "the silk industry of Western Europe for over 1,200 years originated from the treasure hidden in this bamboo tube."[109] This is why Europeans referred to China as *Sĕres* or *Sĕrres*, reflecting their perception of China as the land of silk. Westerners had difficulty understanding the fact that silkworms produce silk, which led to some interesting misconceptions. Some people believed that silk was a type of plant that grew on trees. In the 15th century, an Englishman wrote: "There is a people called Serres, and they have a tree that grows wool-like leaves." As a result, the English often referred to silk as "China wool" (Serres' wool). This idea dates back to ancient times; the Roman poet Virgil wrote:

How the Serres spin, their fleecy forests in a slender twine. ("The Chinese spin the wool from their forests into fine threads.")

As late as the 16th century, Lyly's writings still mentioned strange legends, claiming that silk shirts could cause the skin to bleed![110]

---

[109] *Encyclopadiadia Britanica*, vol. 20 (14th ed.), pp. 664 - 666.
[110] She Kunshan, *Chinese Characters in English*, in the 1st issue of *Wen Xun*, page 7.

Later, as maritime trade between China and Western Europe flourished, the variety of silk products exported from China gradually increased. Loanwords for Chinese silk products became popular in Britain, such as *Canton crape* (广东绉纱) or *China-crape* (中国绉纱), *pongee* (本机绸), *Chefoo silk* (芝罘绸), and *Shantung silk* (山东绸). Additionally, words like *pekin* referred to Beijing satin, and *nankeen* referred to Nanjing yellow cotton fabric, further expanding the use of loanwords from silk to cotton products.[111]

Another major cultural export from China, besides silk, is porcelain, and as a result, the name *China* became synonymous with porcelain. However, *Sĕrres* was used as the export product to represent the country, while *China* was used as the country name to represent the export product. The word China and its Latin form *Sinae*, Greek *Thinai*, and Sanskrit *Cina* all share the same origin. While some have suggested that the name might be the name used by Malay Archipelago navigators in the 4th century BC to refer to the coast of Guangdong,[112] I personally agree with the theory that it is a phonetic counterpart to "Qin" (秦).[113][114] When porcelain was first introduced

---

[111] Ibid., pages 6 - 7.

[112] Berthold Laufer, *The Name China*, T. P. s. II, XIII (1912), pp. 719 - 726.

[113] Paul Pelliot, *Deux Intinĕraires de Chine en Inde*, B. E. F. E. O. IV (1901), pp. 143 - 149, and also *T. P. s.* II, XIII (1912), 727 - 742 (as mentioned before).

[114] In Volume Five of the *Records of the Western Regions of the Great Tang Dynasty*, there is a conversation between King Harsha of the Kingdom of Kanyakubja and Xuanzang. The king said, "I have once heard that in the country of Mahacina there is the Son of Heaven of the Qin King... Is the Great Tang country this one?" Xuanzang replied, "Yes. 'Cina' was the title of the former king's country, and 'Great Tang' is the name of my sovereign's country. In the past, before ascending to the throne, he was called the Qin King. Now that the Qin King has succeeded to the throne, he is called the Son of Heaven...". "Cina" is the equivalent pronunciation of "China" (Qin).

to Europe, the English referred to it as *chinaware*, meaning "ware from China." Over time, the term *chinaware* evolved to mean "ware made of china" (porcelain), and eventually, the word was shortened to *china*. Now, the distinction between *China* (the country) and *china* (porcelain) in English is merely a matter of capitalization. However, in spoken English, *Chinaman* (Chinese person), *chinaman* (porcelain seller), and even *chinaman* (porcelain figurine) are all pronounced the same, with only the vowel in the second syllable differing due to stress, as [ə] or [æ].

Chinese porcelain was first introduced to Europe in the 16th century by the Portuguese. Unlike the English, who vaguely referred to it as "Chinaware," they specifically named it *porcellana* (later becoming *porcelain* in English), meaning "shell," as they compared the glossy, milky white texture to the delicate appearance of shell inlay.

It wasn't until the 18th century that the British ceramic industry began to develop, initially relying on a large import of Chinese porcelain. As ceramic production grew, many technical terms related to it entered the English language. At first, the British imported essential materials such as *kaoling* (kaolinite, a clay mineral, with the chemical composition $Al_2Si_2O_5(OH)_4$) and *petuntze* (little white bricks). *Kaoling* is derived from the translation of *Gao Ling* from the northwest of Jingde Town in Jiangxi province. This clay is also known as *china-clay*, *porcelain-clay*, or *china-metal*. *Petuntze* is another type of raw material but is less valuable than *kaoling*. The proper blend of these materials produced porcelain, with the best quality using equal parts of both, while more ordinary porcelain used three parts *kaoling* to six parts *petuntze*, and the coarsest porcelain required one part *kaoling* to three parts *petuntze*.[115] After the porcelain was made, the next step was to add color, leading to terms for porcelain glaze such as *china-glaze*, *china-paints*, *china-blue*, and *china-stone*. Initially, the British focused on imitating the designs found on Chinese porcelain, so motifs such as the *chilin or kylin* (麒麟), *fenghwang or phoenix* (凤凰), and *willow pattern* were copied. The willow pattern was introduced to Britain by Thomas Turner in 1780. This design was very popular, and Japanese merchants seized the opportunity to mass-produce similar patterns and sell them cheaply to the common people in Britain and the United States.[116]

The third major cultural export from China is tea. This beverage's contribution to world civilization is as significant as that of silk and porcelain. The tea-drinking culture began to flourish in China during the Tang Dynasty.[117] However, Zhang Hua's *Bo Wu Zhi (Encyclopedic Records and Tales)* already had the words "Drinking real tea makes people less sleepy." It can be seen that people were already aware of its invigorating and thirst-quenching properties in the Jin Dynasty. The foreign popularity of tea can be seen in a legend that further

---

[115] *Encylopadia Britanica,* vol. 5, p. 549, china-clay: *The Oxford Dictionary*, II, p. 351, and also V, p. 652.

[116] She Kunshan, *Chinese Characters in English*, in the 1st issue of *Wen Xun*, pages 7 - 9.

[117] In Feng Yan's *Records of What Feng Yan Saw and Heard*, it is recorded: "When Li Jiqing was sent to console the people in the south of the Yangtze River, drinking tea had just begun to prevail at that time. Lu Yu came to see him. After sitting down, Lu Yu personally brewed tea, named the different kinds of tea aloud, and made distinctions and explanations. Lord Li secretly despised him in his heart. After drinking tea, Li ordered his servant to take out thirty coins to pay the 'tea doctor.'" According to the record, Lu Yu lived in seclusion by the Tiao River in the early years of the Shangyuan period (760 A.D.), so drinking tea prevailed in the middle of the 8th century.

emphasizes its stimulating effect. It is said that the Indian monk Bodhidharma vowed to meditate with his eyes open for nine years. After three years, he found that his eyes kept closing, so he cut off his eyelids and continued his meditation. After six years, when he was exhausted and nearly falling asleep, he plucked a leaf from a tree beside him and put it in his mouth. Immediately, he felt rejuvenated and achieved his original goal of staying awake for nine years.[118]

The first tea traders in Europe were the Portuguese.[119] They came to China in the late 16th century to buy tea, using the Mandarin pronunciation "cha." Later, the Dutch took control of the tea trade in the Far East. These Dutch traders concentrated in the Southeast Asia region, so the people of Xiamen first shipped tea from China to Bantan[120] in Java, from where it was then transported to Europe on Dutch ships. In the Xiamen dialect, tea is called $[\text{te} \nearrow]$, and the Dutch also pronounced it as *téh*. As a result, Europeans who drank Dutch tea, such as the French, Germans, and Danes, adopted the Xiamen pronunciation (e.g., French *thé*, German *Tee* or *Thee*, and the earlier European pronunciation *tā*). Meanwhile, countries like Russia, Poland, and Italy, which drank mainland tea, retained the official

---

[118] *Encyclopadia Britanica*, vol. 21 (14th ed.), p. 857.

[119] Regarding the earliest record of tea, in 852, the Arabic word "sēkh" was seen in *Relation des Voyages faits par les Arabes et les persons daps l'Indie et à la Chine dans le IX e Siècle de l'ere Chritienne*. In Reinaud's translation, Volume I, page 40, it was also written as "Chai Catai". See *Ramusio Dichiaratione*, in Volume II, page 15. Refer to Hobson-Jobson, new edition, pp. 905 - 908.

[120] Bantan, which is now written in Latin letters as Bantam, was the former territory of the Sultan of Java and was the most important trading port with Europe from the 16th to the 18th century. It is now in ruins.

pronunciation (e.g., Italian *cia*, Russian чай[tʃˈaːi], Portuguese *o chá*). The English initially used the official pronunciation (e.g. Thomas Blount's 1674 work spells it as *cha*), but later, due to their quantity purchase of Dutch tea, they dropped *cha* and switched to *tea*. The earliest appearance of *tea* in English was in a 1615 letter by Wickham, an employee of the East India Company, and Samuel Pepys spelled it *tee* in his diary entry of September 28, 1600.[121] At first, the English regarded tea as an extremely precious beverage, but over time it became a common necessity for ordinary people. The English no longer relied solely on Dutch tea merchants and began to travel to China themselves to procure local specialties. The growing variety of tea types led to the following four lines of poetry:

> *What tongue can tell the various kinds of tea?*
> *Of Black and Greens, of Hyson and Bohea;*
> *With Singlo, Congou, Pekoe and Souchong,*
> *Cowslip the fragrant, Gunpowder the strong.*

Bohea refers to the "Wuyi" tea from Fujian, *Pekoe* is "Baihao," *Congou* refers to "kung fu tea," *Hyson* is "Xichun," *Cowslip* is "Niushe," and *Gunpowder* is similar to what we call "Gaomo'er." In addition to these, other types such as *Twankay* ("Tunxi"), *Keemun* ("Qimen"), *Oolong* ("Wulong"), *Young Hyson* or *Yüchien* ("Yuqian") were also introduced into English. Beyond these, there were terms like

---

[121] W. W. Skeat, *A Concise Etymological Dictionary of the English Language*, p. 545, Encyclo padia Britanica, vol. 22 (14th ed.), p. 857.

brick-tea, *tile-tea*, and *tisty-tosty*, which refer to differences in texture and shape.

Some English people believed that drinking tea made one weak, so they referred to habitual tea drinkers as *tea-spillers* or *tea-sots*. The word "tea" also gave rise to an idiom: "to take tea with," meaning to argue with someone, especially one with a hostile or adversarial tone. This may have originated from the Shanghai practice of "settling a dispute over a cup of tea in a teahouse." As tea culture became popular in Britain, many new terms and items were introduced into daily life, such as *tea cloth, teapot, teacup, teakettle, tea urn, teaspoon, teatable, teatray, teaset, tea rose, tea biscuit, tea gown, tea party* or *tea fight*, and *tea service*, all of which arose after tea culture spread to Britain. The term and the practice of *tea party* we have used in China recently are just like calling beef juice "*beef tea*." They are examples of how Chinese words, after traveling abroad, returned to China with a bit of foreign influence.[122]

In addition to tea, we have many other plants and products that were introduced to the UK and the US. Among flowers and plants, there are terms like *china-aster, china-rose, china-berry, china-pink* (carnation), and others. For fruits, there are *china-orange*, also called *mandarin orange, loquat, litchi, kumquat,* and *whampee*. For vegetables, there are *pakchoi, petsai* or *Chinese cabbage, china-squash* (pumpkin), *china-pea, china-bean* (cowpea), and others. In the realm of medicinal herbs, we have *ginseng, galingale* (a type of

---

[122] She Kunshan, *Chinese Characters in English*, in the 1st issue of *Wen Xun*, pages 9 - 12.

ginger),[123] *chinaroot* (a medicinal root), and more. Furthermore, there is *china-grass* or *china-straw* (ramie), which is said to be the strongest fiber in nature, as well as *tung oil* or *wood-oil* (from the tung tree), which became a major export during the Anti-Japanese War and was almost the sole product China used to earn foreign currency.

Next, let's consider some terms related to commerce and maritime life. When Westerners began trading with China, they first had to understand Chinese units of measurement and currency. Some terms, such as "sycee" (a type of gold or silver ingot), "liang" (weight unit), and "li" (distance unit), were directly borrowed into English using "sound substitution." "Sycee" originally referred to the patterns on silver but later became synonymous with "yuanbao" (gold or silver ingot). However, because trade between China and Britain began moving from Southeast Asia to the Chinese mainland, some British merchants, too lazy to translate, simply used familiar Malay terms,

---

[123] Gaoliang ginger is now called Liangjiang in Guangdong. In the Han Dynasty, there was Gaokang County, and in the Three Kingdoms period, it was named Gaoliang Prefecture. It is now Gaozhou in Guangdong. The westward spread route of this word in the Middle Ages is generally believed to be Chinese (Cantonese) - Persian - Arabic - French - English. It has a very long history in England. *The Oxford Dictionary* states that "galingale" probably comes from the Chinese "koliang kiang", which means "mild ginger from ko", a prefecture in the province of Canton. Besides being used as medicine, this kind of ginger is mainly used as a spice in cooking. All cooks in medieval Europe had to know how to use this indispensable flavoring ginger. The English poet Geoffrey Chaucer (1340 - 1440) once described in his *Canterbury Tales* that his cook had the special skill to make chicken stewed with ginger, saying:
"A cook they hadde with hem for the nones,
To boille the chiknes with the marybones,
And poudre-marchant tart, and galingale."
However, as early as 350 years before Chaucer, the word "Galingale" had already been found in the English language. It is also written as "galangal." Refer to Rev. G. A. Stuart, *Chinese Materia Medica*, pp. 31 - 33. According to Professor Ma Jian, the Arabs translated Gaoliang ginger as "khulin jān", which became "galingal" when it spread to Germany and then changed to "galingale" after spreading to England.

such as *teal* (silver taels), *catty* (weight unit, about 600 grams), and *picul* (weight unit for bulk goods), which all come from this practice. Regarding maritime life, there are words like *typhoon* (a direct transliteration of "da feng (大风)," meaning "great wind"), which we've already discussed. In addition, words like *sampan* (a small boat) and *tanka* (Chinese boat-dwelling people) provide a snapshot of the lives of floating communities. Since Shanghai became an international trading hub after it opened as a treaty port in the 22nd year of Daoguang (1842), the term *Shanghai* in English has accumulated various meanings. It refers not only to a breed of chicken (said to lay double-yolked eggs), a type of oil (possibly tung oil), and a kind of gun, but also to an act of kidnapping. When a ship was short of sailors, it often goes ashore to find a person, gets him drunk with medicinal liquor, and makes him do hard work on the ship. This active form was called "to shanghai," and the victim was called "to be shanghaied." Another specialty of Sino-Western communication in Shanghai is Pidgin English. This language is called *pidgin* or *pigeon English* by the British and Americans. It is believed that *pidgin* is a corrupted version of the word "business," which Chinese speakers couldn't pronounce correctly, leading to *pidgin*. Others say it was influenced by the Portuguese word *occupacção* (with the first two syllables lost), and this word is also spelled as "pigeon". *Pidgin English*[124] is indeed the crystallization of the mixture of Chinese and

---

[124] "Some people... pidgin English". In the 1950 edition, it was written as "Because the Chinese people couldn't pronounce 'business' correctly, it was wrongly pronounced as 'pingin', and then through repeated mispronunciations, it became 'pigeon'! 'Pigeon English.'"

English. It naturally emerged when a Chinese who didn't know English and an Englishman who didn't know Chinese wanted to exchange ideas. It uses Chinese grammar and a limited number of misread English words to form a makeshift language tool. When used, both sides supplement it with gestures and various facial expressions, adapting to the situation. One example of a word created in this way is *cumshaw*, which some believe to be a Cantonese translation of "thank you," but it's more likely a mispronunciation of *commission*. The term *cumshaw* means not only "gift" or "small account," but it also carries the meaning of "commission."[125]

Additionally, many terms from China's modern history or official system have entered English. These include *Taiping* (Taiping Heavenly Kingdom), *Boxer* (Boxer Rebellion), *Kuomintang* (Nationalist Party), *yamen* (government office), *tupan* (provincial governor), *tuchun* (military governor),[126] *tsungli* (prime minister), *tipao* (local police), and others. Those named after the playthings exported from our country include *tangram* (a seven-piece puzzle), *fire-cracker*, *gold-fish*, *Chinese-tumbler* (a balancing toy), *Chinese-lantern* (paper lantern), and so on. Even gambling games, symbols of "native culture," such as *fan-tan* (a betting game) and *mahjong*, have become familiar terms in Anglo-American social circles. The term *chopsuey* was initially just an ordinary dish of "mixed stir-fry," and etymologically, it is just the transliteration of "za sui (miscellaneous chopped-up bits)." But now it has become the general name for

---

[125] She Kunshan, *Chinese Characters in English*, in the 1st issue of *Wen Xun*, pages 12 - 14.
[126] There are also two words, "tuchunate" and "tuchunism", derived from this word.

66

Chinese cuisine. In fact, large restaurants in New York, such as Yangcheng (Canton), Ding Hao, and Shanghai Restaurant, also use "chopsuey house" as their signage. A major obstacle for foreigners eating Chinese food was the use of chopsticks. Initially, they were translated as "nimble sticks," but now the term *chopsticks* has become the most common term. One example of a term from Chinese popular culture entering English is *feng-shui* (风水, the traditional Chinese practice of arranging environments). The word *joss*, originally borrowed from the Portuguese word *Deos* (god) in Pidgin English, came to specifically refer to the idols of gods in China. Therefore, the term *Joss-house* refers to a Chinese temple, and *Joss-stick* refers to incense sticks used in worship.[127]

China is famously known as the "Land of Etiquette," and our traditional customs and rituals have left a deep impression on Westerners. Sometimes, they feel that we are overly rigid with formalities. The French humorously referred to all these elaborate rituals as *Chinoiserie*. This term quickly caught the attention of the British, who borrowed it and transformed it into *chinesery*.[128] Furthermore, sometimes, in order to maintain face or avoid embarrassing someone, we may refrain from expressing disagreement at the moment. The British have a term for this type of hypocrisy, calling it the *Chinese compliment*. Speaking of "saving face," it is

---

[127] She Kunshan, *Chinese Characters in English*, in the 1st issue of *Wen Xun*, pages 14 - 16.
[128] *Concise Oxford French Dictionary*, p. 163, a; *The Oxford Dictionary*, II, p. 354; *Webster's Dictionary*, pp. 468 - 469. Xiang Da said: "The word 'Chinoiserie' began in the 18th century, and at that time its meaning referred to a Chinese fashion. There is a special chapter discussing it in Reichwan's 'China and Europe'."

perhaps one of our most notable contributions to the English language. There is an idiom in English: to *save one's face*. According to the *Oxford Dictionary*, the origin of this phrase is:

Originally used by the English community in China, with reference to the continual devices among the Chinese to avoid incurring or inflicting disgrace. The exact phrase does not appear to occur in Chinese, but "to lose face" and "for the sake of his face" are common.

However, *Webster's Dictionary* recognizes *to lose face* as a widely used phrase in America.[129]

In old etiquette, one practice that foreigners found especially difficult to adjust to was the kowtow. In the *Oxford Dictionary*, the word *kowtow* is humorously described as:

The Chinese were determined they should be kept in the constant practice of the koo-too, or ceremony of genuflection and prostration.[130]

In reality, Chinese people do not frequently kneel and kowtow! The poet Guo Jiasheng (courtesy name Qinshi) from Wuqing wrote a poem about the kowtow bug: "In a shape as tiny as a bean, it never rests. Before shedding its black shell, it already seems full of shame. All living beings should be upright and unyielding. Why does this little bug only keep kowtowing? As long as it can be pardoned and set free for the moment, who knows what judgments it harbors secretly? If it could recognize the approaching disaster, once enraged, it really

---

[129] *The Oxford Dictionary*, IX, p. 137; *Webster's Dictionary*, p, 1460, C.
[130] *The Oxford Dictionary*, V, p. 753.

should rise up against it like a sworn enemy."[131] This poem may reflect the aspirations of some Chinese who believe that all living beings should be upright and unyielding. There is also a famous historical anecdote related to the kowtow during the Qing Dynasty. In the 21st year of Jiaqing (1816), Lord Amherst, a British envoy, visited China. He refused to perform the kowtow during his audience with the Qing Emperor, and as a result, the Qing court ordered him to return to Britain, with the words, "From now on, there is no need to send envoys from afar, only to endure the toilsome journey." This dispute over "kowtowing" is evidenced by the imperial edict sent by Emperor Jiaqing of the Qing Dynasty to the King of Britain regarding Lord Amherst's visit to China:

"...When your envoy first arrived in Tianjin, I ordered officials to host a banquet. But when the envoy thanked us, he did not follow the proper ceremonial rites. I considered that a foreign envoy might not be familiar with the proper rituals, and thus I showed leniency. So I specifically ordered my ministers to inform your envoys, when they were about to arrive in the capital, that when the envoys came to pay their respects in the fifty-eighth year of the Qianlong reign, they all kowtowed according to the etiquette. How could there be any changes this time? Your envoys told our ministers in person that they would follow the etiquette and perform the kowtow when the time came and would not violate the protocol. Our ministers reported this to me accordingly. Then I issued an edict, arranging for your envoys to have

---

[131] *Poetry Collection of the Wintergreen House*, Volume Three, Chapter Seven.

an audience on the seventh day of the seventh month. On the eighth day, a banquet was held and rewards were bestowed in the Hall of Rectitude and Brightness, and then food was offered in the Garden of Shared Delights. On the ninth day, they were to take their leave, and on that same day, they were allowed to visit Longevity Hill. On the eleventh day, rewards were distributed at the Gate of Supreme Harmony, and then they went to the Ministry of Rites to attend a banquet. On the twelfth day, they were sent off on their journey home: The dates and specific etiquette for performing the ceremonies had all been informed to your envoys in detail by our ministers. On the day of the audience on the seventh day of the seventh month, your envoys had already arrived at the palace gate. As I was about to ascend to the throne hall, your chief envoy suddenly claimed to be seriously ill and unable to move. Thinking that the chief envoy could fall suddenly ill, I only allowed the deputy envoys to enter for the audience. However, the two deputy envoys also claimed to be ill at the same time. There could be no rudeness greater than this! I did not reprimand them severely and ordered them to return to their country on that very day...."[132]

According to legend, there were also some under-the-table dealings by Chinese officials involved. Anyway, this is an interesting anecdote about "kowtow" in the history of Chinese diplomacy. There's also the word *chin-chin*, which originally came from the Chinese

[132] *The Veritable Records of Emperor Renzong of the Qing Dynasty*, Volume 320, Chapter Five, Wang Xianqian's *Donghua Record*, Jiaqing 42, Chapter One; Harley Farnsworth MacNair, *Modern Chinese History selected Readings*, Shanghai, 1923, pp. 11 - 13.

phrase "qing qing(请请, please, please)." According to the *Oxford Dictionary*, *chin-chin* is defined as "a phrase of salutation," and in the example it cites:

We soon fixed them in their seats, both parties repeating chin chin chin, chin, the Chinese term of salutation. [1795 Symes, Embassy to Ava 295(Y.)]

Here, "chin chin (qing qing)" clearly means *please take a seat*, not a greeting. However, over time, it evolved into a form of respect or a greeting.

On the thirty-sixth day from Charing-cross, a traveler can be making his chin-chin to a Chinese mandarin. (1885 Paul Mall G. 15 Apr.4/1)

It later even became a verb, meaning "to salute or greet":

She "*chin-chins*" the captain and then nods her pretty head. (1959 All Y . Round No . 1, 18 .).[133] The word *chin-chin* clearly strays far from its original meaning in the process of misinterpretation.

The examples mentioned above of Chinese words borrowed into English and vice versa are just the beginnings of the study on Chinese loanwords. I hope that future researchers will find inspiration from these examples and delve deeper into this topic. Finally, I'd like to quote Palmer's words to conclude this chapter:

---

[133] *The Oxford Dictionary*, II p, 352, Hobson -Jobson, pp, 200 - 201.

From the analysis of loanwords, one can observe cultural contact and ethnic relations, much as archaeologists use the distribution of pottery, decorative wares, and weapons to draw conclusions.[134]

We should recognize the importance of loanwords in linguistic studies, but we must also avoid the error of far-fetched interpretations. The correct conclusions can only be reached through profound knowledge, meticulous methods, and prudent attitudes.

---

[134] L. R. Palmer, *Modern Linguistics*, p. 159.

Chapter 5 Geographic Names as Markers of Ethnic Migrations

"Geographic name research is indeed one of the most fascinating pursuits for linguists, as these names often provide important evidence that can supplement and confirm the accounts of historians and archaeologists."[135]

In the western part of the UK, many geographic names contain elements from the Celtic language. For instance, names like *Pendle Hill, Penhill, Penkridge*, and *Pentrich* feature the Welsh term *pen*, meaning "head." These geographic names are mostly found in Dorsetshire, Wiltshire, Worcestershire, Staffordshire, Derbyshire, and Lancashire. This distribution suggests, "At least in western Britain, there were significant remnants of populations that spoke Celtic. Now, let's take a remarkable example. In the northeastern corner of Dorsetshire, within the Cranborne Chase forest, adjacent to a feature called *Grimm's Ditch*, there is a cluster of Celtic geographic names. This entire area is surrounded by the remains of ancient British settlements." This conclusion was reached by Zachrisson in his recent study, *Romans, Celts, and Saxons in Ancient Britain*.[136]

---

[135] L. R. Palmer, *Modern Linguistics*, p. 168.
[136] L. R. Palmer, *Modern Linguistics*, p. 169.

Another example is the word *Avon*, a Celtic term meaning "river." "In Manx[137], it is written as *Aon*, in Gaelic[138] as *Abhainn* (pronounced *avain*). We can also find its ancient readings such as *amhaim* or *auwon*. This term became the proper name for many rivers in England, Scotland, France, and Italy. For instance, the *Stratford Avon* flows through Warwickshire and Worcestershire. The *Bristol Avon* divides Gloucester and Somerset. In Gloucestershire, there is also a smaller *Avon* near Berkeley Castle. The *Hampshire Avon* flows from Salisbury to Christchurch, with another branch reaching the sea at Lymington. Similarly, in Devon, Monmouth, Glamorgan, Lanark, Stirling, Banff, Kincardine, Dumfries, and Rose, there are several rivers called Avon or Evan."[139] Collectively, this trail of Celtic geographic names stretches from Bohemia across Europe to Britain, encompassing cities like Vienna, Paris, and London.[140]

The Scandinavian colonization of England can also be illuminated through the study of geographic names. For instance, the term *Ingleby* (meaning "village" or "farm" in English) reveals the intensified Scandinavian settlements in Yorkshire. As Mawer noted, "Unless the Scandinavian population once held a dominant presence

---

[137] Manx, which is now often referred to as Manx or Manx Gaelic, is spoken by the residents on the Isle of Man in the Irish Sea. They have relatively few contacts with the outside world and retain many primitive features. It belongs to the Goidelic branch of the Celtic language family.
[138] Gaelic, translated as "盖尔语" in Chinese nowadays, is spoken by the residents in the northwest of Scotland and belongs to the Celtic language family.
[139] Isac Taylor, *Words and Places*, p. 153.
[140] Leonard Bloomfield, *Language*, p. 464.

in these areas, with only occasional remnants of the original inhabitants, such a term would have no meaning."[141]

Most of the remnants of loanwords from the culture of the conquered ethnic groups in the language of the conquerors are geographic names. In the United States, the cultural remnants of Indians have gradually diminished, but many geographic names derive from indigenous terms. Examples include *Massachusetts, Wisconsin, Michigan, Illinois, Chicago, Milwaukee, Oshkosh, Sheboygan, Waukegan,* and *Muskegon,* among others.[142]

From the geographical evolution of China, many geographic names also reveal traces of ancient ethnic migrations and interactions. For instance, in the *Book of Han: Treatise on Geography,* under Zhangye prefecture, there is a record of Liqian (骊靬) County, which was located south of present-day Yongchang County in Gansu. In Qianzhan's *New Commentary on the Treatises on Geography,* Volume 12, the entry on "Liqian (骊靬) County" states: "*Shuowen Jiezi* refers to it as Liqian (骊靬), *Biography of Zhang Qian* calls it Maoxuan (氂轩), and *Records of the Western Regions* refers to it as Liqian (犁靬). The county was established for the Liqian (骊靬) people who surrendered." The *Records of the Grand Historian: Biography of Dayuan* refers to the place as Lixuan (黎轩), while the *Book of Later Han: Records of the Western Regions* calls it Lijian (犁鞬), indicating

[141] L. R. Palmer, *Modern Linguistics,* p. 170.
[142] L. Bloomfield, *Language,* p. 464. See also Aifred Louis, *California Place Names of Indian Origin* (1916 Berkeley, University of California Press).

the same location. Regarding the name Liqian (骊轩), F. Hirth suggested it corresponds to Rekem.[143] Shiratori Kurakichi proposed it to be a transliteration of (A)lek(s)an(dria).[144] Other interpretations also exist.[145] Kuwabara Jitsuzō remarked, "Although the explanation of the name Liqian is not yet settled, there is no academic disagreement today that refers to a geographic name within the Roman Empire or one of its territories."[146][147] Additionally, in the *Book of Han: Treatise on Geography*, there is mention of Kucha County. Yan Shigu annotates: "This county was established for the people of the Kingdom of Kucha who surrendered and settled here, hence the name." The *New Commentary on the Geographical Records*, Volume 13, identifies this county as present-day Mizhi County in Shaanxi. Ancient Kucha (Kuči) was located in what is now Kuqa (Kuča) County in Xinjiang. The existence of Kucha County in Mizhi during the Han Dynasty indicates that some Kucha people had already

---

[143] Hirth, *China and the Roman Orient*, p. 171.

[144] *Research on the Great Qin State and the Zhilin State* carried in the April issue of *Historical Journal* in the 37th year of the Meiji period, pages 25 - 26; and also translated by Wang Gulu, in the 1st volume of *Translation Collection of Papers on the History and Geography beyond the Great Wall*, pages 16 - 18.

[145] See Hirth, *China and the Roman*, p. 170.

[146] Kuwabara Jitsuzo's *On the Western Region People Who Came and Went to China during the Sui and Tang Dynasties*, published in Dr. Naito's *Anthology of Sinology in Celebration of His 60th Birthday*. This article was translated by He Jianmin and titled *Research on the Sinicization of the Western Region People during the Sui and Tang Dynasties*, published by Zhonghua Book Company.

[147] Regarding "Liqian", according to *Western Region Place Names* originally compiled by Feng Chengjun and revised by Lu Junling (published by Zhonghua Book Company in 1980), there are two places recorded in Chinese historical records under the name of Alexandria. One is the country of Alexan dria Prophthasia in the *Book of Han* and the country of Wuyi in the *Book of Wei*, which is now Herat in Afghanistan. The other one is "Liqian" in the *Book of Han* and *Weilue*, "Lijian" in the *Book of Later Han* and *Book of Jin*, and "Lixuan" in the *Records of the Grand Historian, Book of Wei* and *History of the Northern Dynasties*. This name may generally refer to the places colonized by the Greeks or Romans.

migrated to Shaanxi by that time.[148][149] Similarly, in the *Book of Han: Records of the Western Regions*, under the entry for "Wensu Kingdom," Yan Shigu annotates: "North of Liquan County in Yongzhou (Shaanxi province), there is a mountain named Wensu Ridge, so named because people from the Kingdom of Wensu were settled there during the Han Dynasty for farming and herding." The ancient Wensu Kingdom was located in present-day Aksu County in Xinjiang, and the name Wensu Ridge reflects this migration.[150]

At the end of the Western Jin Dynasty, during the turmoil of the Five Barbarians' invasion, the Central Plains fell into chaos. Emperor Yuan of Jin fled south and established his court in Jiankang. Many people from the Central Plains, unable to endure the ravages of foreign rule, migrated to the south. Initially, they regarded their move as temporary, with the intention of returning to their homeland. However, after over two centuries without recovering the Central Plains, their aspirations to return faded, and their descendants fully integrated as southerners. This migration was a pivotal event in the history of the Chinese people. However, because it was a spontaneous mass movement unrelated to government mandates, official historical

---

[148] Kuwabara Jitsuzo's *On the Western Region People Who Came and Went to China during the Sui and Tang Dynasties*, published in Dr. Naito's *Anthology of Sinology in Celebration of His 60th Birthday*. This article was translated by He Jianmin and titled *Research on the Sinicization of the Western Region People during the Sui and Tang Dynasties*, published by Zhonghua Book Company.

[149] The county of Kucha in the Han Dynasty, as verified by the historical geographer Tan Qixiang, was located outside the Great Wall north of Yulin City in today's Shaanxi Province.

[150] Kuwabara Jitsuzo's *On the Western Region People Who Came and Went to China during the Sui and Tang Dynasties*, published in Dr. Naito's *Anthology of Sinology in Celebration of His 60th Birthday*. This article was translated by He Jianmin and titled *Research on the Sinicization of the Western Region People during the Sui and Tang Dynasties*, published by Zhonghua Book Company.

records provide little detail. Although later historians are aware of this migration, they often lack clarity on its specifics. If we intend to understand the migration through existing historical records, the only way is to trace the clues from the states, prefectures, and counties established for the sojourners at that time.

At the time, for the common people who migrated to the south, there was a system of establishing states, prefectures, and counties based on their old native places. (For example, during the early Jin Dynasty, Lanling prefecture and Dongguan prefecture [151] were originally located in present-day Shandong. However, when the inhabitants of these regions migrated to what is now Wujin County in Jiangsu, sojourning prefectures named South Lanling and South Dongguan were established in the area. This arrangement was referred to as "sojourning prefectures." Similarly, sojourning states and counties followed this pattern, as will be further discussed below.) The original intention behind these arrangements was to encourage displaced populations to remember their homeland and aspire to return north. However, by examining the names and locations of these geographic names of the sojourning administrative regions, we can trace the patterns of this ethnic migration. Records of such sojourning states, prefectures, and counties are detailed in Shen Yue's *Book of*

---

[151] Dongguan mentioned here refers to the Dongguan Prefecture established by dividing the Langya Prefecture and Qi Prefecture in the late Eastern Han Dynasty. It was relocated to the south of the Yangtze River during the Eastern Jin Dynasty as an administrative region for refugees. This relocated prefecture was abolished during the Qi Dynasty of the Southern Dynasties. In the Tang Dynasty, Bao'an County located west of today's Shenzhen was renamed Dongguan County. In the Song Dynasty, it was moved to the north of today's Shenzhen, which is today's Dongguan City in Guangdong Province.

Song: Records of States and Prefectures, Xiao Zixian's *Book of Southern Qi: Records of States and Prefectures*, and the *Book of Jin: Geographical Records* compiled by people in the Tang Dynasty. By systematically compiling these records, analyzing their locations, and dating their establishment, the traces of this migration can be largely reconstructed. Tan Qixiang's article, *The Ethnic Migration Following the Yongjia Rebellion in the Jin Dynasty*[152], adopts this approach. Using modern administrative divisions, he classified the sojourning states, prefectures, and counties recorded in the *Book of Song: Records of States and Prefectures* for nine provinces: Jiangsu, Anhui, Hubei, Jiangxi, Hunan, Sichuan, Henan, Shaanxi, and Shandong. He compiled detailed tables listing the original locations ("native sites") and the sojourning locations ("migrant sites") of these divisions and noted differences across the Eastern Jin, early Song, and Southern Qi dynasties. According to his findings:

Jiangsu Province: The province received more migrants than any other, due to the imperial capital being located within its boundaries. The *Book of Song* lists 23 sojourning prefectures and 75 sojourning counties in the province. Among these, the majority of migrants came from northern provinces, with Shandong contributing the largest share (15 prefectures and 39 counties), followed by Hebei (1 prefecture and 5 counties), Henan (1 prefecture and 2 counties), Shanxi (3 counties), and Shaanxi (1 prefecture and 1 county). Gansu contributed none. Migrants from Jiangsu and Anhui's Huainan (the

---

[152] The 15th issue of *Yanjing Xuebao* (1934), pages 51 - 76.

area south of Huai River) region also relocated to Jiangnan (south of the Yangtze River) and Jiangbei (north of the Yangtze River). For Jiangsu itself, there were 3 prefectures and 21 counties, while Anhui had 3 prefectures and 3 counties. Migrants concentrated in areas like Jiangning (now known as Nanjing), Zhenjiang, and Wujin in Jiangnan, and in Jiangdu and Huaiyin in Jiangbei.

Anhui Province: Migrants from northern provinces to Anhui mainly came from Henan (8 prefectures and 54 counties), followed by Hebei (1 prefecture and 6 counties), with fewer from Shandong and Shanxi (3 counties each). No migrants came from Shaanxi or Gansu. Moreover, people from both the north and south of the Huai River within Anhui Province itself and Jiangsu Province also mostly migrated to areas north and south of the Yangtze River. Anhui established 4 prefectures and 13 counties, while Jiangsu established 1 prefecture and 6 counties. The number of migrants received in the area north of the Yangtze River was greater than that in the area south of the Yangtze River, which was the opposite of the situation in Jiangsu Province. Those who settled as refugees in the area south of the Yangtze River were all gathered in a corner near Wuhu in the lower reaches, while those in the area north of the Yangtze River were scattered between the Yangtze River and the Huai River. From Chuzhou and Hezhou all the way to Yingzhou and Bozhou[153],

---

[153] Chu refers to Chuzhou, which was established by changing Nanqiao Prefecture in the Sui Dynasty, and its administrative seat was located in today's Chuzhou City in Anhui Province. He refers to Hezhou, with its administrative seat in today's He County in Anhui Province. Ying refers to Yingzhou, with its administrative seat in today's Fuyang City in Anhui Province. Bo refers to Bozhou, with its administrative seat in today's Bozhou County in Anhui Province.

sojourning prefectures and counties were established everywhere...
Nowadays, there are Dangtu and Fanchang counties in the area south
of the Yangtze River, and both of their names were derived from the
sojourning counties established during the Eastern Jin Dynasty.
According to records, Dangtu originally belonged to Huainan
Prefecture in the Western Jin Dynasty and is now the land of Huaiyuan
County; Fanchang originally belonged to Xiangcheng Prefecture and
is now the land of Linying County in Henan Province. Just from the
names, one can still imagine how the people from Henan and the area
south of Huai River migrated to the area south of the Yangtze River at
that time.

Hubei Province: Hubei Province can be divided into three
regions for discussion: The upper reaches of the Yangtze River region
(around Jiangling and Songzi): Migrants mainly came from Shanxi,
Shaanxi, and Henan, as well as people from the Huai River region in
Jiangsu and Anhui. The lower reaches of the Yangtze River region
(around Wuchang and Huangmei): Migrants mostly came from Henan,
along with people from the north of the Huai River in Anhui. The Han
River basin (from Yunxi and Zhuxi to Yicheng and Zhongxiang,
centered around Xiangyang): The number of migrants received in this
region is twice that of the other two regions in the province. The
largest number of migrants come from Shaanxi, followed by Henan,
Gansu, Hebei, Shanxi, Anhui, and Sichuan... Nowadays, there is
Songzi County within the province, and its name also originated from

---

Generally speaking, these refer to the areas north of the Yangtze River in today's Anhui
Province.

the sojourning county established during the Eastern Jin Dynasty. According to records, Songzi originally belonged to Anfeng Prefecture in the Western Jin Dynasty[154] and is now the land of Huoqiu County in Anhui Province.

Jiangxi and Hunan Provinces: These two provinces, south of Anhui and Hubei, were far from the Central Plains, and thus received fewer migrants, mostly concentrated in their northern areas.

Sichuan Province: Sichuan hosted over ten sojourning prefectures and several dozen sojourning counties. However, the situation is quite simple: Most migrants came from Shaanxi, Gansu, and northern Sichuan itself, with very few from Henan. Except for Pengshan, all sojourning divisions were located northeast of Chengdu, along the corridor connecting Sichuan and Shaanxi. Pengshan was also close to Chengdu.

Henan Province: Most of Henan Province belongs to the Yellow River basin, while its southern regions (Nanyang, Guangzhou[155], and Xinyang) lay in the Huai River and Han River basins. The Liu Song and Xiao Qi dynasties both occupied the Huai River and Han River basins, so they also established sojourning prefectures and counties there to settle the refugees from the northern regions. Most of these

---

[154] Anfeng was an ancient county name, located at the junction of the southeastern part of Henan Province and Anhui Province. In the Western Han Dynasty, its administrative seat was between today's Gushi County in Henan Province and today's Huoqiu County in Anhui Province. During the Liang Dynasty of the Southern Dynasties, its administrative seat was moved eastward to the north of Anfeng Pond in today's Shou County in Anhui Province and was abolished in the Ming Dynasty. There is Anfengtang Town beside Anfeng Pond in today's Shou County.

[155] Guangzhou was located in the southeastern part of Henan Province, and its administrative seat was in today's Guangshan County in Henan Province.

refugees came from the northern part of Henan Province itself, and among the areas of Wan, Deng, Dan, and Bi[156], some came from Shaanxi, Gansu, and the southern part of Hebei Province.

Shaanxi Province: To the south of Zhongnan Mountain in Shaanxi Province lies the Han River Basin, known as Hanzhong. It was occupied by the Eastern Jin Dynasty, the Song Dynasty, and the Qi Dynasty. Migrants to this area mainly came from Gansu, Sichuan, and northern Shaanxi.

Shandong Province: Although Shandong was entirely part of northern China, it also hosted sojourning divisions, as the Liu Song Dynasty controlled much of the province southeast of the Yellow River. If we divide the province's territory into three regions, the eastern Denglai Peninsula[157] had nothing to do with inflow and outflow. The area northwest of the Yellow River was an outflow area, and the middle section was an inflow area. Migrants to Shandong primarily came from Hebei, with some from northern Henan and Shanxi.

This article can be regarded as a systematic and concrete example of "tracing ethnic migrations through geographic names." Due to

---

[156] Wan, Deng, Dan, and Bi refer to Nanyang City, Xichuan County, Dengzhou City, and Biyang County in the southwestern part of Henan Province and also cover some areas in the northwestern part of Hubei Province. Wan is today's Nanyang City; Deng County was located north of today's Xiangfan City; Danshui was located west of today's Xichuan County and got its name because it was adjacent to the Danshui River; Bi refers to Biyang, which is located in today's Biyang County. Bi is also the name of a river, originating from the northwest of Biyang County in Henan Province, flowing through the southeast of Sheqi County and joining the Tang River.

[157] The Denglai Peninsula. Deng refers to Dengzhou, which is today's Penglai City; Lai refers to Laizhou, with its former administrative seat in Yexian County and renamed Laizhou City in 1988. The Denglai Peninsula is the Shandong Peninsula.

space limitations, this chapter cannot reproduce the tables or list all the geographic names in detail; readers interested in further research can refer to the original text.

Regarding the routes of southward migration taken by the people of the Central Plains, Mr. Tan suggests: "The Han River served as a thoroughfare for people from Shaanxi and Gansu moving southeast. Thus, Nanzheng and Xiangyang became major hubs for the Han River region and gathering points for migrants from Shaanxi and Gansu. The Jinniu Road, also known as the Southern Stilted Road, [158] was a southwest passage for Shaanxi and Gansu migrants, which explains why the sojourning prefectures and counties within Sichuan were located near this route. At the time, the Han Gou[159] had been dug, connecting the Yangtze and Huai Rivers. As a result, Jiangdu at the southern end of Han Gou and its opposite banks, Zhenjiang and Wujin, became hubs for migrants from Shandong and northern Jiangsu. The tributaries of the Huai River mostly flowed southeast, so Henan migrants generally moved southeast into Anhui, rather than directly south into Hubei."

The timeline of migration can be roughly divided into four periods:

---

[158] The Jinniu Road was an ancient road name. It extended from today's Mian County in Shaanxi Province to the southwest, entered Sichuan Province, passed through Chaotian Post and reached Jianmen Pass. It was an important road connecting Hanzhong and Bashu in ancient times. Compared with the North Plank Road from today's Feng County in Shaanxi Province passing through Liuba to Baocheng, it was also called the South Plank Road.

[159] The Han Gou was an ancient canal name. It diverted the water from the south of today's Yangzhou City, passed through the west of today's Gaoyou City to the north, then turned northeast, passed through the Sheyang Lake and flowed into the Huai River. It was not exactly the same as the present canal.

1. "Roughly during the early chaos of the Yongjia era (307–313 A.D.), refugees from Hebei, Shandong, Shanxi, Henan, and the area north of the Huai River in Jiangsu and Anhui crossed the Yangtze and Huai Rivers. This marks the first wave of migration. In the third year of Emperor Yuan's Daxing reign (320 A.D.), the people of Langya[160] who crossed the Yangtze established Huaide County in Jiankang. This was the first move to establish prefectures and counties for the sojourners. Subsequently, sojourning states and prefectures such as Xu, Yan, You, Ji, Qing, Bing, and Si were established on both sides of the Yangtze River. Emperor Ming continued this practice and established additional sojourning prefectures and counties of Xu and Yan in the area south of the Yangtze River.

The Book of Song: Preface, 'Since the barbarian invasions of China, the states of Si, Ji, Yong, Liang, Qing, Bing, Yan, Yu, You, and Ping were all lost at once. The remaining people migrated south and sojourning administrative institutions were established.'

Preface to Southern Xu State, 'During the Yongjia rebellion, refugees from You, Ji, Qing, Bing, Yan states, and the area north of the Huai River in Xu State successively crossed the Huai River, with some crossing the Yangtze River to the Jinling Prefecture. Xu and Yan states were partially governed from the north of the Yangtze River. Sojourning states for You, Ji, Qing, and Bing were also established in the area north of the Yangtze River.'

---

[160] Langya was an ancient prefecture and vassal state name, located in the southeastern part of Shandong Province. It was relocated as an administrative region for refugees to the east of today's Nanjing City in Jiangsu Province during the Eastern Jin Dynasty.

Book of Jin: Treatise on Geography: Post-Preface to Si State, 'When Emperor Yuan (317 - 322 AD) crossed the Yangtze River, sojourning state of Si was also established in Xu state.'

Book of Jin: Treatise on Geography: Post-Preface to Xu State, 'Emperor Ming (322 - 324 AD) established prefectures such as South Pei, South Qinghe, South Xiapi, South Dongguan, South Pingchang, South Jiyin, South Puyang, South Taiping, South Taishan, South Jiyang, and South Lu under Xu and Yan states.'"

2. "At the beginning of Emperor Cheng's reign (325 - 342 AD), internal unrest triggered external invasions, causing widespread chaos between the Yangtze River and the Huai River. Migrants from Huainan and the north who had settled in Huainan fled further south across the Yangtze River. This was the second wave.

Book of Song: Treatise on Geography: Huainan prefecture in Yangzhou: 'Amidst the chaos in the Central Plains and repeated southern invasions by the barbarians, many Huainan residents crossed the Yangtze River. At the beginning of Emperor Cheng's reign, the rebellions of Su Jun and Zu Yue caused chaos between the Yangtze River and the Huai River, and the Hu invaders arrived in large numbers. Even more people migrated south across the Yangtze River. Therefore, the Huainan prefecture and various counties were established in the south of the Yangtze River for the sojourners.'

Southern Xu State, 'In the fourth year of Emperor Cheng's Xianhe reign (329 AD), Grand Minister Chi Jian relocated Huainan migrants to the Jinling prefecture.'

Southern Yu State, 'In the fourth year of Xianhe (329 AD), Yu State was established for the sojourners, with its administrative seat in Wuhu.'"

3. "After the reigns of Emperor Kang and Mu (343 - 361 AD), with the decline of the Hu people and the chaos of the Di people, the Central Plains suffered continuous years of war, and the Guanzhong and Longyou areas were the most severely devastated. Many people from Shaanxi and Gansu moved south into the Han River basin. During this time, Huan Wen had subdued Shu, and some barbarians fled south into Sichuan. This was the third wave.

Book of Song: Treatise on Geography: Yong State, 'With the decline of the Hu people and the chaos of the Di people, many migrants from Yong and Qin states moved south to Fan and Mian. During Emperor Xiaowu's reign (373 - 396 AD), Yong State was established as a sojourning state in Xiangyang, with additional sojourning prefectures and counties.'

Qin State, 'It was re-established by Emperor Xiaowu of Jin, with its administrative seat in Xiangyang. During the reign of Emperor An, it was in Hanzhong and Nanzheng.'

Western Jingzhao and Fufeng Prefectures, 'At the end of the Jin Dynasty, the displaced people from the Sanfu Region (Three-Adjunct Regions of the Capital) established these sojourning divisions when they moved out of Hanzhong.'

An'guo Prefecture of Yi State, 'It was established for refugees entering Shu during Emperor Ai's reign (362 - 363A.D.).'

Huaining and Jinxi prefectures were established by Emperor An of Jin for migrants from Qin, Yong, Guan, and Long regions."

4. "During the Liu Song Dynasty, Emperor Wu (420 - 422 A.D.) reclaimed areas such as Guanzhong and Luoyang, restoring parts of Qing, Ji, Si, and Yan states. However, after Emperor Wu's death, the Northern and Southern Dynasties invaded each other, and the Song people suffered repeated defeats. During the reign of Emperor Shaodi (423 A.D.), Si State was lost. By Emperor Wen's reign (424 - 453 A.D.), the Wei people launched a large - scale southward invasion, reaching as far as Guabu and southeast of Liuhe County. By Emperor Ming's reign (465 - 472 A.D.), the four states north of the Huai River, as well as Yu State and the area west of the Huai River, were all lost to the Northern Court. As a result, many of their people crossed the Huai River to the south. Also, during Emperor Wen's reign, the Di people attacked each other several times, and many displaced people from Guanzhong and Longyou took refuge in Liangzhou and Yizhou. This was the fourth wave.

Book of Song: Treatise on Geography: Si State, 'At the beginning of the Jingping era of Emperor Shaodi (423 A.D.), Si State was once again occupied by the northern barbarians. At the end of Yuanjia era of Emperor Wen (453 A.D.), it was re-established as sojourning state in Runan.'

The Beihuai Prefecture, Beijiyin Prefecture, and Dongguan Prefecture in Southern Yan State were all established as sojourning divisions after losing the area north of the Huai River at the end of the Song Dynasty.

Yan State, 'At the end of the Song Dynasty, after losing the area north of the Huai River, the Yan State was established as a sojourning state and was temporarily administered in Huaiyin.' Also, the Dongping Prefecture was established as a sojourning prefecture in Huaiyin, and the Jinan Prefecture was established as a sojourning prefecture in Huaiyang. In the fifth year of the Taishi period (469 A.D.), the Gaoping Prefecture was established as a sojourning prefecture on the border of Dangtu County in Huainan.

Xu State, 'During the reign of Emperor Ming, the area north of the Huai River was occupied by invaders, and the Xu State was established as a sojourning state and was administered in Zhongli[161].'

Qing State, 'During the reign of Emperor Ming, after losing the area north of the Huai River, the Qing State was established as a sojourning state on Yuzhou[162].'

Regarding the Fengyi Prefecture in Yong State and the Fengyi Prefecture in Qin State, the refugees from the Sanfu Region (Three-Adjunct Regions of the Capital) fled from Xiangyang and Hanzhong, and these prefectures were established as sojourning regions during the Yuanjia period.

The South Xinba Prefecture and the South Jinshou Prefecture in Yi State were established in the Yuanjia period for the refugees who flowed into the area south of the Jianmen Pass.

---

[161] Zhongli was an ancient county name, located northeast of today's Fengyang in Anhui Province. A prefecture was established here during the Eastern Jin Dynasty.
[162] Yuzhou (also written as Yu'zhou) was located in the Yuntai District of Lianyungang City in Jiangsu Province. It was originally in the sea. Due to the continuous eastward movement of the coastline, it was connected to the land in the Qing Dynasty and is now an important part of Lianyungang City.

In the *Book of Qi: Treatise on Geography*, regarding the Liang State, it is recorded that 'During the Yuanjia period of the Song Dynasty... The Di and other barbarians attacked each other several times, and many refugees from Guanzhong and Longxi took refuge and submitted to the rule here.'"

From the material above, we can form a relatively clear picture of the number of migrants received by various regions, their migration routes, and the timeline of their movements. This information supplements gaps in official historical accounts. Thus, I believe Tan's article serves as an exemplary case of combining historical geography and linguistics.

Differences in the historical and contemporary distribution of ethnic minorities can also be revealed through geographic names. Taking the Zhuang people as an example, according to Rui Yifu's *A Study of the Naming of Animals and Insects Among Southwest Ethnic Minorities*[163], the modern distribution of the Zhuang people includes the following areas:

Guangxi: Shangsi, Mengshan, Liujiang* [164] , Fengshan, Longsheng, Yongfu, Zhongshan, Tianxi*, Xiuren*, Guixian*,

---

[163] Published in the 1st and 2nd issues of Volume 2 of *Anthropology Bulletin* of the Institute of History and Philology, Academia Sinica.

[164] The ones marked with * are old county names. The comparison with the current county and city names is as follows:

Liujang was an old county name in Guangxi. In 1951, it was merged with Luorong County and Zhongdu County to form Luzhai County.

Xiuren was an old county name in Guangxi. Its administrative setup was abolished in 1951, and its areas were incorporated into Lipu County and Luzhai County respectively.

Yibei was an old county name in Guangxi. In 1951, it was merged with Si'en County to form Huanjiang County. In 1986, it was renamed Huanjiang Maonan Autonomous County.

Guode was an old county name in Guangxi. In 1951, it was merged with Pingzhi County to form Pingguo County.

Wangang was an old county name in Guangxi. Its administrative setup was abolished in 1952, and its areas were divided and incorporated into Fengshan, Donglan, Tianyang, Tiandong and other counties.

Xiangdu was an old county name in Guangxi. In 1951, it was merged with Zhenjie County to form Zhenxiang County. In the same year, Zhenxiang County was merged with Longming County to form Zhendu County. In 1957, it was renamed Tiandeng County.

Tongzheng was an old county name in Guangxi. In 1951, it was merged with Funan County and Suilu County to form Fusui County.

Pingzhi was an old county name in Guangxi. In 1951, it was merged with Guode County to form Pingguo County.

Jingde was an old county name in Guangxi. In 1951, it was merged with Tianbao County to form Debao County.

Huaxian was an old county name in Guangxi. In 1959, it was renamed Huazhou County. In 1994, it was renamed Huazhou City.

Haikang was an old county name in Guangdong. In 1994, it was renamed Leizhou City.

Wan County was a historical county name in Hainan, Guangdong. It was established as Wan'an County in the Tang Dynasty, renamed Wanning County in the Five Dynasties and Southern Han Dynasty, renamed Wan County in 1912, renamed Wanning County again in 1914, and renamed Wanning City in 1996. The old name is used in the text.

Luorong was an old county name in Guangxi. In 1951, it was merged with Liujiang County and Zhongdu County to form Luzhai County.

Si'en was an old county name in Guangxi. In 1951, it was merged with Yibei County to form Huanjiang County.

Guixian was an old county name in Guangxi. In 1988, it was renamed Guigang City.

Suilu was an old county name in Guangxi. In 1951, it was merged with Tongzheng County and Funan County to form Fusui County.

Yongchun was an old county name in Guangxi. Its administrative setup was abolished in 1952, and its areas were divided and incorporated into Heng County, Binyang County and Yongning County.

Longjin was an old county name in Guangxi. In 1951, it was merged with Shangjin County to form Lijiang County. In 1952, it was renamed Longjin County again. In 1961, it was renamed Longzhou County.

Chongshan was an old county name in Guangxi. In 1951, it was merged with Zuo County to form Chongzuo County.

Yangli was an old county name in Guangxi. In 1951, it was merged with Wancheng County and Leiping County to form Daxin County.

Zuo County was an old county name in Guangxi. In 1951, it was merged with Chongshan County to form Chongzuo County.

Zhenjie was an old county name in Guangxi. In 1951, it was merged with Xiangdu County to form Zhenxiang County. In the same year, Zhenxiang County was merged with Longming County to form Zhendu County. In 1957, it was renamed Tiandeng County.

Mingjiang was an old county name in Guangxi. It was incorporated into Ningming County in 1952.

Tianbao was an old county name in Guangxi. In 1951, it was merged with Jingde County to form Debao County.

Zhenbian was an old county name in Guangxi. It was renamed Mubian County in 1953 and renamed Napo County in 1965.

Fengchuan and Kaijian were both old county names in Guangdong. In 1952, the two counties were merged to form Fengkai County.

Sanjiang, Luocheng, Yibei*, Nandan, Hechi, Guode*, Hengxian, Lingyun, Donglan, Tiandong, Wangang*, Tianbao*, Xiangdu*, Tongzheng*, Pingzhi*, Jingde*.

Guangdong: Maoming, Huaxian*, Xinyi, Dianbai, Lingshan.

Guizhou: Libo.

However, Li Rong, in the third section of his *Ethnic Groups and Languages*, titled *Investigating the Ancient Geographic Distribution*

Yining was an old county name in Guangxi. Its administrative setup was abolished in 1951, and its areas were divided and incorporated into Longsheng, Lingchuan and Lingui counties.
Rong County was an old county name in Guangxi. It was renamed Rong'an County in 1952.
Tianhe was an old county name in Guangxi. It was incorporated into Luocheng County in 1952. In 1983, Luocheng County was renamed Luocheng Mulao Autonomous County.
Xiang County was an old county name in Guangxi. In 1952, it was merged with Wuxuan County to form Shilong County. In 1960, Shilong County was renamed Xiangzhou County.
Huile was cited by the author from Xu Songshi's "The History of the People in the Yuejiang River Basin" (published by Zhonghua Book Company in 1939) as quoted by Li Rong. After checking Xu's book, it was also written as Huile. There was a map of Guangdong and Guangxi attached to the front of the book, marking the names of various counties. On the map, to the south of Wenchang and Qiongdong and to the north of Wanning and Lingshui in the eastern part of Hainan Island, there was "Huile". At that time, the text was written from right to left, so "Huile" on the map was actually "Lekui". Xu mistakenly wrote it as "Huile" in the book.
Lekui County was established in the Tang Dynasty. In 1959, it was merged with Qiongdong County to form Qionghai County. In 1992, it was renamed Qionghai City.
Guishan was an old county name in Guangdong. It was renamed Huiyang in 1911. The old name is used here.
Haiyang was an old county name in Guangdong. It was renamed Chao'an in 1914. The old name is used here.
Qianjiang was an old county name in Guangxi. It was incorporated into Laibin County in 1952.
Xilong was an old county name in Guangxi. In 1951, it was merged with Xilin County to form Longlin County. In 1953, the Longlin Autonomous County of Various Ethnic Groups was established. In 1963, Xilin County was separated to set up a county on its own, while the name of the Longlin Autonomous County of Various Ethnic Groups was retained.
Nadi was suspected to be a misprint of "Napo". Napo was merged with Zhenbian County in 1953 and renamed Mubian County. In 1965, it was renamed Napo County.
Cangpei was suspected to be a misprint of "Cangwu". There is Fuliu in the southwest of today's Cangwu area.
Nama was an old county name in Guangxi. In 1951, it was merged with Longshan County to form Mashan County.

of the Zhuang Through Geographic Names [165] , references Xu Songshi's *The History of the People in the Pearl River Basin*[166] and lists Zhuang geographic names containing "Na," "Dou," "Gu," and "Liu."

Among them, those containing the character "Na" include:

Duna (Panyu), Nafu (Xinhui), Nazhou (Zhongshan), Nafu Market (Taishan), Naluo Village (Qingyuan), Naluo Market (Gaoyao), Nakang (Xinxing), Nawu (Yangchun), Naji Market (Enping), Nabolang (Kaiping), Nayue (Yangjiang), Nahua (Dianbai), Nalou (Huaxian), Naluo (Wuchuan), Naliang (Shicheng), Nalang (Hepu), Nalian (Lingshan), Naxian (Haikang*), Najia (Xuwen), Nahuan (Qiongshan), Najiatang (Chengmai), Napenling (Lingao), Nasai (Danxian), Nami (Wanxian), Nakang (Yunfu), Nakuan (Qinxian), Naliu (Liujiang), Nama (Luorong*), Naran (Luocheng), Nayan (Laibin), Nalong (Hechi), Nafuo (Si'en*), Naya (Donglan), Nabai (Wuming), Nagam (Binyang), Nachong (Baise), Nalü (Tiandong), Naan (Tianyang), Nanong (Lingyun), Namen (Xilin), Nageng (Zhaoping), Napo (Mengshan), Nadong (Tengxian), Nabo (Yulin), Nagutan (Luchuan), Nali (Pingnan), Napeng (Guixian), Nahuai (Wuxuan), Nadeng (Yongning), Nasi (Suilu*), Naping (Long'an), Nalang (Hengxian), Nawang (Yongchun*), Naxiao (Longjin*), Namin (Chongshan*), Nabu (Yangli*), Nabang (Zuoxian*),

---

[165] The reading report of the *Selected Readings of Famous Linguistic Works* of the Department of Chinese Literature at the National Southwest Associated University, manuscript.
[166] Published by Zhonghua Book Company.

Nazhuang (Zhenjie*), Nakan (Ningming), Naqian (Mingjiang*), Naxia (Shangsi), and Natun (Tianbao*), Naluo (Zhenbian*).

Geographic Names Containing "Du" (都):

Duna (Panyu), Duning and Duzhanba (Shunde), Duhui (Xinhui), Duyanshui (Taishan), Duwan'ao (Gaoyao), Duhu (Xinxing), Duquan (Gaoming), Dutianpu (Enping), Dujiu (Deqing), Dulang (Fengchuan*), Duxu (Kaijian*), Dulongjia (Xinyi), Dufengshui (Wanning), Dumen (Luoding), and Duqi Market (Yunfu), Ducheng Market (Yunan), Du'anshui (Shixing), Duli Tang (Yangshuo), Dulao (Yining*), Dunai Tang (Longsheng), Dule (Liujiang), Dule (Luorong), Dusu (Luocheng), Dugan (Mengshan), Du Tian (Huaiyuan), Duzao Bao (Rongxian*), Dule Tang (Xiangxian*), Dulong Market (Yishan), Dugan Ai (Tianhe*), Duli Tang (Si'en), Dubang Jiang (Tengxian), Dujie (Rongxian), Dubu (Huaiji), Dubei (Xingye), Dubang (Pingnan),.Dulu (Guixian), Dutong (Chongshan), Duai (Zuoxian), Dujie (Zhenjie*).

The character "Du" (都) is sometimes written as "Duo" (多). For example, there is a place called Duluping (都卢坪) to the north of Guiding County in Guizhou Province, which was referred to as Duole (多乐) in the *Book of Tang*.[167] Examples in Guangxi and Guangdong include:

Duoan Market and Duolang Market (Tianbao), Duoluo Mountain (Lingshan), Duoxuntu (Wenchang), Duoyi Ridge (Huitong), Duoni

---

[167] The original annotation in Xu Songshi's *The History of the People in the Yuejiang River Basin.*

Village (Huile*[168]), Duohui Village (Wanxian) and Duomeigong (Lingshui).

Geographic Names Containing "Gu" (古):

Guzhao (Nanhai), Gulouchang (Panyu), Gulou (Shunde), Gudou Mountain (Xinhui), Guzhen (Zhongshan), Gutang (Sanshui), Gulingzi (Taishan), Gulai (Qingyuan), Guchangping (Fogang), Guyang (Qujiang), Guxia Village (Renhua), Guzao Village (Guishan*), Gunitang (Boluo), Guyunyue (Heyuan), Guzhenshan (Heping), Gulou (Haiyang*), Gugou Village (Jieyang), Guchan (Huilai), Guyuanjia (Dapu), Gubashui (Gaoyao), Gulun Village (Xinxing), Guchong (Yangchun), Guli (Guangning), Guboling (Kaiping), Gulao Market (Heshan), Guopeng (Deqing), Guling (Fengchuan), Gufeng (Kaijian), Guding Market (Xinyi), Guliupo (Wuchuan), Guli (Hepu), Guxian (Lingshan), Gulan Market (Luoding), Guwu Fan (Yunfu), Gumianjia (Yunan), Gulupu (Nanxiong), Gulouping (Xingning), Guli Village (Qinxian), Gusen Dong (Fangcheng), Gulou Mountain (Raoping), Guzhu (Guilin), Guding (Yangshuo), Guqiao (Yongfu), Guluo (Yining), Guliudong (Quanxian), Guman (Longsheng), Gulian (Liujiang), Guding (Luorong), Gushan Dong (Luocheng), Gudan (Liucheng), Guzhao (Huaiyuan), Gulian (Laibin), Gulong (Rongxian), Guchen (Xiangxian), Guosuo (Yishan), Guman (Tianhe), Guyong (Hechi), Gulai (Si'en), Guli (Wuming), Gula Market (Binyang), Gulü Mountain (Qianjiang*), Guli (Shanglin), Gusui (Xilong*), Guwen

---

[168] Li Fanggui, *The Native Language of Longzhou*, valley, ravine; and also the original annotation in Xu Songshi's aforementioned book: "These six characters, such as 'lü' and 'lu', mean 'mountainous area'."

(Pingle), Gulun (Hexian), Guben (Lipu), Gusha (Xiuren), Guzan (Zhaoping), Gulan (Cangwu), Guli (Tengxian), Guquan (Rongxian), Guwei (Cenxi), Guleng (Guiping), Gusuan (Pingnan), Gumeng (Guixian), Gulei (Wuxuan), Gutong (Yongning), Gubo Mountain (Hengxian), Gula Market (Yongchun), Guliang (Chongshan), Gumin (Yangli), Gulong Market (Zhenjie), Guliu (Shangsi).

Geographic Names containing the character "Liu" (六):

Liuhe (Taishan), Liutian (Fengchuan), Liupingshan (Yangjiang), Liushuang (Maoming), Liu'an (Xinyi; noted by Xu Songshi as a Yao name derived from Zhuang), Liuleipo (Huaxian), Liupu (Hepu), Liulan (Lingshan), Liufu (Qinxian), and Liuma (Fangcheng), Liuding (Liujiang), Liuzuo (Luorong), Liuliao (Liuren), Liuhe (Huaiyuan), Liuwei (Laibin), Liudou (Rongxian), Liuwai (Xiangxian), Liubo (Yishan), Liusang (Hechi), Xialiu (Si'en; noted as a Yao name derived from Zhuang), Liuchang (Donglan), Liuhong (Nadi*), Liuchu (Wuming), Liuhe (Laibin), Liuche (Qianjiang), Liubian (Shanglin), Liuna (Baise), Liulian (Tiandong), Liuluo (Xilin), Liuzhang (Fuchuan), Liuzhe (Lipu), Liuduan (Xiuren), Liulou (Tengxian), Liuhuai (Rongxian), Liufan'ai (Cenxi), Liuxueling (Huaiji), Liuwang (Yulin), Liuwu (Bobai), Liujingxu (Beiliu), Liuxuan (Luchuan), Liuchen (Pingnan), Liubi (Guixian), Liubang (Wuxuan), Liuxue (Yongning; referred to as "Luxue" in local records), Liuwu (Hengxian), Liulü (Yongchun), Liuma (Zhenjie), and Liuge (Shangsi), Liutuo (Wuming), Liukun (Binyang).

Other variations of "Liu" in place names include:

As "Lu" (禄): Lujing (Nanhai), Luma (Taishan), Lubu Market (Gaoyao), Lucun (Sihui), Lutang Village (Gaoming), Ludong (Heshan), Luyuan Village (Yunfu), Baolu (Liucheng), Luqiao (Luocheng), Fulu (Tianhe), Luping (Lingyun), Silutang (Cangpei*), and Lukuan (Wuxuan).

As "Lu" (渌): Lushan (Fengchuan), Lushui Village (Lingshan), Lufu (Qinxian), Lupao (Donglan), Lulang (Shanglin), Lubu (Nama*), Luwan (Baise), Luxie (Tiandong), Lufengxu (Tianyang), Ludantang (Xilin), Luding (Xiuren), Lumeng (Yongning), Lulou (Suilu), and Luwu (Yongchun).

As "Lü" (绿): Lügun (Deqing), Lüling (Dianbai), Lüju (Lipu), Lüyan (Tengxian), Lüyin (Rongxian), Lü'e (Bobai), and Lüdipp (Beiliu).

As "Lu" (菉): Nalufan (Maoming) and Dalu Market (Fangcheng).

As "Lu" (陆): Luyin (Hechi).

The characters "Liu" (六), "Lu" (禄), "Lu" (渌), "Lü" (绿), "Lu" (菉), and "Lu" (陆) in these names are all transliterations of the Zhuang word luːk √ , meaning "valley" or "mountainous land."[169] Similarly, "Na" (那) is a transliteration of the Zhuang word na √ ,

---

[169] Li Fanggui, *The Native Language of Longzhou*, luːk √ valley, ravine; and also the original annotation in Xu Songshi's aforementioned book: "These six characters, such as 'lu' (渌) and 'lu' (禄), mean 'mountainous area'."

meaning "field" or "wetland."[170] "Du" (都) or "Duo" (多) may be transliterations of the Zhuang prefix tu ╫, while "Gu" (古) is likely a transliteration of ku ┐ , both of which serve as geographic-name articles in Zhuang.

When comparing the distribution of geographic names containing "Na," "Du," "Gu," and "Liu" in Guangxi and Guangdong with Rui Yifu's account of the modern geographic distribution of the Zhuang, it is evident that the Zhuang historically occupied a much larger territory within these two provinces. Though their modern settlements have shrunk, the enduring geographic names highlight the historical footprints of the Zhuang.

When geographic names near the border were translated into Chinese, the translators, not understanding the original meanings, often created absurd and humorous mistakes. There are two contrasting examples in Yunnan Province. Along the border between Yunnan and northern Myanmar, there are two rivers. According to the Chinese names, one is called Enmaikai River and the other is called Mailikai River.[171] If we trace their origins, the first river is called

---

[170] Li Fanggui, *The Native Language of Longzhou*, field; paddy field, rice-field. Xu Songshi's original annotation: "Na means field, Nahuai means oxen field, and Naxiao means thatched field." Li Rong quoted the *China Provincial Map* published by the Shenbao Press and stated that Tianyang County in Guangxi Province is also named Napo, and thus said: "It can be seen that 'na' means field, which is undoubtedly the case."
[171] "Another one is called the Mali Hka River." This was added in the 1989 edition.

nma $_1$ ˥k'a˩↓ in the Kachin [172] language, meaning "bad river," referring to a river that is difficult to navigate. The second river is called mǎli ˥k'a↓ in Kachin, meaning "river with many trees." The word "开" (kai) is a phonetic transcription of k'a↓, meaning "river" or "stream." The translation mistakenly puts "开" (kai) and "江" (means river in English) in both names, which directly translates to "Enmai River River" and "Maili River River." In the western part of Yunnan, in the Xinping County area, within the Huayao Baiyi (now known as the "Inland Dai")[173] region, there is a river called the Nandu River. Nandu River is a translation of nam↓ tu˥ in the Huayao Baiyi language. The word "南" (nan) is a phonetic transcription of *nam* in Tai languages [174] (including Dai), which originally means "river" or "water." The translation puts "南" (nan) and "河" (river) together, leading to the direct translation "River Crossing River." From these two examples, we can infer not only the different distributions of the Kachin and Baiyi peoples but also their different "word orders." The Kachin language places the modifier "开" (k'a)

---

[172] Shantou language, which is the Jingpo language. "Shantou" was the old name used by the Han people to refer to the Jingpo ethnic group. The Jingpo ethnic group and the Kachin people in Myanmar belong to the same ethnic branch.

[173] Huayao is another name for the Yi ethnic group in the Xinping area of Yunnan Province. It got its name because the women of this ethnic group tie colorful belts around their waists. According to the current understanding, Huayao and Baiyi do not belong to the same ethnic group.

[174] Tai language is a general term for the languages in the Zhuang-Dai language branch. This name was put forward by the French linguist Henri Maspero in 1911 and was later accepted by the linguistic community.

after the noun, while the Baiyi language places the modifier "南" (nam) before the noun, clearly showing the two distinct word orders.[175]

Finally, I would like to mention two famous geographic names in Myanmar during the War of Resistance against Japanese Aggression. When the Yunnan-Myanmar road was open, the cities of Myitkyina $[\text{myit} \dashv \text{kyi} \dashv \text{na} \dashv]$ and Rangoon (also known as yan $\dashv$ kung $\dashv$) became well-known, both militarily and commercially. However, very few people know the etymology of these names. Myitkyina $[\text{myit} \dashv \text{kyi} \dashv \text{na} \dashv]$ in Burmese means "beside the great river." "Myit" is the phonetic transcription for "great river," and "kyina" means "beside" or "next to." Geographically, the city is located on the upper reaches of the Irrawaddy River (also known as the Ayeyarwady River), and the name clearly reflects its location beside the river. The term "支那" (Zhī nà) have nothing to do with the phonetic translation of "China." Rangoon yan $\dashv$ kung $\dashv$ in Burmese means "without enemies." There is a historical story behind this place's name. Before the reign of King Alaungpaya of Myanmar, this place was originally called Da Gon, which means "pagoda spire" and was originally a place name of the Mon ethnic group. During the period of King Aungzeya (Alaung Paya Dynasty), the Mon people

---

[175] All are based on the records of the southwestern border languages that I have investigated myself. Xiang Da said: "There is also an example in the 'Book of the Barbarians': Volume 2 states that 'The Nuoshui River originates from Tubo... and is called the Nuoyi River.' In Tibetan, 'nuo' means black and 'yi' means water, and it is the same in the Mo language, that is, the Black Water."

(also known as Talaing) invaded and reached the Burmese capital, Shwe Bo (translated as "Golden King"). Alaung Paya led his troops to resist and drove the enemies back. When they reached Da Gon, the enemies had already scattered and vanished. In commemoration of this victory, the place was renamed Rangoon to celebrate the fact that "there were no enemies." During the Pacific War, Rangoon was also briefly occupied by the Japanese forces, but eventually, they were driven out without a trace. Thus, the original meaning of the name Rangoon serves as a kind of prophetic metaphor for the eventual defeat of the Japanese invaders during the War of Resistance against Japanese Aggression.[176][177][178]

---

[176] All are based on the records of the southwestern border languages that I have investigated myself.

[177] Regarding the part about Myanmar place names, it was adjusted and supplemented by Mr. Wang Danian, who specializes in Myanmar language and culture, in the 1989 edition.

[178] The phenomenon of sojourning prefectures and counties also existed in the north, although the situations were not exactly the same. For example, Yunzhouxi Village in Wenshui County, Shanxi Province, where Liu Hulan was from, was located to the west of Yunzhou Village. Yunzhou Village was the former site of Yunzhou and was changed to Shuozhou at the end of the Northern Wei Dynasty. There is Gaoche Village south of Jiaocheng County in Shanxi Province, which should be the remains of the Gaoche ethnic group (another name for the Tiele ethnic group) that moved south from the northern desert and settled down. In the suburbs of Beijing nowadays, there are Tunliu Camp, Zhangzi Camp and so on, which are the remains of the population migration from other provinces to fill the suburbs of Beijing in the early Ming Dynasty. A similar situation is recorded in the entry of "Longquan County in Suizhou" in Volume Four of *Yuanhe County Annals* compiled by Li Jifu in the Tang Dynasty: "Wu'er City was located forty li northwest of the county. At first, Helianbobo defeated Liu Yu's son Liu Yizhen in Chang'an and captured his people. Then he built this city to house them and named it Wu'er City." In the eyes of the Helian family of the Xiongnu Tiefo tribe that established the Xia regime during the Sixteen Kingdoms period, the people from the Central Plains, especially those who moved south during the Jin Dynasty, were all regarded as "Wu people". Capturing the soldiers and civilians of the Eastern Jin Dynasty and building a city to house them separately for management can also be regarded as sojourning in terms of people living in groups in a different place.

Qian Daxin also pointed out such a phenomenon in the article *There Was No 'Nan' Character in the Prefectures and Counties Relocated for Refugees in the Jin Dynasty* in Volume Six of *Shi Jia Zhai Yang Xin Lu*: "After the Jin Dynasty moved south, the prefectures of Xu, Yan, Qing and others were established between the Yangtze River and the Huai River as the sojourning prefectures, but the character 'Nan' was not added. After Liu Yu destroyed the

Southern Yan and recovered the former territories of Qing and Xu, he established the prefectures of Beiqing and Beixu to govern them, while the names of the sojourning prefectures remained the same." "Establishing Beiqing and Beixu" was actually to restore the original names and administrative systems of Qingzhou and Xuzhou. Because the sojourning Qingzhou and Xuzhou still existed and the character 'Nan' was not added when they were relocated, the character 'Bei' was added to the restored administrative systems instead to make a distinction.

The changes of place names are just like a cultural history, which have great potential for in-depth exploration. There is a record in *The Spring and Autumn Annals: The Second Year of Duke Ai*: "Zhao Yang of the State of Jin led his troops and Han Da of the State of Zheng led his troops, and they fought at Tie, and the troops of the State of Zheng were defeated." The corresponding record in *Zuo Zhuan* is: "Climbing onto Tie, he saw that the troops of the State of Zheng were numerous." Du Yu of the Jin Dynasty annotated: "Tie is the name of a hill." And he also said: "Tie is to the south of Qi City." Tieqiu or Tieshan was located in the northwest of Puyang County in today's Henan Province. According to the general rules of place name naming, it was very likely that iron was produced there or had been produced there before, and the place name was derived from its special product. From a rational analysis, if it was indeed named after the product, the time when iron production began must have been earlier than the second year of Duke Ai of Lu. From this, we can explore the starting era of iron smelting in China. According to the entry of "Wenshui County in Taiyuan Prefecture" in Volume Thirteen of *Yuanhe County Annals*, today's Wenshui County in Shanxi Province was renamed Wenshui County from Shouyang County in the tenth year of the Kaihuang period (590) of the Sui Dynasty. In the first year of the Tianshou period (690) when Wu Zetian became the empress, it was renamed Wu Xing County. Fifteen years later, after Wu Zetian passed away, Li Xian (Emperor Zhongzong of the Tang Dynasty) restored the title of the Tang Dynasty, and Wu Xing County was renamed Wenshui County again. Whether it was changed at the suggestion of Wu Zetian or the officials of the central government at that time, or changed by the local people to flatter her, this fact at least has considerable weight in resolving the dispute over whether Wu Zetian's ancestral home was in Shanxi or Sichuan.

Chapter 6 Surnames and Alternative Names as Clues to Ethnic Origins and Religious Beliefs

The Chinese nation was originally formed through the integration of numerous ethnic groups. Although each ethnic group has undergone significant sinicization, clues to their origins can still sometimes be traced through surnames. Historical and contemporary examples of this phenomenon are readily observable. For instance, the Yuchi (尉迟) family was a prominent clan during the Tang Dynasty. It is said that the royal family of Khotan before the Tang Dynasty belonged to the Vijaya clan. Based on research by M.A. Stein and Sten Konow, the *Vijaya* mentioned in Tibetan texts corresponds to Viśa in Saka [179]. The surname Yuchi is a transliteration of Viśa, suggesting that people from Khotan who settled in China adopted Yuchi as their surname. Regarding the Yuchi individuals who resided in Chang'an during the Tang Dynasty, their origins can be categorized into three groups: 1) Those descended from the Yuchi tribe of the Northern Wei Dynasty, which had already undergone deep sinicization (e.g., Yuchi Jingde and Yuchi Kuiji); 2) Those who came to China during the Sui and Tang periods as hostages (e.g., Bazhina and Yiseng, mentioned in Zhang Yanyuan's *Records of Famous Paintings of Past Dynasties*); 3) Those whose lineage and origins remain unclear (e.g., Yuchi Sheng, who has biographies in the *Old Book of Tang* 144, *New Book of Tang* 110, and *Cefu Yuangui* 692).

---

[179] Saka refers to the Sakya dialect of the Tibetan language.

According to Konow's research in *Studies on Khotan*, Yuchi Sheng corresponds to Vijaya Sambhava in Tibetan texts, while his brother, King Yuchi Yao of Khotan, is identified as Vijaya Bohan, equivalent to Viśa Vahanx in Khotanese.[180]

Similarly, regarding the Bai family of Kucha, Feng Chengjun, based on the names Suvarna-puspa ("Golden Flower") and Haripuspa ("Lion Flower") of two Kucha kings, speculates that Bai is a transliteration of *puspa*.[181] Other examples from the Tang Dynasty include the surname Kang, originating from the Kingdom of Kang (Samarkand); the surname Mi, derived from the *Maymurgh* of *Records of the Western Regions*; the surname Cao, from the Kingdom of Cao (Kabudhan or Kabudhangekath, northeast of Samarkand, as noted in *Records of the Western Regions* and Arabic geography); and the surname An, from the Kingdom of An (Bukhara).[182] These examples allow us to infer their Central Asian origins from the surnames.

The Murong (慕容) surname was originally a Xianbei (proto-Mongolic) name. Its descendants, due to a reluctance to reference their origins, are divided into two branches: the Rong family in Dongguan, Guangdong, and the Mu family in Penglai, Shandong. Although they appear unrelated, both trace back to a common ancestor. Xiang Da

---

[180] Xiang Da, *The Civilization of Chang'an and the Western Regions in the Tang Dynasty*, pages 6 - 8.
[181] Feng Chengjun, *Translated Collections of Historical and Geographical Researches on the Western Regions and the South China Sea*, page 11, citing *On the Bai Surname of Qiuci Again* in the 2nd issue of Volume 2 of *Academic Quarterly of the Women's Normal University*.
[182] The previously cited book, pages 12 - 24.

noted, "I once met an elderly scholar from Gansu named Mu Shouqi, who claimed to be a descendant of the Tuyuhun branch of the Murong family." Thus, the Mu surname also has descendants in Gansu.

Surnames and alternative names can also reflect religious beliefs. Chinese Muslims, for instance, have adopted common Han surnames such as Zhang, Wang, Liu, Yang, Jin, Cui, Li, Zhou, and Cao, alongside unique Muslim surnames such as Hui, Ha, Hai, Hu, La, Sai, Hei, Na, Xian, Ya, Yi, Tuo, Tuo, Yi, Yu, Mai, Jian, Bai, Gai, Mu, Duo, Zhang, Ba, Ke, Sa, Xi, Ding, Min, Zhe, Sa, Hu, Sa, Kao, Yu, Bai, and others. There are also semi-Muslim surnames like Ma, Ma, Bai, Man, Lan, Hong, Ding, Gu, Wan, and Mu. Pure Muslim surnames are often rooted in Islamic genealogies, while semi-Muslim surnames are adapted from Han surnames.[183] These surnames sometimes allow for the identification of a person's Islamic faith. This is evident in folk sayings like the one popular in Northwest China: "Nine out of ten Muslims are surnamed Ma, and the remaining one is likely Ha." In Yunnan, a similar proverb states, "Zhangs are Han, Lis are Luoluo, but most Muslims are surnamed Ma." These folk traditions reflect the common practice of deducing religious affiliation or ethnic origin from surnames. Let us now present a few examples to illustrate the origins of Hui ethnic surnames:

The surname *Sa* originates from the descendants of Sa'dullah, the title of a prominent figure in the Yuan Dynasty. "Sa'dullah" is the Arabic term for "Sa'd" (meaning "good fortune") and "Allah"

---

[183] See Kobayashi Gen's *Huihui*, pages 331 - 337.

(meaning "God"), which together can be translated as "Divine Fortune." Sa'dullah's courtesy name Tianxi corresponds well with the original meaning of the Arabic surname. The surname *Ding* originates from the descendants of Ding Henian of the Yuan Dynasty. According to Yuan Dynasty scholar Dai Liang's *Jiuling Mountain Collection*, there is a *Biography of Gaoshi* written by Ding Henian that states, "Henian was a person from the Western Regions. His great-grandfather was Alaoding, his grandfather was Shansi Ding, and his father was Zhimalu Ding. He also had a cousin, Jiayamo Ding." However, Qing scholar Yu Yue in *Tea Fragrance Room Sequel* notes, "Henian did not mention his surname. However, from his great - grandfather downwards, the last character of their names was Ding. No one knows what this means. As a result, people in the world mistakenly believe that Ding was his surname, which is incorrect. According to Qian Daxin's *Supplement to the History of Yuan Dynasty: Treatise of Literature*, there is also one volume of *Haichao (Seaside Nest) Collection*, one volume of *Aisi (Grief and Remembrance) Collection*, and one volume of *The Sequel* attributed to Ding Henian, but these mistakenly associate him with the Ding surname. The character *Ding* is derived from the Arabic word *din*, meaning "retribution." In all religions, the concept of cause and effect (karma) is fundamental, and Arabs use *din* to refer to religion. The name *Alaoding*, a transliteration of Ala-ud-Din, means "Honor of Religion"; *Shansi Ding*, a transliteration of Shams-ud-Din, means "Sun of Religion" (this is the same name as the Prince of Xianyang in the Yuan Dynasty, Saidianchi, whose other name was Shansi Ding); *Zhimalu*

106

Ding, a transliteration of Jamal-ud-Din, means "Perfection of Religion" (this is also the name of a scholar from the Western Region, Zhamaluding, who composed the *Wan Nian Li (Perpetual Calendar)* in the fourth year of Zhiyuan period); *Jiayamo Ding*, a transliteration of Diyam-ud-Din, means "Exemplar of Religion." Henian, a Confucian scholar, had been heavily sinicized, which is why he adopted the surname *Ding*. The surname *Ma* comes from the shortened version of *Ma Sha Yi Hei*. *Ma Sha Yi Hei* is the transliteration of the Arabic name *Shaikh Muhammad*. "Shaikh" in Arabic means "elder" and is a respectful title for elder or distinguished individuals. It is written in English as *Sheik* or *Sheikh*. Arabs typically place their title before their name, but in China, to accommodate linguistic conventions, people often reversed the order, so it became *Ma Ha Ma Sha Yi Hei*, commonly shortened to *Ma Sha Yi Hei*. Over time, this led to the surname Ma, with Sha Yi Hei becoming the given name. This is the reason why many Hui people in the northwest and southwest of China have the surname *Ma*.[184] Additionally, surnames like *Ha*, originating from Hasang; *Na*, from Nasudadin[185]; and *Sai*, from Saidianchi Shams-ud-Din... all have traceable origins.

The use of alternative names reflecting religious beliefs can be seen in the case of Yuwen Hu, a prominent figure during the Northern Zhou Dynasty. His childhood nickname was *Sabao* (萨保). In a letter to his mother, Lady Yan, recorded in the *Book of Zhou*, he wrote:

---

184 The above three examples were kindly provided by Professor Ma Jian. Special thanks are hereby given!
185 Kobayashi Gen, the previously cited book, page 332.

"Having been apart from your knees for thirty-five years, receiving the form and breath of life, I understand the mother-child bond. Who is like *Sabao*? How could I be so unfilial?"

Sabao (萨保) is a reference to *Sabao* (萨宝), a name associated with the *Ala* religion. During the Northern and Southern Dynasties, the practice of using religious names was common among the Chinese or sinicized ethnic groups beyond the Great Wall, with many names related to Buddhism. For example, Yuwen Hu's brother, Yuwen Dao, had the nickname *Pusa* (菩萨), which is another example of this practice.[186] Xiang Da noted: "According to research, the title of the Zoroastrian official 'Sabao' already existed in the Sui Dynasty. In the *Book of Sui: Treatises of Government Officials*: 'In Sabao in Yongzhou was regarded as a seventh-rank official; for those in various states with more than two hundred Hu households, the Sabao was regarded as a ninth-rank official.' *Sabao* (萨保 or 萨宝), is the transliteration of the Uighur word *sartpau*, which means 'leader of a caravan.' Scholars such as Fujita Toyohachi, Haneda Ko, and Kuwabara Jitsuzo have thoroughly discussed this issue, so I will not repeat it here." Xiang Da further commented: "*The Book of Sui: Treatises of Government Officials* discusses the Qi official system, saying: 'In the Honglu Temple, there were two *Safu* in the capital, and in every state, one *Safu*.' The title *Safu* is also derived from *sartpau*."[187] According to

---

[186] He Jianmin's translation of *Research on the Sinicization of the Western Region People during the Sui and Tang Dynasties* [Zhonghua Book Company, 1939], page 60.
[187] Xiang Da, *The Civilization of Chang'an and the Western Regions in the Tang Dynasty*, pages 82, 83.

Fujita Toyohachi in *Studies on the Western Regions* (*Historical Journal*), *Sabao* is the transliteration of the Sanskrit term *sarthavaho*, meaning 'leader of merchants' or 'leader of a caravan'. Kuwabara Jitsuzo, citing Haneda Ko's research and Radloff's writings[188], stated that in Uighur, the leader of a caravan was referred to as *sartpau*, which is closely related to *Sabao*.[189] Based on these various sources, we can infer from Yuwen Hu's childhood nickname that he had connections to the *Ala* religion.

In the *History of Yuan Dynasty*, Volume 121, *Biography of Subutai* with the appended *Biography of Ulaghatai* states: "In the first year of Emperor Xianzong's reign, Emperor Shizu led a campaign to the southwest against various barbarian tribes including the southwestern Yi, Wuman, Baiman, and Guiman, and appointed Ulaghatai to oversee the military affairs... In the autumn of the Jia Yin year, he arrived at Kunze, capturing the king of the country, Duan Zhixiang, and his chieftain, Mahelaxi." According to the text, "Mahelaxi" is a transliteration of the Sanskrit word *Maharaja*, meaning "Great King," which is sometimes written as "摩诃罗差" (Móhē Luóchā). Because the Mongols often transliterated the "j-" sound as "", it was translated as "剌昔" ("laxī"). In one version, "剌昔" was written as "剌者", which makes it even closer to the pronunciation of *raja*.[190] Buddhism had been popular in Dali for a

---

[188] Ueda Kazutaka, *Fragments of the Lotus Sutra in Uighur Script*, published in the September issue of *Toyo Gakuho* in the fourth year of the Taisho period, page 397.

[189] He Jianmin's translation of *Research on the Sinicization of the Western Region People during the Sui and Tang Dynasties*, page 122.

[190] I would like to thank Shao Xinheng (Xun Zheng) for his enlightenment on this point!

long time, and even today, remnants of the Acharya religion[191] are found in the western part of Yunnan. Therefore, judging from the name, Mahalaxi, the chief of Duan Zhixiang in the early Yuan Dynasty, was undoubtedly a Buddhist.

Since the spread of Christianity in China, many names have reflected religious influences. For example, in the Yuan Dynasty, individuals such as Kuerijisi, Ma Zuchang, and Zhao Shiyan can be identified as Christians based on their names or the names of their ancestors. In the *History of Yuan Dynasty*, Volume 134, *Biography of Kuerijisi* states: "Kuerijisi, of the Mongol Anchidai tribe. His great-grandfather was Basibuhua... his grandfather was Huyahuxin... and his father was Yaoshimou... He served as a vice-director in the central secretariat and was presented to Emperor Shizu." According to Zhang Xinglang, Kuerijisi is a transliteration of *Geogius*, which indicates that he was a Christian. We can tell he was a Christian not only from his own name, but also from the transliteration of his grandfather Huyahuxin (Hoham Hoshaiah) and his father Yaoshimou (Joachim), which provide conclusive evidence. [192] Furthermore, another biography of Kuerijisi in the *History of Yuan Dynasty* (Volume 118) states: "Kuerijisi... After the ascension of Emperor Chengzong, he was made Prince of Gaotang. The northwest was unstable, and he requested to go and pacify it... In the winter of the second year, enemy

---

[191] Acharya, a transliteration of the Sanskrit word "Acatya", means teaching disciples and correcting their behaviors, that is, a tutor. Here it refers to Buddhism that follows these norms.
[192] See the supplementary notes to Chapter Three of Zhang Xinglang's *Introduction to The Travels of Marco Polo*, the printed version in 1924, the first kind of *Shoushutang Complete Works*.

troops came in full force, and after three battles and three victories, Kuerijisi continued to pursue the enemy northward, into dangerous territory. However, his cavalry was unable to keep up, and his horse stumbled, causing him to be captured. The enemy tried to entice him to surrender, but he refused and died in captivity... His son Shu'an was young at that time, so an imperial edict was issued that his younger brother Muhunan should inherit the title of Prince of Gaotang." According to Chen Yuan, "Recent research shows that Kuerijisi is the King George mentioned in *The Travels of Marco Polo*. The basis is the first letter sent by Archbishop Giovanni da Montecorvino in Yanjing on January 8, 1305 (the 9th year of Dade period in the Yuan Dynasty), which is currently preserved in Rome. The position, deeds, year of death, and the orphan of the Christian King George described in the letter are all consistent with those of Kuerijisi, the consort and Prince of Gaotang. Recently, because Kuerijisi was the chief of the Ongud tribe (also known as Yonggu), and the names of his brothers and sisters recorded in the official biography in the *History of Yuan Dynasty* are all Christian names, people have determined that he is the King George in *The Travels of Marco Polo* and the first letter of Giovanni da Montecorvino. However, apart from his brothers and sisters, his father, Aibuhua, and his uncle, Junbuhua, were also devout Christians."[193] In 1935, Egami Namio discovered various Nestorian tombstones inscribed with Syriac in the area around Bailing Temple.

---

[193] Chen Yuan, *Research on the Sinicization of the Yuan Western Region People*, citing *Histoire de mcn Jobeleka* III, the 4th issue of Volume 1 of *National Studies Quarterly* of Peking University, page 597.

One stone was connected to Kuerijisi, the Prince of Gaotang, reading: "This is the tomb of Kuerijisi, a servant of God and a believer in the Catholic Church. Amen." This serves as further evidence. As for Ma Zuchang being a Christian, Zhang Xinglang provided three pieces of evidence to prove he was a Christian: "(1) In the *History of Yuan Dynasty*, many members of the Ongud tribe have Christian names, and Zuchang was from the Ongud tribe. (2) In the *Spiritual Way Stele* of his great-grandfather Yuehenai written by Ma Zuchang, which describes the family names: there are 25 names in the Han style, one in Mongolian, and 14 Christian names. (3) Yuehenai's grandfather was named Bazaomayelishu, and this name was particularly common among the Nestorian faction."[194] In addition to what Zhang Xinglang had listed, Chen Yuan supplemented five more pieces of evidence. The fourth one states that Yelikewen of the Yuan Dynasty probably included factions from Rome, Greece, and Nestorius. What faction did Ma Zuchang's ancestors belong to? According to the *Genealogy of the Ma Family*, the opening sentence clearly states: "The ancestors of the Ma family were from the noble Nestorian clan in the Western Regions. The first one to come to China was Haram Meshech." This indicates that Ma Zuchang's ancestors belonged to the Nestorian faction of Yelikewen and had held high-level religious positions. [195] Now, combining the views of Zhang and Chen and referring to Ma

---

[194] Chen Yuan's previously cited article citing the notes to Chapter Fifty-nine of Volume One of Zhang Xinglang's *The Travels of Marco Polo*, the 4th issue of Volume 1 of *National Studies Quarterly* of Peking University, page 592.
[195] Chen Yuan's previously cited article, the 4th issue of Volume 1 of *National Studies Quarterly* of Peking University, pages 593, 596.

Zuchang's *Epitaph of the Late Minister Mr. Ma*[196] and Huang Xian's *Genealogy of the Ma Family*[197], apart from the names *Bazaomayelishu* (recorded in the *Genealogy* as *Bosuoma Yelisdu*) and *Haram Meshech*, we can also cite the following names: Yue Hunan (written as *Yue Hunai* in the *Epitaph*), Xilijisi (written as *Xiligusi* in the *Epitaph*), Miedoushila, Baoluchi (written as Baolushi in the *Epitaph*), Aolahan, Yueshimou, Quelixisi, Yagu, Yeliha, Yuenan, Yishuo, etc. These are all Christian names. Also, in the *History of Yuan Dynasty*, Volume 180, *Biography of Zhao Shiyan* states: "Zhao Shiyan, courtesy name Zijing, his ancestors were from the Ongud tribe. His great-grandfather was Tekoah... His grandfather was Anthony... His father was Hosea... Shiyan served under nine emperors... He had five sons, three of whom were prominent: Yejuntai, followed by Yuelu (Julius), and Bohu." Although Zhao Shiyan's own name is fully sinicized, the three generations before him and his descendants all used Christian names, so it can undoubtedly be concluded that he came from a Christian family.[198] In modern times, several well-known figures can also be identified as Christians simply by their names. For example, in the sports world, there are people like Fu Baolu and Ma Yuehan (John); in academia, there are Hong Weilian and Zhao Luorui; in the Foreign Language Department of the Southwest Associated University in

---

[196] The Hongzhi engraved edition collected by the Peking University Library, "The Collected Works of Ma Shitian" is the base copy for the Siku Quanshu. There are many corrections by the imperial librarians. Xiligusi is written as Xiligusi as in the inscription. And Kuolijisi was corrected by the imperial librarians to Keliejisu.

[197] Huang Jin, *The Collected Works of Jinhua*, Volume 43, pages 1 - 5, the version of *Series of the Four Treasuries*.

[198] See Chen Yuan's previously cited article, the 4th issue of Volume 1 of "National Studies Quarterly" of Peking University, page 623.

Kunming, there are Ma Baolian and Chen Bide (Peter). Even if you have never met them personally, you can infer from their names that they have likely been baptized.

Finally, I would like to briefly introduce the so-called "father-son linkage naming system". This is a cultural feature of the Tibeto-Burman-speaking tribes. It can help determine familial relationships within the tribe through both physical traits and language, and resolve several historical disputes regarding tribal affiliations. In general, within this tribe, the last one or two syllables of the father's name often overlap with the first one or two syllables of the son's name. There are roughly four variations of this system:

1.**ABC → CDE → DEF → FGH**

En heng nuo → Nuo ben pei → Ben pei guo → Guo gao lie

2.**A□B → B□C → C□D → D□E**

Gong ya long → Long ya gao → Gao ya shou → Shou ya mei

3.**ABCD → CDEF → EFGH → GHIJ**

Yizun Laoshao → Laoshao Duzai → Duzai Azong → Azong Yiqu

4.**□A□B → □B□C → □C□D → □D□E**

A zong A liang → A liang A hu → A hu A lie → A lie A jia

While minor deviations occur within individual branches, these naming patterns generally adhere to the formats outlined above.

I have written three articles [199] on this topic, documenting examples from various tribes:

---

[199] *On the Father-Son Linkage Naming System of the Tibeto-Burman Ethnic Groups*, published in the combined 3rd and 4th issues of Volume 1 of *Frontier Humanities* published

Burmese branch: Three cases

Xifan[200] branch: Two cases

Luoluo branch: Seven cases

Minjia[201] branch: Six cases

The six tribes covered the Burmese, Chashan, Mexie[202], Luoluo, Aka[203], and Minjia tribes. Their distribution spans from Yunnan's Dali, Yao'an, Yunlong, Weixi, Lijiang, Pianma, Shijia [204], Wuding,

---

by the Frontier Humanities Research Office of Nankai University in March 1944; *On the Father-Son Linkage Naming System of the Tibeto-Burman Ethnic Groups Again*, published in the 9th issue of Volume 3 of *Frontier Administration Review* published in September 1944, pages 18 - 21; *On the Father-Son Linkage Naming System of the Tibeto-Burman Ethnic Groups for the Third Time*, published in the combined 1st and 2nd issues of Volume 2 of *Frontier Humanities* published in December 1944. See Appendix I of this book.

[200] Xifan has three interpretations. (1) It was the former name for the Pumi ethnic group in ancient Chinese documents. The Pumi ethnic group is mainly distributed in the northern part of Yunnan Province, and its distribution area overlaps with that of the Ersu people in Muya County, Sichuan Province. Pumi language is said to belong to the Qiangic branch by one view, and to the Tibetan branch by another. (2) Sun Hongkai's "Ersu Shaba Script" (in "Illustrated Records of Ancient Chinese Ethnic Minority Writing Systems", China Social Sciences Press, 1990) states: "The Ersu Shaba Script is a writing system used by a part of the people who call themselves Ersu (formerly known as Xifan)." The Ersu people are distributed in Liangshan Prefecture and Ya'an area in Sichuan Province, and their language belongs to the Qiangic branch of the Tibeto-Burman language family. The Pumi people are related to the Ersu people, but they don't seem to be of the same ethnic group. (3) The Tibetan people who speak the Namuyi language and are distributed around Xichang in Sichuan Province were also called Xifan in the old days.

[201] Minjia was the former name for the Bai ethnic group. There is a saying that it was the name given by the Han military households who were stationed in the Erhai area to the local Bai ethnic households who had lived there for generations.

[202] Mexie was the common name used by the Han people in the old days to refer to the Naxi ethnic group. In the literature of the Tang and Song dynasties, they were called Moxie Man, and after the Yuan and Ming dynasties, they were called Moshe, Mosuo, Mosha, Moxie, Mosuo and so on in the literature. In modern times, they were mostly called Moshe.

[203] Aka, that is, the Ka people, is one of the ethnic minorities in Laos. There were 870,000 people in 1987. The Ka language belongs to the Mon-Khmer language family of the Austroasiatic language family.

[204] Shijia was the name of a village. It belonged to Tengyue Hall in Yunnan Province in the Qing Dynasty. It was located on the north side of the Xiaojiang River, a tributary of the Nmai Hka River in the territory of present-day Myanmar, west of Pianma in Lushui County. When China and Myanmar demarcated the border in 1960, it was assigned to Myanmar.

Mengzhe[205], Menglian, south to Myanmar, and north to the Shuixi[206] region of Guizhou, Mianning in Sichuan, and the Daliang Mountains in Xikang[207]. Through the application of this language and cultural exchange, I have resolved several historical ethnic issues.

Some historians and Western scholars studying Orientalism or the history of the Baiyi people, such as Hervey de Saint-Devis, Parker, Rocher, and Cochrane, believe that the Nanzhao and Baiyi peoples are closely related and should belong to the Tai family (泰系). They even argue that Nanzhao was a kingdom established by the Baiyi people. According to the *Ancient History of Ancient Siam* originally written by Damrong Rajanubhab and translated by Wang Youshen:

According to records from China, five independent regions of the Tai people merged to form one kingdom during the Tang Dynasty, known as Nanzhao. The capital of Nanzhao was Angsai, which is today's Dali Prefecture in Yunnan. The Tai people of Nanzhao were known for their strength and had invaded Tang territory and Tibet several times but eventually made peace with the Tang in the Buddhist year 1420 (877 A.D.). The king of Nanzhao married a Tang princess,

---

[205] Mengzhe, now known as Mengzhe, belongs to Menghai County in Xishuangbanna Autonomous Prefecture.

[206] Shuixi, in the Yuan Dynasty, there were the names of Shuidong and Shuixi for the Tusi in Guizhou Province. The area under the jurisdiction of Shuixi was roughly equivalent to the present Bijie area. In the early Qing Dynasty, the Shuixi Pacification Commissioner was established. The historical name is used here.

[207] Xikang was an old provincial name. It was located between present-day Sichuan Province and the Tibet Autonomous Region. The Chuanbian Special Administrative Region was established in 1914, and it was changed to Xikang Province in 1928. Its provincial capital was Ya'an. In 1950, the area west of the Jinsha River was changed to Qamdo Prefecture. In 1955, Xikang Province was abolished. The area east of the Jinsha River was incorporated into Sichuan Province, and Qamdo Prefecture was incorporated into the Tibet Autonomous Region.

and from that time onward, the royal family began to intermingle with the Han ethnic group, and the Tai people gradually forgot their customs and habits, assimilating into Chinese culture. Despite this, the Tai people maintained their independence until the reign of Kublai Khan, Emperor Shizu of Yuan. In 1254 (Buddhist year 1797), he led a large army to conquer the Tai kingdom, advancing into Myanmar. From that time onward, the Tai people's original land was gradually incorporated into China.

Regarding this view, we will not argue further, but just examining the genealogy is enough to prove it incorrect.

According to the *Unofficial History of Nanzhao* compiled by Yang Shen, which quotes *The Ancient Records of Bai*, the genealogy of the ancestors of the Nanzhao Kingdom is as follows:

Biao Ju Di – Di Meng Ju – Meng Ju Du...

From there, the lineage continues for thirty-six generations, down to

Xi Nu Luo – Luo Sheng – Sheng Luo Pi – Pi Luo Ge – Ge Luo Feng – Feng Jia Yi – Yi Mou Xun – Xun Ge Quan – Quan Long Sheng, Quan Li Sheng – Sheng Feng You – Shi Long – Long Shun – Shun Hua Zhen

The historical records of Nanzhao are preserved in the works of Jiang Bin, *A Brief Record of the Origins and Development of Nanzhao*. Jiang Bin, from Xiangyuan, served as an official in Yunnan during the early Jiajing period in the Ming Dynasty and obtained works such as *The Ancient Records of Bai* and *The Records of Nanzhao* by local

117

scholars. He wrote this book, which was printed in the Jiajing era and is now preserved in the Peking University Library.

If we accept the father-son name connection system as a cultural characteristic of the Tibeto-Burman peoples, and as my late friend Tao Yunkui observed, there is no such phenomenon in the Baiyi genealogy from the Cheli Xuanwei Office that he had seen, then, after reviewing the Nanzhao Meng family's genealogy, the argument presented earlier can be easily disproven.

As for the genealogies of the other five kingdoms outside of Nanzhao, most also use the father-son linkage naming system, such as:

Mengxi Kingdom (4 generations):

Xi Fushou – Qieyang Zhao (brother) – Zhao Yuan – Yuan Luo

Yuexi Kingdom (2 generations):

Bo Chong – Yu Zeng (brother's son)

Langqiong Kingdom (6 generations):

Feng Shi – Luo Duo – Duo Luo Wang – Wang Pian – Pian Luo Yi – Yi Luo Jun

Tengdan Kingdom (5 generations):

Feng Mie – Mie Luo Pi – Pi Luo Deng – Deng Luo Dian – Dian Wen Tuo

Shilang Kingdom (4 generations):

Wang Mu – Wang Qian (younger brother) – Qian Bang – Bang Luo Dian[208]

Later, the Duan clan in Dali was deeply sinicized, and this cultural trait became less prominent. However, Duan Zhixiang's son was named Xiangxing, and his grandson was named Xingzhi, unintentionally revealing traces of the father-son linkage naming system. As for the Gao clan, which established the "Great China," they also continued to observe this custom. Their genealogy is as follows:

Gao Zhisheng – Gao Shengtai – Gao Taiming – Gao Mingqing

Descendants of the Gao clan served as local officials in Yao'an Prefecture during the early Qing period, continuing to use the father-son linkage naming system. According to the *Yunnan Tongzhi (General Annals of Yunnan)*, Volume 135, Page 17, compiled in the 20th year of Guangxu, citing the *Old Chronicles*, it says:

At the beginning of the Shunzhi era, Gao Wengying submitted his loyalty and was still granted a hereditary position. Upon Gao Wengying's death, his son Yinghou inherited it; after Yinghou's death, his son Houde succeeded him. In the third year of the Yongzheng reign, Gao Houde was dismissed for illegal actions and was exiled to Jiangnan.

According to the *Biography of the Baiyi* in *Yunlong Ji Wang (Records of Yunlong in the Past)* within volume 19 of *Yunnan Bei*

---

[208] The genealogy of the Six Zhaos was determined by referring to Fan Chuo's *Book of the Barbarians*, *New Book of Tang: Biographies of the Southern Barbarians* and Yang Shen's *Unofficial History of Nanzhao*.

Zheng Zhi (Yunnan Historical Records for Reference), there is a record stating:

At first, the Yi people had no surnames. A Miao man had four sons, who began using the father's name as their surname: the eldest was Miao Nan, the second was Miao Dan, the third was Miao Wei, and the fourth was Miao Zhi. Miao Dan had five sons: Dan Jia, Dan Ti, Dan Niao, Dan Deng, and Dan Jiang. Among the five sons, only Dan Jia had a son named Jia Deng.

This is clearly another piece of evidence for the father-son linkage naming system. However, the original text's reference to "Baiyi" (摆夷) should be a mistake for "Boyi" (僰夷)[209] or "Baiyi" (白夷)[210], referring to Baizi[211] or Minjia. I have previously mentioned that the Tai people do not have this cultural trait, and based on the distribution of the indigenous peoples of Yunnan, Yunlong only has the Bai people, not the Baiyi, so I felt confident in making this textual correction. If my judgment is correct, then by comparing this material with the genealogies of the Duan clan of Dali, the Gao clan of "Great China," and the Gao clan of Yao'an, we can find cultural evidence, in

---

[209] Boyi was an ancient ethnic group name in China, also known as Baiyi, Baiyi, Baiyi, etc. Before the middle of the Ming Dynasty, it referred to the ancestors of the Bai ethnic group. After the late Ming Dynasty, it referred to the Dai ethnic group in Dehong area, Yunnan Province. It refers to the latter here. It should be related to the Bo people who had the custom of hanging coffins in Gong County, Sichuan Province, but they were not of the same branch.
[210] Baiyi refers to the Dai ethnic group in the Dehong area. Because they preferred white in clothing colors, they were also called Baiyi.
[211] Baizi was the former self-appellation of the Bai ethnic group.

addition to linguistic classifications, to help clarify the ethnic identity of the Minjia.[212] However, the evidence does not stop there.

In July 1944, a group of thirty-three people, invited by Ma Jinsan (Chongliu), Yan Danfu (Xu), Chen Xunzhong (Fuguang), and Wang Meiwu (Shu), went to Dali to collect materials from local county records. On the way back, one of my companions, Wu Qian, obtained two valuable pieces of evidence related to the father-son name system in Xiaguang, Dali. The materials he found were: One was the *Inscription and Epitaph of the Virtuous Yang Sheng*, from the third year of Chenghua in the Ming Dynasty (1467), written and with incantations inscribed by Yang Wenxin, a monk practicing esoteric Buddhism in Longguan, in the 3rd year of the Chenghua reign of the Ming Dynasty (1467). The original stele is located at Moping at the foot of the Xieyang Peak in Xiaguan, Dali. The other one was the *Genealogy of the Zhao Clan of Taihe and Longguan,* , written by Xu Tingduan, a successful candidate in the highest imperial examination and the supervisor of the Nanjing Imperial College, also known as the Hermit of Yangxuan Mountain, on a lucky day in February of the 6th year of the Tianshun reign (1462). In the first material, we find:

Yang Xian – Yang Xianqing – Yang Qingding

In the case of the grandfather and grandson, all three generations maintained the father-son linkage naming system, but this custom did not continue beyond Qingding. Wu Qian commented: "Qingding was

---

[212] Li Fanggui once assumed: "The Minchia and some minor dialects may also belong to this (Tibeto-Burman) groups". See Languages and Dialects, The Chinese Year Book, Shanghai, 1938 - 1939 issue, p. 49:

a person from the Hongwu period in the Ming Dynasty. Around the 15th year of Hongwu, the Deputy General Lan Yu and Mu Ying led an army to conquer Dali and established official positions and military guards.[213] Qingding was appointed as the chief of the local area. This shows that during the Yuan Dynasty, the Duan clan in Dali and the Yang clan still followed the father-son linkage naming tradition . However, as more Han people migrated to the region, the local indigenous people gradually became sinicized, and the Yang clan abandoned their old practice of father-son linkage naming system. This is one of the reasons why the custom was abandoned."

In the second material, we find the following:

Zhao Fuxiang – Zhao Xiangshun – Zhao Shunhai

Again, for three generations, the father-son linkage naming system was followed, but after Zhao Ci (the son of Shunhai), this cultural trace is no longer seen. Wu Qian commented: "The Zhao clan, from Zhao Fuxiang to Zhao Xiangshun and Zhao Shunhai, followed the father-son linkage naming system for three generations. It is likely that several generations from the first ancestor, Zhao Yongya, to Zhao Fuxiang also did the same. Unfortunately, their names have been lost

---

[213] *History of Ming*, Volume 313, Biographies 202, the entry of "Yunnan Tusi: Dali": "In the fifteenth year of the Hongwu period, Zuo General Lan Yu and Right General Mu Ying, who were in charge of the southern expedition, led their troops to attack Dali... Dali was completely pacified. Therefore, Dali Road was changed to Dali Prefecture, garrisons were set up, and a Commanding Office was established... In the sixteenth year, Wang Zhi, Marquis of Lu'an, Qiu Cheng, Marquis of Anqing, and Zhang Long, Marquis of Fengxiang were ordered to supervise the troops and go to Pin Dian in Yunnan to repair the city walls, build military forts, set up postal stations, and settle the people. In the twentieth year, an imperial edict was issued to Cao Zhen, Marquis of Jingchuan, and the Sichuan Military Commission to select 25,000 elite soldiers, provide them with military weapons and farm tools, and have them cultivate the land in Pin Dian in Yunnan to wait for expeditions."

and cannot be verified. After Zhao Shunhai's son, Zhao Ci, the father-son linkage naming system was discontinued. Zhao Ci lived at the end of the Yuan Dynasty and the beginning of the Ming Dynasty. Because he practiced Tantric Buddhism, during the Hongwu period, he once accompanied Wuji, a monk from the Gantong Temple, to pay homage to the emperor. This is comparable to the Yang clan of Longguan, who, starting with Yang Sheng in the Hongwu period, also stopped using the father-son linkage naming system. This can be used as a reference. Therefore, it is clear that the indigenous people of Dali followed the father-son linkage naming system until the Yuan Dynasty, but after the Hongwu period of the Ming Dynasty when Lan Yu, Mu Ying, and others conquered Dali, the number of Han settlers increased, and the local people began to gradually assimilate into Han culture, abandoning their ancient customs. This is undeniable."

By comparing these two pieces of evidence with the genealogies of the Duan clan of Dali, the Gao clan of "Great China," and the Gao clan of Yao'an, we can draw three new conclusions:

First, from this cultural trace, we can infer that a portion of the indigenous people in Dali and the surrounding counties in western Yunnan had a historical connection with the Tibetan-Burmese peoples.

Second, the location of the *Inscription and Epitaph of the Virtuous Yang Sheng* is at "Mexie Ping" at the foot of Xiayang Peak in Xiaguang, Dali. When comparing this geographic name with the surname systems described by Yu Qingyuan in *Notes from Weixi* and the 34 generations of father-son linkage names in the *Mu Clan Genealogy* from Lijiang (see Appendix I), I believe this is no coincidence. At the very least, it can be said that the ancestors of Yang Sheng had a blood relationship with the broader Tibetan-Burmese ethnic group.

Third, from previous studies by scholars such as Terrien de Lacouperie, H. R. Davies, Ding Wenjiang, Ling Chunsheng, and others regarding the ethnic affiliation of the Minjia, based on this cultural feature, I believe these theories are worth reconsidering. To date, only Li Fanggui's hypothesis that the Minjia language belongs to the Tibetan-Burmese group seems closest to the facts.

Chapter 7 Kinship Terminology as a Mirror of Marriage Systems

In primitive societies, the use of names played a significant role. When people shared the same name, it was often believed that they were essentially the same. For instance, calling a woman "sister" could lead to treating her as such, thus prohibiting marriage. This is a fine line. Therefore, if a tenth cousin and a first cousin are addressed with the same term, the fear of incest naturally extends to the latter.[214] To facilitate the explanation, let me use the kinship terms of the Heiyi people from the village of Hetaoqing near Kunming as an example.

In the kinship terminology of these Heiyi people, we find the following:

Elder brother, elder male cousins on the paternal side, elder male cousins on the maternal side through the mother's sister, husband's elder brother, wife's elder brother (?), etc., are all called ˧mu˧.

Younger brother, younger male cousins on the paternal side, male cousins on the maternal side through the mother's sister, husband's younger brother, etc., are all called ȵɔ˧zu˧.

Elder sister, elder female cousins on the paternal side, elder female cousins on the maternal side through the mother's sister, husband's elder sister, wife's elder sister, etc (?), are all called ˧vi˥.

---

[214] Robert H. Lowie, *Primitive Society*, 1920. The Chinese translation by Lu Shuxiang, *Primitive Society* [The Commercial Press, 1935; Jiangsu Education Publishing House, 2006], page 19, the original page is 16.

Younger sister, younger female cousins on the paternal side, younger female cousins on the maternal side through the mother's sister, husband's younger sister, etc., are all called ŋɔ˧˥ mɔ˥:.

Male cousins on the maternal side through the mother's brother, wife's younger brother, etc., are all called a˥ ɣɯ˥ ɬa˥ (one's parents use the same term to address the wife's father).

Female cousins on the maternal side through the mother's brother and the wife's younger sisters are both called a˥ ɣɯ˥ mɔ˥ (one's parents use the same term to address the wife's mother).

Male cousins on the paternal side through the father's sister are called a˥ ni˥ zu˥ (the wife's parents use the same term to address one's father).

Female cousins on the paternal side through the father's sister are called a˥ ni˥ mɔ˥ (the wife's parents use the same term to address one's mother).[215]

If we carefully consider these kinship terms, we can immediately identify three issues: 1) Why are the children of paternal uncles, maternal aunts called the same as one's own siblings, and also confused with the siblings of one's husband? 2) Why are the children of the maternal uncle called the same as the wife's siblings, and also

---

[215] The materials used here are taken from Gao Huanian's *A Study of a Kind of Heiyi Language in the Vicinity of Kunming*.

126

used by the husband's parents to address the wife's parents? 3) Why aren't the term for the children of the paternal aunt confused with those of other siblings, but the wife's parents use them to address the husband's parents? To answer these questions, we need to examine the relationship between cousins and cousin marriage in preferential mating.

In sociological terms, the children of brothers and sisters of the same sex—i.e., the children of siblings of the same sex—are referred to as "parallel or identical cousins." In the language of primitive people, they are usually also called siblings. On the other hand, the children of brothers and sisters of different genders—i.e., the children of siblings of the unlike sex—are referred to as "cross cousins." In the language of primitive people, the term for these cousins usually indicates a more distant kinship. Cousin marriage, which was favored in primitive societies, was almost entirely restricted to cross cousins, while parallel cousins were prohibited from marrying due to incest taboos. Cross-cousin marriage, such as marriage between a man and his maternal uncle's daughter or paternal aunt's daughter, theoretically allows two possibilities: one where a man can marry either his maternal uncle's daughter or his paternal aunt's daughter, and another where a nephew can marry his maternal uncle's daughter, but a nephew cannot marry his paternal aunt's daughter. The latter option is the more common practice.[216] The Heiyi marriage system follows this type. Because of this, the terms for parallel cousins are the same, while

---

[216] Lyu's translation of *Primitive Society*, p. 32, original p. 27.

the terms for cross cousins are different. Additionally, since they do not practice the "exchange method" of marriage, and oppose "returning of flesh and bone" (meaning the taboo against a nephew marrying his paternal aunt's daughter), the children of the wife's younger siblings and those of the maternal uncle use the same terms, while the children of the paternal aunt are clearly distinguished. The reason why the parents-in-law of the husband's side address those of the wife's side as cross cousins, and the parents-in-law of the wife's side address those of the husband's side as cousins on the father's side through the sister is the same.

This method of marriage is widely distributed. It can be found in Western Australia and near Lake Eyre, Melanesia, Fiji, and throughout South Asia, where it is most prevalent, with detailed descriptions found among the Toda[217] and Vedda[218] peoples. It is also found among various ethnic groups in India and Indochina, such as the Mikir[219] people of Assam. The same practice is reported in Sumatra, Siberia (Koryak[220], Kanchadal[221], and Tungus peoples), British Columbia's

---

[217] The Toda people, an ethnic minority in India, live in the Nilgiri mountain area in Madras. There were about 1,000 of them in 1978. The Toda language belongs to the Dravidian language family.

[218] The Vedda people, an ethnic minority in Sri Lanka, retain remnants of a matriarchal society and number only a few hundred people. The Veddah language belongs to the Indo-Aryan language group.

[219] The Mikir ethnic group, also known as the Arun people, has four regional endogamous tribes, which are further divided into several exogamous groups. There were 230,000 of them in 1978. The Miju language belongs to the Tibeto-Burman language family.

[220] The Koryak people are distributed in the northeastern part of Russia. They are divided into two groups, namely reindeer-herding nomads and coastal fishermen. There were less than 8,000 of them in 1979. The Koryak language belongs to the Chukchi-Kamchatka language group of the Paleoasiatic language family.

[221] The Kamchadal people, that is, the Kamchatka people, are distributed in the northeastern part of Russia.

northern coast in North America, Central California, Nicaragua, and other areas. In South America, the Chibcha[222] people's women use the same term for their husband and their paternal aunt's son. Similarly, this practice is the standard marriage system in many parts of South and East Africa, including among the Hottentot [223], Herero [224], Basutos[225], and Makonde[226] peoples.[227]

Under this system, the principle is that a person marries the daughter of his mother's brother, and thus the maternal uncle becomes his father-in-law. As a result, among many ethnic groups practicing this marriage system, the terms for maternal uncle and father-in-law are often the same. For example, in the three border languages of Yunnan-Burma that I have studied — Shantou (Kachin), Chashan (A-chit), and Langsu (Maru)[228] — and also in the Liangshan Luoluo language studied by Lin Yaohua — this is the case:

---

[222] The Chibcha people, also called the Muisca people, are a branch of the Indians in northern Latin America. There were 270,000 of them in 1978. Their language belongs to the Chibchan language family.

[223] The Hottentots, which means "stutterers" and is a derogatory term used by Dutch colonists for the local people, call themselves the Khoikhoin. They are mainly distributed in Botswana and Namibia. There were 137,000 of them in 1978. The Hottentot language belongs to the Khoisan language family.

[224] The Herero people, also known as the Ovaherero people, are mainly distributed in Namibia and Angola. There were 45,000 of them in 1960. Their language belongs to the Niger-Congo language group of the Niger-Kordofanian language family.

[225] The Basotho people, that is, the Sotho/Basotho people, are similar to the Mbanderu and Himba ethnic groups. They are mainly distributed in South Africa and Lesotho, with a population of over 3 million. Their language belongs to the Niger-Congo language group.

[226] The Makonde people, an ethnic group in East Africa, are distributed in Tanzania and Mozambique, with a population of 100,000. Their language belongs to the Niger-Congo language group.

[227] Lyu's translation of *Primitive Society*, p. 33, original p. 27.

[228] Langsu people call themselves Lang'e or Leqi. The Langsu language is used by the Langsu branch of the Jingpo ethnic group and belongs to the Burmese branch of the Tibeto-Burman language family.

	Shantou (Kachin)	Chashan (A-chit)	Langsu (Maru)	Liangshan Luoluo
Maternal uncle, father-in-law	kə˧tsat˧	juk˧p'ɔ˧	jauk˧ p'ɔ˧	ogni
Maternal aunt, mother-in-law	kə˧ni˧	juk˧mi˧	juak˧mi˧	Gni gni

Additionally, the Fijians and Veddas also follow this pattern. In traditional Chinese usage, a son-in-law calls his father-in-law "maternal uncle" and refers to himself as " guǎn shēng " (馆甥 loaged son-in-law), but unfortunately, the Heiyi language in the example above does not fully align with this system of address. They call the father, wife's father, and husband's father all a˧ vɣ˧; the mother, wife's mother, and huaband's mother all a˧ jɛ˧; but they call the maternal uncle a˧ɣɯ˧, and the maternal aunt a˧ɬa˥, distinctly different from the terms for the wife's father and wife's mother.

This cousin-marriage system also shows inconsistencies. For example, the case of the Heiyi in Kunming is similar to that of the Han people but different from that of the Liangshan Luoluo, who belong to the same ethnic group. According to research by Lin Yaohua, "the

Luoluo practice reciprocal cross-cousin marriage, but they prohibit any form of marriage between parallel cousins." Therefore, "the children of maternal aunts and paternal uncles are called by the same term, and are regarded as siblings or *ma dzz gni mo;* thus, marriage between them is considered incestuous." In their kinship terms, paternal cross-cousin brothers are called *a bər zin*, maternal cross-cousin brothers are called *ogni zin*, paternal cross-cousin sisters are called *a sa*, and maternal cross-cousin sisters are called *o gni a mi*. Although they have their respective distinctions, there is also the term *ozie a sa* which can be used as a general term for cross - cousin siblings. Moreover, the direct terms for maternal cross-cousin brothers, wife's brothers, and the male parents-in-law of both sides are all *ozie*, while direct terms for sisters-in-law and the female parents-in-law of both sides are *a mĩ a sa*, and terms for daughters-in-law, nieces, and daughters of sisters are all *sa mo*.[229] This reflects that in the Liangshan Luoluo society, the practice of cross-cousin marriage follows a "swap" method, without the taboo of "returning of flesh and bone," which contrasts with the marriage system of the Heiyi in Kunming.

There are two other marriage systems worth noting. One is the system practiced by the Mazateco[230] people in Mexico. In this society, marriage is prohibited between both parallel and cross cousins. This restriction applies to second cousins and third cousins alike. However, individuals with the same surname, provided they are not cousins, are

---

[229] Lin Yueh-Hwa, *Kinship system of the Lolo*, H. J. A. S. IX, 2, June, 1946, pp. 94-99.
[230] The Mazatec people, now written in the Latin alphabet as Masatecs. There were 150,000 of them in 1978. Their language belongs to the Oto-Manguean language family.

allowed to marry.[231] Their kinship terms do not distinguish between parallel and cross cousins; for example, paternal male cousins and cross cousins (maternal and paternal) are both referred to as nøʔé and paternal female cousins and cross cousins (maternal and paternal) are both referred to as ntičha, which corresponds to the actual social practices of the society. Secondly, in the matrilineal societies of the Trobriand Islands[232] in Melanesia, there exists a marriage system that is the opposite of the Chinese system. This group is restricted by the law of clan exogamy, strictly prohibiting marriage with the daughter of one's maternal aunt. They consider marriage with paternal female cousins and paternal cross cousins (female) as preferential mating, while marriage a maternal cross cousin is not strictly prohibited but is considered undesirable.[233]

Levirate and sororate, like the cousin marriage system, also tend to create certain kinship terms. Sapir once pointed out that their influence has two aspects: On the one hand, under both systems, paternal uncles (father's brothers) often become stepfathers, and maternal aunts (mother's sisters) become stepmothers, so it is natural to use the same terms to refer to them. On the other hand, the children of brothers are equivalent to one's stepchildren, and the children of sisters are also considered in the same way. Sapir found examples of

---

[231] Florence H. Cowan, *Linguistic and Ethnological Aspects of Mazateco Kinship*, Southwestern Journal of Anthropology III, 3, 1947, pp. 252, 255, 256.
[232] The Trobriand Islands, now known as the Kiriwina Islands, are located among the Coral Islands in Papua New Guinea.
[233] B. Malinowski, *The Sexual life of Savages*, London, 1932, (3rd edition), p. 82.

this in the language of the Wishram[234] people in southern Washington state. The second way these marriage customs manifest their influence in language is particularly interesting. Because uncles may eventually take the place of the father and assume a paternal role, they are often referred to directly as "father," without any distinguishing terms. For the same reason, a mother's sisters are referred to directly as "mother." Similarly, the children of brothers are treated and addressed as one's own children, and the children of sisters in the same manner. Furthermore, since men often marry their wife's sisters, it is natural to use the same term to refer to both the wife and the wife's sister. Similarly, women can use the same term for their husbands and potential husbands (brothers of the husband). The Yahi[235] people in the northwest of California use this kind of kinship terminology. This style of kinship terminology, like the levirate and sororate marriage customs, is widespread across the world. The seemingly mysterious situation — where a person can have twelve "fathers" and twelve "mothers" — can be satisfactorily explained by these systems.[236]

---

[234] The Wishram people, who live on the north bank of the Columbia River in Klickitat, Washington State, USA, call themselves the Tlaklait people, speak the Chinook language, and make a living by fishing for salmon. There were still 125 of them in 1960.

[235] The Yahi people, a branch of the Indians who speak the Hokan language family, lived in the area of the Pit River in Sacramento, California, USA. The last Yahi named Ishi died in 1906.

[236] B. Malinowski, *The Sexual Life of Savages*, London, 1932, (3rd ed.), p. 45, the original pages are 37-380.

In the Thonga[237] of Africa, we also encounter cases where a nephew or stepson inherits a widow, and in the Miwok[238] culture, men can marry the children of their wife's brothers. The latter custom is quite significant because it influences Miwok kinship terminology. According to Gifford, at least twelve terms reflect the influence of this system. For example, the term *wokli* not only refers to the brothers and sisters of a wife but is also used to refer to the children of her brothers. Gifford concluded that this custom was an old tradition among the Miwok people, as many kinship terms suggest the existence of this marriage practice, yet none of the terms indicate the influence of cousin marriage.[239]

However, relying solely on kinship terms to deduce marriage systems can be risky. For example, the kinship terminology of the Trung people in Gongshan, Yunnan, has some peculiarities. They use the term a˩ ke˩ for father's younger brother, husband of father's sister, mother's brother, wife's father; a˩ ɲi˥ for wife of father's younger brother, father's sister, wife of mother's brother, and wife's mother; ik˥ta˥p'o˥ma˥ for elder sister and elder maternal

---

[237] The Tonga people, also called the Batonga people, are distributed in the Zambezi River basin, with a population of over 1 million. Their language belongs to the Niger-Congo language family.
[238] The Miwok people, a branch of the North American Indians, are distributed in California, USA. In 1970, combined with the Maidu people, they numbered more than 2,500 in total. Their language belongs to the Penutian language family.
[239] Lyu's translation of *Primitive Society*, page 46, the original page is 38.

aunt; and ik ˥ ta ˦ p'o ˥ ma ˥ ta ˪ də ˦ for younger sister and younger maternal aunt.[240]

This could, at a stretch, be interpreted by speculative ethnologists as a relic of the "consanguine family." However, it is not that simple, and we must proceed with caution.

Lewis H. Morgan believed that the evolution of human marriage passed through three stages: the first stage was complete promiscuity, the second stage was consanguine family, and the third stage was group marriage. "Consanguine family" refers to brother-sister marriage, but with limitations on parent-child relations. Morgan cited the fact of sibling marriage in ancient times as evidenced by the kinship terminology of the Hawaiians. Their system of kinship terms is simpler than that found in most other barbarian tribes. While most primitive tribes make a conscious effort to distinguish between maternal and paternal relatives, the Hawaiians not only did not make such distinctions, but they used the same term to refer to all relatives of the same generation, without differentiating between close and distant kin. For example, the term *makua* refers to both parents and includes their siblings, with gender distinctions made by adding words like "male" or "female." Based on this, Morgan inferred that terms like "uncle" and "father" were the same because, in the past, uncles were originally fathers' brothers and were also fathers. They were equally close to the "mothers" (i.e., their sisters). Likewise, a person's

---

[240] See the author's *A Preliminary Exploration of the Qiuyu Language in Gongshan*, the third mimeographed paper of the Institute of Liberal Arts of Peking University, printed in Kunming in August 1942.

nephews, nieces, and children were all called "children" because their sisters were also their wives or their brothers' wives. This reasoning could be extended further. Morgan argued that while marriage systems may change, the kinship terms reflecting these systems remain conservative and can serve as ancient records, much like fossils, of social institutions.[241]

Herr Cunow has presented a strong rebuttal to Morgan's logic. He argued: "Morgan only saw the broad kinship terms of the Hawaiian system that cover blood kindred but failed to notice the distinction between affines (in-laws) and affinities. They have specific terms for brothers-in-law and sisters-in-law, and even for the relationship between the parents of the husband and the parents of the wife (the parents-in-law). If Hawaiian kinship terms represent a consanguine family system, then what would these terms mean? If siblings marry, then my wife's brother would be my brother, and her parents would be my parents, or at least my parents' siblings."[242]

However, Morgan's fundamental mistake was in wrongly assuming that a word translated as "father" in the native language means "the one who gave birth to me" in the minds of the natives. He thought that Hawaiians would not call an uncle "father" unless, at some point in the past, the uncle had had sexual relations with his sister and thus was possibly "the one who gave birth to me." But this is a complete misinterpretation of the evidence. In fact, they did not call the maternal uncle "father"; rather, they used the same term for

---

[241] Lu's translation of *Primitive Society*, page 68, the original pages are 56-57.
[242] Lu's translation of *Primitive Society*, page 70, the original page is 58.

both the maternal uncle and the father, a term which has no exact counterpart in our language. Furthermore, this linguistic confusion is not necessarily based on having had sexual relations with the same woman, which is an arbitrary assumption that could lead to unconscious misinterpretations. The simple and correct explanation for the Hawaiian kinship system is Cunow's interpretation: it is merely a stratification of blood kindred by generation.[243]

Let's return to discussing the kinship terms of the Trung. We should note that although they mix terms for father's younger brother, husband of father's sister, mother's brother, wife's father, wife of father's younger brother, father's sister, mother's brother's wife, and wife's mother, and sisters and maternal aunts, the following kinship terms are independent and not mixed:

Father: a ˇ pǎi ˇ

Husband: ləŋ ˈ la ˇ

Mother: a ˇ mǎi ˇ

Wife: p ʻo ˈ ma ˈ

Son: a ˇ tɕ ʻial ˈ

Elder brother: ik ˈ ɹa ˇ də ˈ maŋ ˈ

Nephew (paternal): a ˇ la ˇ

---

[243] The previously cited book, pages 70, 71, the original pages are 58-59.

137

Younger brother: ik ˥ ɹa ˩ ɑ ˩ d ə̌˥

Nephew (maternal): a ˩ saŋ ˩

Cousin (paternal): a ˩ uaŋ ˩ a ˩ tɕʻ ial ˥

Based on Cunow's criticism of Morgan, we should not hastily infer from the mixed terms discussed in the previous section that the Trung people once practiced consanguineous marriage.[244]

To summarize the chapter's discussion, we can say that kinship terms in a society can indeed serve as supporting evidence for studying marriage and family systems in primitive societies. However, when applying them, it is essential to carefully consider other cultural factors to avoid falling into arbitrary and erroneous conclusions.

---

[244] Zhang Qiaogui's *The Cultural History of the Dulong Ethnic Group* (Yunnan Nationalities Publishing House, 2000), when discussing the marital status of the Dulong ethnic group, states: "In the fixed marriageable groups, several brothers from Clan A can form spousal relationships with several sisters from Clan B simultaneously or successively. However, men from Clan B cannot marry women from Clan A as wives, but can only marry women from Clan C as wives, effectively preventing the backflow of bloodlines and thus forming circular exogamous groups." It also says, "The restriction that blood cannot flow backward is very strict."

Chapter 8 Conclusion

Chapters 2 to 7 form the basic content of this book. Clearly, it cannot encompass all issues related to language and culture; instead, it selects some common examples, threads them together, and provides brief explanations. The conclusions presented below are merely generalizations drawn from the materials covered in those chapters.

Firstly, language is a product of social organization and evolves along with the process of social development. Thus, it should be regarded as a form of social ideology. For example, the history of the word *fee* reflects a pastoral society where livestock was considered property; the transition of the word $t'\,\text{ɬeɬ}$ from meaning "fire drill" to "matchstick" reflects the Athabascan people's past practice of fire drilling. The Trung people of Gaoligong Mountain and the Nootka tribe of North America both refer to marriage as "buying a woman." Although modern social customs have changed, traces of marriage as a transaction remain evident. In the *Shuowen Jiezi*, characters derived from the radical 贝 (shell) are all related to money, demonstrating that before the Qin Dynasty abolished the use of shells as currency in favor of coins, there was a monetary system involving shells and precious tortoise shells. This shows that the objective social life of an era determines the content of its language; it can also be said that the content of language reflects various aspects of the social life of that time. Social phenomena, ranging from economic life to all aspects of social consciousness, are embedded in language. The Yafetian (Yafety)

139

school of linguistics, led by Nikolai Yakovlevich Marr (1864–1934), places special emphasis on the study of semantics because semantic changes occur in response to social and economic conditions—they are dynamic, not static. [245][246] Thus, the history of semantic development is inextricably linked to the history of social evolution.

Secondly, language is not isolated but connected to many other aspects. No social phenomenon exists or develops independently without being influenced by other phenomena. Interconnections and mutual influences among various phenomena are necessary for progress along a defined trajectory. Since language is a product of social organization, it naturally adheres to this principle. Therefore, linguistic research must not be confined to the study of language itself or limited to existing linguistic data. Instead, the scope of study must be broadened to connect linguistic phenomena with other social phenomena and consciousness. Only then can the functions of language be fully understood, and the principles of linguistics be effectively illustrated. The materials discussed in the previous six chapters are not restricted to traditional dialects or the Han-centric

---

[245] Appendix *Soviet Linguistics* of the Japanese translation of *Introduction to Archaeology* by Hayakawa Jiro, in the tenth year of Showa (1936), pages 271 - 294.
[246] Nikolay Yakovlevich Marr (1865—1934), a renowned Russian-Soviet linguist, successively served as a professor at the University of St. Petersburg and Leningrad University, and was elected as an academician of the Russian Academy of Sciences and then the Soviet Academy of Sciences. He achieved remarkable accomplishments in the study of Caucasian languages. He combined the Semitic, Hamitic and Caucasian (also called Yaphtic) language families and named them the Noetic language family because, according to the Bible, Noah had three sons, namely Shem, Ham and Japheth. His "New Theory of Language", which held that language was part of the superstructure and had class nature, had a significant influence on the Soviet linguistic circle in the 1930s and 1940s. Chinese scholar Miao Lingzhu once wrote *New Soviet Linguistics* (Tianxia Book Company, 1950) to systematically introduce it. In 1950, Stalin criticized the views that language was part of the superstructure and had class nature in *Marxism and Problems of Linguistics*.

"national language." The examples I have used aim to encompass various aspects across time and space, with particular emphasis on the spoken languages of domestic ethnic minorities and culturally less-developed foreign groups. Examining the connections between language and a specific ethnic group or some ethnic groups often provides valuable insights into earlier patterns of population distribution and migration. Furthermore, the cultural elements reflected in language are evidently beneficial for understanding culture itself. The chapter on loanwords in this book includes a substantial amount of material and is relatively extensive. It provides numerous examples of mutual connections and influences between Chinese and other languages from the 1st to the 20th century. Marr once stated, "Unhybridized languages simply do not exist."[247] This idea finds preliminary support in the evidence from the Chinese presented in this chapter. For further research, it is necessary to expand the study of borrowed and loaned words in Chinese, arrange them chronologically, and examine their connections to various cultural aspects from a historical materialism perspective. Such research is inseparable from the history of Sino-Western exchanges. In other chapters, we also observe that language is closely related to geography, surname studies, and anthropology. By leveraging the connections between language and these fields to study historical or social phenomena, we can achieve greater accuracy when analyzing the conditions, time, and place of specific events.

---

[247] *Soviet Linguistics*, page 282.

Thirdly, linguistic evidence can assist in dating cultural elements. Language, like culture, is composed of various elements from different periods. Some of these elements can be traced back to a distant, obscure past, while others have emerged only recently due to contemporary developments or needs. If we can establish the relationship between cultural changes and linguistic changes, we can estimate the relative chronology of cultural elements. The degree of precision or ambiguity in these estimates depends on the specific circumstances. Using this method, language provides us with a "stratified matrix" for clarifying the sequence of cultural changes. Its relationship to cultural history is, roughly speaking, akin to the role of geology in paleontology.[248] The Yafetian school of linguistics also emphasizes the paleontological analysis of language, linking stages of linguistic development with stages of social and economic structures.[249] This new research direction is no longer like Indo-European linguistics, which focuses solely on comparing the structural forms of static language phenomena. This book does not delve into methods for analyzing linguistic stratification, determining the chronological order of linguistic elements, or reconstructing earlier pronunciations. However, the examples provided, such as shizi (师子, lion), shibi (师比, a kind of ornament), biliuli (璧流离, colored glaze), putao (葡萄, grape), and muxu (苜蓿, alfalfa), reflect cultural exchanges from the Han Dynasty or earlier, while terms like moyao

[248] Edward Sapir, *Time Perspective in Aboriginal American Culture*, pages 51 - 54.
[249] *Soviet Linguistics*, pages 286 - 291.

(没药, myrrh) and huluba (胡卢巴, fenugreek) only appear in Chinese records as late as the 10th or 11th centuries. These layers of cultural influence are quite evident. In the same language, for example, in Tibetan loanwords, for "talc" (滑石) and "jade" (玉石), the character "stone" (石) in the former has a -k ending, while the latter does not. For "tongs" (铗子) and "duck" (鸭子), the character "铗" has a -p ending, while the character "鸭" does not. This clearly shows that they were borrowed from Chinese into Tibetan at different times. These examples illustrate how linguistic data can help in determining the chronology of cultural elements. The importance of linguistic and written evidence in the study of social history was noted by Lev Vygotsky, who remarked, "Our knowledge of primitive society derives largely from language; many words have been passed down from antiquity." [250] However, it is crucial to note that linguistic changes occur much more slowly than cultural changes and written forms change even more slowly. Certain cultural elements may have long since disappeared, but their remnants can still be preserved in language and script. When dating cultural elements, we must not only distinguish their stratified sequences but also recognize that the timeline of linguistic changes generally lags behind cultural changes. For instance, this book uses examples from *Shuowen Jiezi* to explore social structures. While the text was compiled during the Han Dynasty, many of its characters were not newly created at that time, nor do they

---

[250] Page 7 of the *Brief History of Social Development* published by Jiefang Press, citing Chapter Two of *Lectures on Political Economy*.

entirely reflect Han societal structures. For example, we cannot conclude from the character 斬 ("to execute") in *Shuowen Jiezi* that the gruesome punishment of dismemberment was still practiced during the Han Dynasty.[251] Similarly, we cannot infer from the oracle bone inscriptions for 臣 ("servant") and 奚 ("slave") that slavery only began during the Shang Dynasty. When using linguistic evidence to study history, it is essential to consider the broader social context of the time. For example, the ritual systems of the Shang Dynasty reveal two distinct schools: the old school, represented by Wuding, which adhered to established traditions, and the new school, led by Zujia, which embraced innovation. In terms of the divination practices, divining travels and stops, as well as recording the daily itinerary of the king, are practices of the new school; whereas divining announcements, the fortune of ten days or a year, the year's harvest, solar and lunar eclipses, dreams, childbirth, illness, pregnancy, death, rain, and various other affairs, are more prevalent in the old school, and rarely seen in the new school. These differences reveal contrasting views on human and natural phenomena. Interestingly, the abundance of old school records provides us with more historical data. For instance, Wuding's frequent divinations concerning the fertility of queens and the health of princes have left us with a wealth of

---

[251] In the *Book of Later Han: Biographies of Eunuchs: Biography of Lü Qiang*, it is recorded that "He submitted a memorial stating affairs and said: '... (Cao) Jie and others... poisoned people, envied the loyal and the good, and had the disaster like that caused by Zhao Gao, yet they were not punished by being torn apart by chariots...', etc. This is just a rhetorical exaggeration in the text and cannot be taken as evidence that the cruel punishment of being torn apart by chariots was still in use.

information about the names of his wives and children. However, we cannot conclude that Wuding alone practiced polygamy or that it only began with him. Similarly, the new school may have engaged in polygamy but simply did not record it. Knowing the differences in divination matters between the two factions, for the divination matters of the old faction, we should consider this as a general phenomenon in the Shang Dynasty, which has been accidentally preserved, rather than a special phenomenon of a particular time or king.[252] This perspective is essential for those using linguistic evidence to interpret history.

Fourthly, cultural changes can sometimes influence phonetics or morphology. As mentioned in Chapter 1 of this book: "This compilation attempts to discuss the relationship between language and culture from the perspective of word meaning, with a heavier emphasis on semantics and less involvement in phonetics and grammar." However, in practice, it is not entirely free of these aspects. For instance, when discussing loanwords, we cited the French words *camouflage* and *rouge* as examples where phonetic changes occurred when borrowed into English. Similarly, pure phonetic loans in Chinese exhibit similar phenomena. Moreover, loanwords of phonetic-meaning integrations and phonetic-meaning combinations, new phonetic-compound, and descriptive forms also demonstrate how the Chinese adapt loanwords to fit the structure of their own language after contact with foreign cultures. Such examples are even more

---

[252] Preface to *Oracle Bone Inscriptions of Yinxu*, Part A by Dong Zuobin, pages 10 - 11, the second volume of *The Archaeological Reports of China - Xiaotun*, 1948.

abundant in other languages. For example, the Minomin[253] language of Native American tribes in North America lacks voiced stops, trills, or lateral sounds, so they adapt the English word *automobile* into [atamo: pen]. Similarly, the Tagalog[254] language of the Philippines, which lacks the [f] sound, transforms the Spanish word *fiesta* into *[pi'jesta]*.[255] In English, words like *tuchun* ("warlord"), *Shanghai* ("Shanghai"), and *chin-chin* ("please-please") were borrowed from Chinese, but constructions such as *tuchunate* ("warlord system"), *tuchunism* ("warlordism"), *to be shanghaied*, and *chin-chins* have been Anglicized in their grammatical structure. Additionally, the French word *rouge* ("red") originally only functioned as an adjective and noun. However, in English, it has given rise to new usages, such as the verb *to rouge* (to apply rouge), and sentences like "She is rouging her face,"[256] with the verb usage not existing in the original French. These examples illustrate how local phonetics and grammar often influence loanwords. Conversely, can a language change semantics, phonetics, or grammar after contact with foreign cultures? This is certainly possible. Regarding semantics, this book has already provided several examples, but here we can add a few more intriguing ones. For instance, in the Navajo language of Native Americans, the

word for "horse" is now ⱡʃ?, but comparative evidence and analyses of certain Navajo compound words reveal that this term

---

[253] The Minominee people, with a population of 4,300 in 1976, lived in reservations in Wisconsin, USA. Their language belongs to the Algonquian language family.
[254] Tagalog, also known as the Tagalog language.
[255] L. Bloomfield, *Language*, page 446.
[256] Ibid., page 453.

originally only meant "dog." Before contact with European culture, dogs were the only domesticated animals for the Navajo people, so after the introduction of horses from Europe, they inevitably referred to horses as "dogs." Similarly, the Navajo word bé · š , which originally meant "flint," has now come to mean "metal," also due to European influence. New compound words derived from these terms, such as ɫ ʃʼ ʔɣéɫ ("saddle," – rɣéɫ meaning "burden") and bé · šèà · ("iron bucket," – éà · ʔ meaning "basket"), would not make sense or even form compounds if based on the original meanings of ɫ ʃʼ ʔ and bé · š . Furthermore, modern Navajo refers to maize as nà · d á · ʔ . Ethnographic evidence shows that maize was a recent agricultural acquisition from their neighboring Pueblo[257] people, who were historical enemies. Linguistic analysis and comparative studies also confirm this conclusion. The etymology of nà · d à · ʔ , unknown to contemporary Navajo speakers, derives from nà · – ("enemy") and -d à · ʔ ("food"). Historical evidence shows that the literal meaning of nà · d á · ʔ is "enemy's food."[258]

---

[257] The Pueblo people, also translated as the Pueblos or the Pueblo Indians, lived in the southwestern United States. There were 30,000 of them in 1970. They spoke various languages belonging to the Aztec-Tanoan language family and the Penutian language family.
[258] Harry Hoijer, *Linguistic and Cultural Change*, *Language*, Volume XXIV, No. 4, pages 341, 343, 1948.

Cultural changes may not influence local phonetics as extensively as semantics, but we can still find examples that illustrate this point. In the Chiri cahua[259] dialect of the North American Apache[260] language, the phonemes /l/ or / $\overset{\text{z}}{\text{z}}$ / traditionally only occur in medial or final positions. However, when Chiri cahua speakers borrowed the Spanish words *lôco* ("crazy") and *rico* ("rich"), they adapted them to *lo'gò* and *ži'gò*, respectively, placing /l/ or / $\overset{\text{z}}{\text{z}}$ / in initial positions, a previously unattested phonetic environment. Additionally, compound words derived from these terms exhibit the same phonetic shifts. Moreover, the presence of /l/ or / $\overset{\text{z}}{\text{z}}$ / in word-initial positions slightly disrupted the phonetic equilibrium of the Chiri cahua language. Certain sounds that never previously occurred following /l/ or / $\overset{\text{z}}{\text{z}}$ / in native words became permissible after this cultural contact, introducing new phonetic structures.[261] In another example, the Longzhou dialect in Guangxi incorporates many words consisting of a Tai root combined with a Chinese loanword. For instance:

- **van** $\downarrow$ **tɕi** $\dashv$ ("day"), where **van** $\downarrow$ is from Tai, and **tɕi** $\dashv$ is from Chinese;

---

[259] Chiri cahua, also known as the Chiri cahua language, belongs to the Athapaskan language group of the Na-Dene language family.

[260] The Apache people, mainly distributed in Arizona and New Mexico, USA, had a population of less than 23,000 in 1970. Their language belongs to the Athapaskan language group of the Na-Dene language family.

[261] Harry Hoijer, *Linguistic and Cultural Change, Language*, Volume XXIV, No. 4, page 343, 1948.

- tçu √ ła:u ⌐ ("bamboo pole"), where tçu √ is from Mandarin, and ła:u ⌐ is from Tai;

- mi ⌐çai ⌐ ("no need"), where mi ⌐ is from Tai, and çai ⌐ ("to use") is from Cantonese.[262]

These examples also reflect the mutual influence between culture and phonetics.

When a grammatical affix frequently appears in loanwords, it can extend to local material, creating new structures. For example, in English, the suffix *-able* (from Latin-French origins) appears in words like *agreeable*, *excusable*, and *variable*. However, in words like *bearable*, *eatable*, and *drinkable* which are formed by its extension, the basic verbs are native. Similarly, French-derived suffixes combined with native English bases to create words like *breakage*, *hindrance*, *murderous*, and *bakery*. In another case, the agentive suffix *-er*, common in Germanic languages, also appears in Spanish, such as in *banco* ("bank") and *banquero* ("banker"). This suffix later extended to Tagalog, where, for example, [ši: paʔ] ("soccer") produced [si'pe:ro] ("soccer player"), coexisting with the native-derived [ma:niʰni:paʔ] ("soccer player").[263] These examples illustrate

---

[262] Li Fanggui, *Longzhou Vernacular*, page 36, 1940.
[263] L. Bloomfield, *Language*, pages 545, 455.

how cultural changes can influence morphology by introducing and expanding grammatical structures.

After completing the summary, I deeply feel that this book has many shortcomings. The most prominent issue is that the language and content do not fully enable the general public to understand it. Secondly, the book does not include enough Chinese examples. As for the viewpoints and methods, there are also some aspects open to discussion. However, the author confidently believes that this small book has preliminarily laid the foundation for a new path in Chinese linguistics. If we aim for further development, I solemnly suggest the following three areas of focus for anyone interested in building a new Chinese linguistics:

Firstly, regarding semantic research, we should no longer adhere rigidly to traditional philological methods. It must be recognized that the meaning of words cannot be isolated from their context. Definitions in dictionaries are often unreliable. We should analyze the "stratified matrix" of semantic evolution across different eras using methods akin to paleontology. Additionally, historical materialist methods should be employed to investigate the social and economic contexts behind the death, transformation, and emergence of word meanings. The scope of material collection should no longer be biased between "elegant" and "vulgar." A wide range of sources, from classics, histories, dictionaries, specialized works, quotes, notes, novels, dramas, and legends, to folk sayings and popular arts, should be comprehensively gathered. In terms of research methods, we should approach from two directions: from the top down, tracing the usage of classical texts to popular speech, and from the bottom up, tracing common vocabulary back to its origins. In this way, we can connect materials from ancient and modern, elegant and vulgar sources. Although such work is highly labor-intensive for an individual, it can be successfully completed with planned and organized collective efforts.

Secondly, over the past twenty-plus years, research on modern dialects has been overly focused on phonetics. While clarifying the phonetic systems of various regional dialects is necessary for creating new phonetic scripts, we must align this with the first suggestion, paying particular attention to vocabulary collection and research. This work should first focus on identifying similarities and differences in how commonly used words appear in various dialects. For example, the words "饮" for "drink" and "食"for "eat" have become obsolete in Beijing dialect but remain active in Cantonese. Similarly, the -m final sounds in classical Chinese words like "xun" (寻), "zen" (怎), and "shen" (甚), as well as the -p final in "zha" (眨), are no longer acknowledged in modern Beijing speech, yet phrases like [ɕyɛ˥ mə ·l] ("zenme", 怎么), "shenme" (甚么), and "zhaba" (眨巴) still circulate. Another example is the size distinction between "fang" (房, room) and "wu" (屋, house), which varies between southern and northern China. In some regions, the term for "smell" is "listen" (听), while in others it is "smell" (闻). The same black color is referred to as "hei" (黑), "wu" (乌), or "xuan" (玄) in different

151

dialects. Similarly, the character "qing" (青) represents blue in some dialects and black in others. Examples like these are too numerous to list one by one. If we want the unification of the Chinese language, we must start by analyzing these contradictions. Furthermore, we need to delve deeply into various industries and social classes, conducting separate investigations into their commonly used terms, and compiling them into categorized vocabularies. Anyone who has studied a foreign language should know that different industries or social classes each have their own set of rich vocabulary. For example, farmers have their own jargon, workers have their own terms, hunters have their own specialized vocabulary, miners have their own terminology, and the jargon of truck drivers is different from that of sailors. The slang used by young students can even make a group of old men gape in astonishment. But these are all lively, active words, not dead words that are kept unused. Don't the various industries and social classes in China also have such vocabularies? But if we let them grow and die on their own, without linguists collecting them and without literary figures applying them, it is like abandoning a treasure while feeling poor. Isn't that wasteful and inefficient? Mao Zedong once said: "Our literary and artistic workers previously did not understand the language of the objects they depicted. You speak the language of intellectuals, while they speak the language of the masses. I've said before, many comrades like to talk about 'popularization,' but what does 'popularization' really mean? It means that the thoughts and emotions of our literary and artistic workers should be in harmony with those of the workers, peasants, and soldiers. And in order to achieve that, we must start by learning the language of the masses. If we don't even understand the language of the people, how can we talk about literary creation?"[264] I believe that in this regard, the task of linguists is even more important than that of literary workers. If everyone works together and follows the approach I have suggested, then the results of linguistic research can provide material for literary workers to draw from. At the same time, the expansion of vocabulary by literary workers can encourage linguists to further explore. This way, through mutual interaction, both fields can develop through their connection.

As for the study of grammar, past achievements have also been insufficient. Although the method of *Ma Shi Wen Tong (Ma's Grammar)* was criticized for being a "Latin grammar applied to Chinese," generally speaking, studies of the grammar of modern Chinese, with a few notable exceptions, still suffer from the same flaw of "applying Latin grammar to Chinese." As for the grammar of various regional dialects, research on that is practically nonexistent! What we should do now is to rigorously use descriptive linguistic methods to analyze the structure of modern Chinese. This must be based entirely on the spoken language of the people, and only then can we establish a correct grammar for the living language. Once the grammar of modern Chinese has been outlined, we can adopt the same descriptive approach to analyze the ancient grammar of previous eras,

---

[264] "Talks at the Yan'an Forum on Literature and Art", Volume V of *Selected Works of Mao Zedong*, page 99 [the 1947 edition published by the Xinhua Bookstore in the Jin-Cha-Ji Border Region].

using a historical perspective. These two tasks should not be mixed or pursued simultaneously.

Thirdly, we should recognize the importance of studying the languages of domestic ethnic minorities. In China, scholars have generally paid little attention to the study of minority languages, and Western scholars have not approached the topic with the same enthusiasm as they have for Indo-European languages. Taking Sino-Tibetan languages as an example, the first work on comparative research of these languages, B.J. Leyden's *On the Languages and Literature of Indo-Chinese Nations* (Asia Researches, X, 1808), was published in the early 19th century. Compared with the contemporary Indo-European linguistic work A. Friedrich Schlegel's *Über die Sprache und Weisheit der Indier* (1808), both occupied an important position in the early stages of comparative studies of their respective linguistic families. Why, then, did Indo-European linguistics make significant progress in the 19th century, while Sino-Tibetan linguistics lagged? The main reasons are as follows:

1.Historically, research on this language family was primarily conducted by Western scholars. Chinese scholars not only lacked interest in this field but were also unprepared for it. The number of European researchers studying Sino-Tibetan languages was far fewer than those studying Indo-European languages.

2.European scholars studying Sino-Tibetan languages were often inadequately prepared. A significant portion of the work was conducted by missionaries. Their contributions were significant, but a missionary usually lived in one place for ten to twenty years, and in the end, could only provide us with some valuable materials, such as dictionaries. Expecting them to do scientific language research would be too demanding.

3. Western scholars studying Sino-Tibetan languages often had other primary interests, with language studies being secondary. For example, B. Laufer focused on cultural transmission, while P. Pelliot concentrated on historical research.

4. Specialists in linguistic studies often had overly broad aspirations, preferring to explore many languages superficially rather than conducting in-depth research on a single one.

5. Finally, many Sino-Tibetan languages lacked written records, necessitating fieldwork to collect data. This type of research requires individuals with thorough training in phonetics, a rare qualification at the time.

For these reasons, it is no surprise that research on Sino-Tibetan languages did not progress significantly. Similar challenges exist in the study of other minority languages in China.

Since the outbreak of the War of Resistance Against Japanese Aggression, some universities and academic institutions relocated to southwestern provinces such as Sichuan, Yunnan, and Guizhou. Researchers engaged in linguistic studies came into direct contact with many ethnic minorities speaking diverse languages, sparking a keen interest in field investigations. Using scientific linguistic methods, they achieved preliminary results despite harsh material conditions (see Appendix IV, *Linguistics in Yunnan*). These achievements represented progress beyond what Western missionaries had accomplished. Now that universities and academic institutions have resumed their original operations, research activities are gradually recovering and developing under the cultural and educational policies outlined in the Common Program of the People's Republic of China. Should research into the languages of domestic ethnic minorities continue? I believe that not only must this work be resumed, but it should also be significantly developed. Two main reasons can be cited:

1.From an academic perspective: Minority languages often preserve the "stratified matrix" of past cultures (as previously discussed), enabling us to analyze the course of social development using methods analogous to those of paleontology. This is particularly true for unwritten oral languages, which retain more of the consciousness and forms of popular language. Just as Marr applied the languages of Caucasian minorities to establish materialist Yafety linguistics, why can't we use the languages of domestic minorities to create a new Chinese linguistics? For example, in comparative studies of Old Chinese, minority languages provide significant insights. Take the Beijing Mandarin word fēng (风) and a term from a Luoluo dialect from Sichuan, brum (wind). At first glance, they seem unrelated. However, knowing that "风" derives its phonetic element from fan (凡), we can infer that the Old Chinese pronunciation included a closed final -m. Since ancient Chinese lacked bilabial fricatives, the initial would have been p-, reconstructing the ancient pronunciation of 风 as *pǐum. Additionally, the character "岚", which takes its sound from "风", is still pronounced as "lam" in modern Guangzhou dialect. This example can, on the one hand, prove that "风" belongs to the category of closing-mouth rhymes, and on the other hand, show that its initial consonant may have evolved from the consonant cluster *pl-. In this way, the Old Chinese pronunciation of "风" can be reconstructed as *plum, and doesn't it then have a close connection with "brum"? If we take the record in Sun Mu's *Jilin Leishi (Matters Related to Jilin Region)* that "风曰孛缆" as additional evidence, this comparison probably won't be too far-fetched. Similarly, consider the Beijing Mandarin word kǒng (孔) and the Thai words klong (tube) and ploang (empty, hollow). They appear unrelated until we find the idiomatic expression "孔曰窟笼" in the *Song Jingwen Biji (Notes of Song Jingwen)*, linking them plausibly. Other examples include "平" in Thai as *plieng*, "兼" as *klem*, and "变" as *plien*, all demonstrating the value of comparative research. From a practical perspective: If we aim to systematically document unwritten minority languages, we must develop a unified phonetic transcription system. The adequacy of the existing Latinized new script and necessary supplements can only be determined through scientific investigations of these languages. In conclusion, the study of domestic minority languages is indispensable and should not stagnate under any circumstances.

2. Setting aside academic considerations, the study of minority languages is equally important from a political perspective. If we wish to unite the domestic ethnic minorities, we must first learn their

languages. Stalin once said, "Minorities are not dissatisfied due to the lack of national unity, but because they are denied the right to use their own languages. Once they have the right to use their own languages, this dissatisfaction will naturally disappear."[265] Mao Zedong also stated, "Chinese Communists should actively assist the broad masses of all minority groups, including their leaders who connect with the people, in striving for their political, economic, and cultural liberation and development, as well as in forming their own armies that support the people's interests. Their languages, scripts, customs, habits, and religious beliefs should be respected."[266] This policy is clearly stipulated in the Common Program of the People's Republic of China (Article 53). To implement this policy, we must first train a group of professionals proficient in minority languages so that we can assist these communities in raising their cultural and political standards. Only by integrating relatively underdeveloped ethnic groups and tribes into the broader trajectory of higher culture can we address the issues on minority groups. Language serves as a critical tool in this process of integration. From an anti-imperialist and anti-invasion standpoint, the importance of studying minority languages becomes even clearer. In the past, China often neglected its minority groups, but imperialist powers with expansionist ambitions have long recognized their strategic value. For instance, decades ago, foreigners compiled comprehensive dictionaries and grammar for languages like

---

[265] *The Marxist Theory of the National Question*, the version published by the Foreign Languages Publishing House in Moscow, page 80.
[266] *On Coalition Government*, the version published by Jiefang Press, page 90.

Tibetan, Burmese, and Baiyi. Even for unwritten languages like Kachin and Lisu, foreign missionaries devised Romanized scripts. With these linguistic tools, imperialists could spread religion, facilitate trade, plot cultural assimilation, and exploit our border communities. The inclusion of valiant Kachin fighters in British military forces during World War II is one example. In the spring of 1943, I met two Chashan friends from Pianma in Dali. They had received eight to nine years of British-style secondary education in Myitkyina and Mandalay, becoming fluent in Burmese and somewhat conversant in English, yet their knowledge of Chinese was limited to a few barely comprehensible phrases in the Lushui dialect. They knew of Caesar, Charlemagne, Napoleon, Livingstone, Queen Victoria, King George, and Churchill, but were unaware of Qin Shi Huang, Emperor Wu of Han, Emperor Taizong of Tang, Zhao Kuangyin, Zhu Yuanzhang, Sun Yat-sen, or Mao Zedong. Once, after I shared a story from the Spring and Autumn period, they were astonished and asked, "The Republic of China has only been around for 32 years. Why are you talking about events from thousands of years ago?" Later, when I brought them to Kunming, I gradually learned their native language, and they managed to speak 50-60% of Mandarin. Over time, they gained a clearer understanding of China and the significance and mission of the national resistance against Japan. During our two-and-a-half months together, I not only gathered valuable linguistic materials, but they also returned to their hometown as excellent military guides. During the War of Resistance Against Japanese Aggression, the Japanese attempted to mimic Hitler's tactics by using

159

language policies to divide the Tai-speaking minority groups in Yunnan, Guizhou, and Guangxi provinces, including the Baiyi, Zhuang, Lü, Shuijia, Yanghuang, and Zhongjia[267]. A traveler to Shilin, Lu'nan County, Yunnan Province, once overheard a local claiming that their ancestors had migrated from Thailand over a thousand years ago. This kind of ideological poison is far more insidious than the spread of cholera by the enemy. To prevent imperialist aggression and to help minority groups integrate into the broader trajectory of higher culture, we must first begin by studying their languages.

Finally, I hope that all linguists nationwide will come together, critically engage with my three proposals, and work in a systematic, planned manner to contribute collectively to building a new Chinese linguistics!

---

[267] The Lü people, presumably the Lü people (written as "Lu" in the Latin alphabet and "Лю" in the Slavic alphabet), mainly lived in Lai Chau Province in the northwest of Vietnam. They were an ancient ethnic group there. There were 1,300 of them in 1973. The Lu language belongs to the Zhuang-Dong language group of the Sino-Tibetan language family.
The Shuijia, that is, the Shui ethnic group.
Yanghuang (羊黄), now known as Yanghuang (佯僙), is the language spoken by those who call themselves "our people" in Pingtang County and other places in the Qiandongnan Buyi and Miao Autonomous Prefecture in Guizhou Province. Yanghuang belongs to the Dong-Shui language branch of the Zhuang-Dong language group. There were more than 30,000 people speaking it in 1982.
Zhongjia, the former name of the Buyi ethnic group.

Appendix 1: The Father-Son Linkage Naming System of the Tibeto-Burman Peoples[268]

Before explaining what the "father-son linkage naming system" is, let me first tell a story:

In the 33rd chapter of Wen Kang's *Heroes of Sons and Daughters*, Auntie An, from the An family, mocks her husband, An, for his tendency to cite classical texts. She recounts a story about a man who always lost at chess and had to invite a skilled player to assist him. The original text says:

There was a man who played a game of incredibly bad chess, always making moves that led to certain defeats. Desperate, he invited an experienced player to guide him. The skilled player first advised him, saying that assisting him was easy, but it would be difficult to do it openly. He told the man, "Wait until you reach a crucial point, and I will speak one riddle. If you follow my instructions, you will no longer lose." This poor chess player was thrilled, and the two of them went together to play against someone. When the game began, the skilled player subtly advised him on his moves. On one occasion, the poor player moved his guard to the left, and the opponent immediately countered with a cannon in the center. He moved his elephant, and the opponent responded with a rook. As the game progressed, the

---

[268] The first draft of this article was originally published in the combined 3rd and 4th issues of Volume 1 of *Frontier Humanities* of Nankai University (March 1944). Later, the follow-up work *On the Patronymic System of the Tibeto-Burman Ethnic Groups Again* was published in the 9th issue of Volume 3 of *Frontier Administration Review* (September 1944), and *On the Patronymic System of the Tibeto-Burman Ethnic Groups for the Third Time* was published in the combined 1st and 2nd issues of Volume 2 of *Frontier Humanities* (December 1944). This appendix is a comprehensive revision and compilation of the above three articles.

opponent's horse crossed the river, and a few more moves would have resulted in a checkmate. The poor player, seeing no way out, was desperate. He looked at the skilled player for guidance. The skilled player then said, "A long spear!" He repeated it several times, but the poor player didn't understand and lost again. When they returned, the poor player complained to the skilled player. The skilled player said, "I gave you such a high-level suggestion, and you didn't follow it. How can you blame me?" The poor player responded, "When did you even suggest a move to me?" The skilled player became anxious and said:

"Did you not hear me say, 'A long spear, reaching through the heavens and earth, (yi gan chang qiang tong tian che di)

Where no one on the ground can act without it, (di xia wu ren shi bu cheng)

In the city, the elder sister goes to burn incense, (cheng li da jie qu shao xiang)

The village mother, (xiang li niang)

Mother long, father short, (niang chang ye duan)

Short and long are shortcuts, (duan chang jie jing)

Respecting virtues at court, (jing de da chao)

The court's ladder, (chao tian deng)

Hidden inside the ladder, (deng li cang shen)

with a clean and pure body, (shen qing bai)

The fair-faced Pan An, (bai mian pan an)

An An delivers rice, (an an song mi)

Rice, flour, oil, and salt, (mi mian you yan)

162

Yama summons Lü Dongbin, (yan wang yao qing lv dong bin)

The guest bird carries a letter, flying south, (bin hong shao shu yan nan fei)

Flying tiger Liu Qing, (fei hu liu qing)

Celebrating the eight scholars, (qing ba shi)

The scholar with the pockmarked face, the nine clever ones, (shi ge ma zi jiu ge qiao)

The clever enemies, (qiao yuan jia)

Every family sees the world's intentions, (jia jia guan shi yin)

Blown by the wind, the fire ignites, (yin feng chui huo)

Burning the warship, (huo shao zhan chuan)

Borrowing arrows from the ship's bow, (chuan tou jie jian)

Every arrow hits the wolf's tooth, (jian jian she lang ya)

Sleeping on a small bed, (ya chuang shang shui zhe ge xiao yao jing)

A mischievous little demon, (jing ling gu guai)

Cunning and strange, (guai tou guai nao)

Angry that the enemy is so wicked, (nao hen chou ren tai bu liang)

The brothers of Liangshan, (liang shan po shang zhong di xiong)

Brothers are generous, younger brothers endure, (xiong kuan di ren)

Enduring with reason, (ren xin hai li)

That is how it should be, (li ying ru ci)

A house is for rent, (ci fang chu zu)

In the backyard of the rented house, there's a loquat tree, (chu zu de na suo fang zi hou yuan zhong zhe pi pa shu)

The leaves of the loquat tree resemble donkey ears. (pi pa shu de ye zi xiang ge lv er duo)

If it's a donkey, you can dismount from the horse. (shi ge lv zi jiu neng xia ma)"

If only you'd listened to me earlier! Had you stopped leaving that left horse staring at the elephant's eye (move path) and instead blocked with the corner check, how on earth did you end up losing because of that single move!. Do you understand now?"

The poor player thought for a long time and finally said, "I understand now. But I'd rather lose than follow your roundabout advice!"

This passage contains a form of wordplay called "top-linking" or "continuing rhymes," where the last word or last two or three words of one sentence are the same as the first word or the first two or three words of the next sentence, either in terms of sound or meaning. For example, the last word of "yi gan chang qiang tong tian che di" (A long spear, reaching through the heavens and earth) is the same as the first word of the sentence "di xia wu ren shi bu cheng" (Where no one on the ground can act without it) . Similarly, the last word "成" (cheng, meaning "to succeed") in "事不成" (meaning "it doesn't work") is the same in sound as "城里" (cheng li, meaning "in the city"). Another example is the phrase "ci fang chu zu" (This house for rent), where the last two words "出租" (chū zū) are the same as the beginning of the following sentence, "chu zu de na suo fang zi hou yuan zhong zhe pi pa shu" (The house for rent has a loquat tree in the backyard), and

164

the last three words of this sentence are the same as the beginning of the next sentence, "pi pa shu de ye zi xiang ge lv er duo" (The leaves of the loquat tree resemble donkey ears). This form of wordplay is popular in folk art and literature. In poetry and songs, there is a style known as "top-link rhyme" or "continuous rhyme" (anadiplosis), which is similar in nature to this word game. For instance, the anonymous poem *Little Peach Blossom* in *Zhongyuan Yin Yun (Phonology of the Central Plains)* uses such a structure:

A heartbroken person writes a heartbroken poem, (Duan chang ren ji duan chang ci)

The words speak of things in the heart, (ci xie xin jian shi)

But when it comes to the end, there's no stopping, (shi dao tou lai bu you zi)

Thinking to myself, (zi xun si)

Thinking of past sincerity, (si liang wang ri zhen cheng zhi)

Sincerity is real, (zhi cheng shi you)

Among those who are affectionate, (you qing shui si)

Who is like that person of mine. (si an na ren er)

Qiao Mengfu also uses continuous rhyme in *Little Peach Blossom*, as found in *Le Fu Qun Yu*[269]. Also, Zheng Dehui's *Zhuan Sha*[270] in the first section of *Zhou Mei Xiang* and Ma Zhiyuan's *Plum*

---

[269] Qiao Mengfu's *Little Red Peach Blossom: In the Style of Linked Pearls*: The falling catkins are separated by the red curtain. The curtain is still, and the double doors are closed. Closing the mirror, I'm shy to look at my face. My brows are knitted. Pointing with my slender fingers, I'm thinking of the date of return. Missing him for leaving me behind, I owe him so much that I'm sick and weak.

[270] Act One, *The Conclusion of the Act of Enticing* in Zheng Dehui's *Mei Xiang*: You say you stroll out of the orchid courtyard. The courtyard is quiet as people are just settling down. Quietly listening, it's the sound of that young man playing the zither. That young man guesses

Wine and *Recalling Jiangnan*[271] in the third section of *Han Palace Autumn*, as well as the poem *Taohua Lengluo (Cold and Fallen Peach Blossoms Cold)* in *Echoes of White Snow* , all employ this structure. Now, let's take *Cold and Fallen Peach Blossoms* as an example.

The peach blossoms are cold, drifting in the wind, (Tao hua leng luo bei feng <u>piao</u>)

Falling and scattering across the small bridge, (<u>Piao</u> luo can hua guo xiao <u>qiao</u>)

Under the bridge, golden fish play in the water, (<u>Qiao</u> xia jin yu shuang xi <u>shui</u>)

Beside the water, a small bird preens its new feathers, (<u>Shui</u> bian xiao niao li xin <u>mao</u>)

The feathers have not yet been wet by the yellow plum rain, (<u>Mao</u> yi wei shi huang mei <u>yu</u>)

Raindrops on red pears look exceptionally delicate, (<u>Yu</u> di hong li fen wai <u>jiao</u>)

---

that I'm seemingly heartless but affectionate. Knowing well what my intention is for coming to listen. After listening quietly until the first watch of the night has passed, even when the night is deep, there's no time to rest. Waiting for what? I quickly move my steps. Passing by the side of the phoenix tree and the golden well. The well railing shelters my body. Casting my shadow, alas, I really dislike the bright moon.

[271] In the third act of Ma Zhiyuan's *The Autumn in the Han Palace, Plum Blossom Wine* and *Recovering the South of the Yangtze River* are connected in the form of linked pearls. *Plum Blossom Wine*:... I return to Xianyang in my imperial carriage. Return to Xianyang, pass through the palace walls. Pass through the palace walls, wind around the winding corridors. Wind around the winding corridors, approach the pepper chamber. Approach the pepper chamber, the moon is dim and yellow. The moon is dim and yellow, the night turns cool. The night turns cool, the cicadas weep in the cold. The cicadas weep in the cold, by the green gauze window. By the green gauze window, I don't want to think about it. *Recovering the South of the Yangtze River*: Ah, if I don't think about it, only those with an iron heart could do so. Even those with an iron heart would shed thousands of sad tears....

Their delicate forms often accompany the drooping willow, (Jiao zi chang ban chui yang liu)

Beyond the willows, two purple swallows fly high, (Liu wai shuang fei zi yan gao)

On the high pavilion, a beautiful woman plays a jade flute, (Gao ge jia ren chui yu di)

Next to the flute, threads are tied and hung with silk, (Di bian qian xian gua si tao)

The silk forms an exquisite fragrance in the shape of Buddha's hand, (Tao jie ling long xiang fo shou)

In her hand, there is a fan facing the river's tide, (Shou zhong you shan wang he chao)

The tide is calm, and the sailboats are steady, (Chao ping liang an feng fan wen)

Steady, she sits in the boat, gently rocking, (Wen zuo zhou zhong qie man yao)

The boat moves toward the West River, as the evening approaches, (Yao ru xi he tian jiang wan)

At the evening window, she sighs in solitude, feeling bored, (Wan chuang ji mo tan wu liao)

She pushes open the screen window to gaze at the desolation, (Liao tui sha chuang guan leng luo)

The snow falls faintly, tapped by the water, (Luo xue miao miao bei shui qiao)

She knocks on the door, asking for the way to Tiantai, (Qiao men jie wen tian tai lu)

The road passes the West River with a broken bridge, (Lu guo xi he you duan qiao)

Beside the bridge, there are peach trees planted. (Qiao bian zhong bi tao)

To discuss this further, works like *The Book of Songs: Already Drunk* from chapters two to the final chapter[272], the song "To the East of Pingling, Pines, and Cypress, Who Cut the Virtuous Duke's Tree?" from the *Book of Song: Treatise on Music*[273], Cao Zijiang's *A Poem to Cao Biao, the Prince of Baima* [274], and Li Bai's *Song of White Clouds:*

---

[272] The whole poem of *Already Drunk* in the *Book of Songs: Major Odes* is as follows: (Chapter One) Already drunk with wine, already filled with virtue. May the gentleman live for ten thousand years and be blessed with great fortune. (Chapter Two) Already drunk with wine, your dishes are already presented. May the gentleman live for ten thousand years and be blessed with bright wisdom. (Chapter Three) The bright wisdom shines brightly, with noble and auspicious endings. With an auspicious ending, there is a beginning. The noble person makes a good announcement. (Chapter Four) What is the announcement? The bamboo and wooden utensils are quiet and fine. Friends are here to assist, assisted with dignity. (Chapter Five) The dignity is very appropriate. The gentleman has filial sons. Filial sons are never in lack, and blessings will always be bestowed upon your kind. (Chapter Six) What is your kind? It's the family at home. May the gentleman live for ten thousand years and always be bestowed with offspring and inheritance. (Chapter Seven) What is the inheritance? Heaven endows you with fortune. May the gentleman live for ten thousand years and have noble servants. (Chapter Eight) What are the servants? They are bestowed upon you, noble men and women. Bestow upon you noble men and women, followed by descendants.

[273] "East of Pingling" in ancient lyrics recorded in Volume Three of in the *Book of Song: Music Record*: East of Pingling, there are pine, cypress and tung trees. I don't know who has kidnapped the righteous man. Kidnapped the righteous man, under the hall. Paying a million coins and two horses. Two horses, it's really difficult. Looking back and seeing the pursuers, my heart is sad. My heart is sad, bleeding profusely. Returning home to tell my family to sell the yellow calf.

[274] Cao Zijian's *A Poem to Cao Biao, the Prince of Baima* has a total of seven chapters. Starting from the second chapter, there is a circular connection between chapters. Here are the second, third chapters and the beginning of the fourth chapter recorded below: (Chapter Two) How desolate is the Taigu Valley! The mountain trees are lush and green. The continuous rain has muddied my way, and the flowing water is vast and crisscrossing. The middle road is completely blocked, so I change my route and climb the high hill. The long slope reaches up to the clouds and the sun. My horse has become black and yellow. (Chapter Three) Even though the horse is black and yellow, it can still move forward. My thoughts are gloomy and can be relieved. What am I thinking about when relieving my gloom? My dear ones are living apart from me. Originally, I planned to be in harmony with them, but in the middle, things didn't go as expected. Owls are crying on the crossbar and yoke, and wolves

Farewell to Liu Shiliu Returning to the Mountains[275] all use similar forms, either repeating the final line of each chapter or repeating the final few characters in each line. These too can be considered examples of "top-linking" style. Why do I start this article with these examples? Because the "father-son linkage naming system" discussed here can be explained through examples of top-linking.

The father-son linkage naming system is a cultural trait of the Tibeto-Burman peoples, which helps establish familial relationships through both physical traits and language. It also provides a solution to several unresolved ethnic affiliation issues in history. Broadly speaking, in this tribe, the final one or two syllables of the father's name are often identical to the first one or two syllables of the son's name. This system generally follows a few patterns:

1.ABC → CDE → DEF → FGH

En heng nuo → Nuo ben pei → Ben pei guo → Guo gao lie

2.A□B → B□C → C□D → D□E

Gong ya long → Long ya gao → Gao ya shou → Shou ya mei

3.ABCD → CDEF → EFGH → GHIJ

Yizun Laoshao → Laoshao Duzai → Duzai Azong → Azong Yiqu

4.□A□B → □B□C → □C□D → □D□E

---

are blocking the road. Flies are confusing black and white, and slanderous words make the close ones become distant. Wanting to return but there's no way, I hold the reins and hesitate. (Chapter Four) Why should I hesitate and stay? My longing has no end...

[275] Li Bai's *Song of White Clouds: Farewell to Liu Shiliu Returning to the Mountains*: The mountains in Chu and Qin are all covered with white clouds. The white clouds follow you everywhere. Follow you everywhere. When you enter the mountains in Chu, the clouds also follow you across the Xiang River. On the Xiang River, with the dress made of usnea, the white clouds urge you to return early.

A zong A liang → A liang A hu → A hu A lie → A lie A jia

Though there may be minor variations within different branches, the overall system rarely deviates beyond these basic patterns.

My interest in this subject initially arose from paper-based materials. In the spring of 1943, I traveled to Jizu Mountain in the western part of Yunnan, where I visited a temple called Xitan Temple. There, I discovered a genealogical record of the Lijiang Mu Chieftains, which piqued my curiosity. After returning, I compiled my travel notes and referred to works by Tao Yunkui, Dong Zuobin, and Ling Chunsheng, and wrote an article *On the Mu Clan Genealogy of Xitan Temple at Jizu Mountain*, published in *Contemporary Review*, Vol. 3, Issue 25. Later, through my own research and materials provided by friends, I gathered more practical, real-world examples. Now, I aim to present both theoretical and real materials in this paper, hoping that anthropologists, ethnologists, and linguists interested in this subject will add further insights or corrections to complete the understanding of this issue.

I will describe this issue under three main sections, six points, and thirteen subtopics:

Burmese ethnic group

1. Burman People (Burma) For this group, I have not obtained direct materials, but I have found evidence of the father-son linkage naming system in Burmese history. For example, during the 2nd to 4th centuries, the Burmese Gupta dynasty also followed this naming practice. Some of the names include:

Pyo—so—ti Ti—min—yi

Yi—min—baik Baik—then—li

Then—li—jong Jong—du—yit[276]

I would also appreciate further contributions from experts in Burmese history.

Chashan (A-chit)

2. Chashan is a tribe living along the northern border of Yunnan and Myanmar. In the spring of 1944, I personally obtained two genealogies from this tribe: one, from a man named Kong Kelang, traced his lineage back forty-six generations; another, from Dong Changshao, traced his lineage back nine generations. The genealogies are listed below:

A. The Kong Family Genealogy:[277]

① Ya ┤be ↓ bawm ┤   ② Ma ┤shaw ⌐bawm ┤

③ Bawm ┤shaw ⌐ chung ┤   ④ Chung ┤shi ┤nin ┤

---

[276] Phayer, *History of Burma*, p.279, as cited in Ling Chunsheng's *A Study of the Bai Man and Wu Man in the Tang Dynasty*, which can be found in the first issue of the first volume of *Anthropology Bulletin* of the Institute of History and Philology.

[277] The phonetic symbols of the Chashan language are slightly revised for the time being according to O. Hanson's *Shantou Script*, but the tone marks are added separately.

⑤ Shi ⊣ nin ⊣ k'ying ⊣ ⑥ K'ying ⊣ da ⌐ə ⊣

⑦ Da ⌐ə ⊣ saw? ⌐ ⑧ Saw? ⌐yaw ⊣ chu ⌐

⑨ Chu ⌐fu ⊣ fek ⌐ ⑩ Fu ⊣ fek ⌐k'um ⌐

⑪ K'um ⌐fu ⊣ zik ↓ ⑫ Zik ↓ k'u ⊣ lam ↓

⑬ K'u ⊣ lam ↓ pe ⊣ ⑭ Shaw ⌐gyaw ⌐xang ⊣

⑮ Xang ⊣ zaw ⊣ byu ↓ ⑯ Byu ↓ zaw ⊣ te ⌐

⑰ Te ⌐maw ⊣ yaw ↓ ⑱ Maw ⊣ yaw ↓ p'yan ↓

⑲ P'yan ↓byaw ⊣ yang ⊣ ⑳ Yang ⊣ lawm ⊣ lik ⊣

㉑ Lik ⊣ ding ↓ chit ⌐ ㉒ Chit ⌐kang ⊣ yan ⊣

㉓ Kang ⊣ yan ⊣ gwi ↓ ㉔ Gwi ↓ chung ↓ chyit ⊣

㉕ Chung ↓ chyit ⊣ yaw ⊣ ㉖ Yaw ⊣ au ⊣ ding ⌐

㉗ Ding ⌐law ⊣ waw ⊣ ㉘ Waw ⊣ law ⊣ jang ⌐

㉙ Jang ⌐law ⊣ bawm ↓ ㉚ Bawm ↓ law ⊣ nu ⌐

㉛ Nu ⌐kyang ⊣ ㉜ Kyang ⊣ bau? ⌐

㉝ Bau? ⌐myaw ⊣ ㉞ Myaw ⊣t'uk ⌐

㉟ T'uk ⌐bawm ↓ ㊱ Bawm ↓ zing ⊣

㊲ Zing ⊣ yaw ↓ ㊳ Yaw ↓ bawm ↓

㊴ Bawm ↓ k'aw ⊣ ㊵ K'aw ⊣ ying ⊣

㊶ Ying ⊣ sau ⊣ ㊷ Sau ⊣ ying ⊣

㊸ Ying ⊣ yaw ↓ ㊹ Yaw ↓ ying ⊣

㊺ Ying ⊣k'aw ↓ ㊻ K'aw ↓lang ⊣

In the forty-six generations listed above, except for generations 1 and 2 which are of the same generation, the rest can represent father-son relationships with names linked. However, the thirteenth and fourteenth generations do not connect. According to Kong Kelang, "Generations above the thirteenth can speak to cattle, dogs, grass, and trees, and have not yet fully become human." This might just be an ancient legend and cannot yet be considered the direct lineage of the Kong family.

B. The Dong Family Genealogy:

① Yawn ⌐sau ⊣   ② Sau ⊣ chang ⌐

③ Chang ⌐lang ⌐

④ Lang ⌐bau ⌐ = Lang ⌐gying

⑤ Bau ⌐zung ⌐ = Bau ⌐ying = Bau ⌐taik ↓

⑥ Zung ⌐ying ⌐   ⑦ Ying ⌐sau ⊣

⑧ Sau ⊣ chang ⌐   ⑨ Chang ⌐sau ⊣ (Dong Changshao)

In this genealogy, the fourth generation has two brothers, and the fifth generation has three brothers, so this branch must have come from the eldest son. According to Dong Changshao, about four hundred years ago, when Pianma was still a wilderness, his first

ancestor, **Yawm ⌐sau ⊣**, came here to clear the land for farming, doing the "hard work of opening up the mountains and forests." The grave of this pioneer is located in Lower Pianma, with a stone stele and carved image. The grave of the fourth ancestor is on the

Cyung ↓ gyung ⊣ mountain in Lower Pianma, and the grave of the

173

fifth ancestor is in Lower Pianma at Aw ˧ yaw ˩ bau ˩ . Neither of these graves has a stone stele. Comparing the Kong and Dong families, it seems that the Dong family came much later than the Kong family. If Changshao's statement is reliable, the Dong family may have moved to Pianma in the late years of the Ming Dynasty during the reign of Emperor Jiajing.

Xifan Branch:

3. The Mexie or Naxi (Moso and Na-khi)[278] — According to Yu Qingyuan's *Notes from Weixi:*

The Mexie do not have surnames. They use the last character of the ancestor's name and the last character of the father's name, adding one more character to form a name that is passed down in succession to indicate closeness or remoteness.

In fact, if we carefully examine the four naming methods mentioned earlier and the three genealogies of the Mosuo people presented below, we can find that what Yu Qingyuan says seems somewhat inaccurate. The materials I have gathered are:

A. The Six Generations Recorded in the Lijiang Mosuo Classics after the Great Flood:

① Zongzheng Lien

② En Heng Nuo

③ Nuo Ben Pei

④ Ben Pei Guo

---

[278] Naxi, that is, the Naxi ethnic group.

⑤ Guo Gao Lie

⑥ Gao Lie Qu[279]

According to Yu's explanation, the third generation here should be "En Nuo Pei," and the fourth generation should be "Nuo Pei Guo," which clearly does not match the facts.

B. The Twelve Generations Recorded in the *Mu Clan's Virtuous Descendants Genealogy* from the Jade Dragon Mountain:

① Tian Xian Cong Cong

② Cong Cong Cong Yang

③ Cong Yang Cong Jiao

④ Cong Jiao Jiao Xian

⑤ Jiao Xian Bi Xian

⑥ Bi Xian Cao Xian

⑦ Cao Xian Li Wei Wei

⑧ Li Wei Nuo Yu

⑨ Nuo Yu Nan Ban Pu

⑩ Ban Pu Yu

⑪ Yu Ge Lai

⑫ Ge Lai Qiu[280]

Since then, it has continued the historical genealogy of the Mu clan. It is said that the first ancestor of the Mu clan was Ye Gunian. Eleven generations before Ye Gunian was the Yuejuan Zhao in the

---

[279] As cited in Dong Zuobin's *New Evidence for the Genealogy of the Cuan People*, which can be found in the second issue of the *Ethnological Research Collection* of the Zhongshan Cultural and Educational Institute.

[280] Refer to Joseph F. Rock, *The Ancient Na-khi Kingdom of south-west China*, Cambridge, 1947, PP. 81-85.

Eastern Han Dynasty, and six generations after him were changed to the Zuo Guo Zhao. Yang Shen's "Preface to the Genealogy of the Mu Clan in Office" said that Ye Gunian was a military officer in the Wude period of the Tang Dynasty, while his descendant Qiu Yang didn't inherit the position until the Shangyuan period of Emperor Gaozong of the Tang Dynasty. However, according to the father-son linkage naming system, after Ge Laiqiu, it should be linked with the line of Qiu Yang, and there shouldn't be Ye Gunian in between as an interval. I rather suspect that Ye Gunian was the sinicized name of either Ge Laiqiu or Qiu Yang. Naturally, more evidence is needed to make a definite judgment on this point.

C. *Mu Clan Genealogy* in Lijiang:

The *Mu clan* has been a hereditary local ruler (Tusi) in Lijiang from the Tang Dynasty (Wu De era) to the early Qing Dynasty. There are four genealogies of this family:

① Yang Shen's *Preface to the Mu Clan Official Genealogy*, written in the 24th year of the Ming Jiajing reign, is now housed in the Lijiang Mu clan collection.

② *Mu Clan Official Genealogy: Image and Generations Study*, published together with Yang's *Preface*, has two versions: one version bears a label inscribed by Chen Zhaozhong of Hainan in the 20th year of Daoguang reign of Qing Dynasty, with a postscript and poems. This version is kept in the Lijiang Mu clan collection; the other version, titled *Mu Family Official Genealogy*, is housed at the Xitan Temple in Jizu Mountain, Yunnan.

③ *Mu Clan Genealogy Stele*, located in the Mu clan graveyard in She Mountain, 10 miles southeast of Lijiang City. It was first engraved in the 22nd year of Daoguang reign of Qing Dynasty.

④ *Supplement to the General Annals of Yunnan: Records of the Southern Barbarians*, with an appendix on the *Mu Clan Official Genealogy*. This draft was compiled in the 27th year of Guangxu reign of Qing Dynasty by Wang Wenshao and others.

The similarities and differences among these four sources are discussed in Tao Yunkui's *On the Distribution and Migration of the Mosuo Clan Names* and my article *Records of the Mu Clan Official Genealogy in Xitan Temple, Jizu Mountain*, so I will not go into further detail here. Now, based on the *Mu Clan Genealogy Stele*, I will present the genealogy as follows:

1.Qiū yáng

2.Yáng yīn dū gǔ

3.Dū gǔ là jù

4.Là jù pǔ méng

5.Pǔ méng pǔ wáng

6.Pǔ wáng là wán

7.Là wán xī nèi

8.Xī nèi xī kě

9.Xī kě cì tǔ

10.Là tǔ é jūn

11.É jūn mù jù

12.Mù jù mù xī

13.Mù xī mù cuō

14.Mù cuō mù lè

15.Mù lè mù bǎo

16.Mù bǎo ā cóng

17.Ā cóng ā liáng

18.Ā liáng ā hú

19.Ā hú ā liè

20.Ā liè ā jiǎ

21.Ā jiǎ ā dé (mù dé)

22.Ā dé ā chū (mù chū)

23.Ā chū ā tǔ (mù tǔ)

24.Ā tǔ ā dì (mù sēn)

25.Ā dì ā sì (mù qīng)

26.Ā sì ā yá (mù tài)

27.Ā yá ā qiū (mù dìng)

28.Ā qiū ā gōng (mù gōng)

29.Ā gōng ā mù (mù gāo)

30.Ā mù ā dū (mù dōng)

31.Ā dū ā shèng (mù wàng)

32.Ā shèng ā zhái (mù qīng)

33.Ā zhái ā sì (mù zēng)

34.Ā sì ā chūn (mù yì)[281]

35.Mù

---

[281] According to J.F. Rock's aforementioned book, pp. 136–153, after Mù Yì, the consecutive naming system continued with the following generations: Ā chūn Ā sú (Mù Jìng), Ā sú Ā wèi (Mù Yáo), Ā wèi Ā huī (Mù Xīng), and Ā huī Ā zhù (Mù Zhōng). After Mù Zhōng, the system was abandoned, and the names Mù Dé, Mù Xiù, Mù Ruì, Mù Hàn, Mù Jìng, Mù Yìn, Mù Biāo, Mù Qióng, and Mù Sōngkuí marked the end of the use of the consecutive naming system. This source differs from the *Genealogical Records of the Mù Family*.

36.Mù sōng

37.Mù rùn

38.Mù jí

39.Mù rén

The naming system for the 39 generations above follows a consecutive name pattern. The first and second generations use the first style, the second to sixteenth generations use the third style, and the seventeenth to thirty-fourth generations use the fourth style. Although the surname "Mu" was granted during the early Ming period, the traditional practice of father-son linkage names was not easily changed at that time. Instead, the original name's last character was added after the surname "Mu" to form the full name, such as "A Jiǎ A Dé" also being called "Mu Dé". It was not until the Kangxi period of Qing Dynasty, starting from "Mu Pǔ", that this cultural characteristic was no longer visible.

D. Yongning Tusi's Genealogy:

According to the *Yongbei Zhili Hall Annals* (Volume 3, pages 36 to 41), the first two generations of the Yongning Tusi family also followed the father-son linkage naming system:

1. Bǔ dū gè jí 2. Gè jí bā hé

However, starting from the third generation, Bǔ chè (1413), and the fourth generation, Nán bā (1425), this cultural trace disappeared. From the fifth generation, Ā zhí (1458), the descendants began to use

"Ā" as their surname. This trend of Sinicization began during the Yongle period of Ming Dyanasty.[282]

Luoluo Branch

4. Luoluo (Lolo) According to the available materials, I have seen seven versions of the genealogy of this tribe:

A. Ding Wenjiang (V.K. Ting) *Cuan Wen Cong Ke (A Collection of Lolo Writings) The Chronicle of the Emperors*, which covers the thirty generations before the flood:

1. Xī mǔ zhē

2. Zhē dào gōng

3. Gōng zhú shī

4. Shī yà lì

5. Lì yà míng

6. Míng cháng jué

7. Cháng jué zuò

8. Zuò ā qiē

9. Qiē yà zōng

10. Zōng yà yí

11. Yí yà jì

12. Jì pò néng

13. Pò néng dào

14. Dào mǔ yí

15. Mǔ yí chǐ

16. Chǐ yà suǒ

---

[282] See J.F. Rock's aforementioned book, pp. 377–381.

17. Suǒ yà dé

18. Dé xǐ suǒ

19. Xǐ suǒ duō

20. Duō bì yì

21. Bì yì dǔ

22. Dǔ xǐ xiān

23. Xǐ xiān duó

24. Duó ā dà

25. Dà ā wǔ

26. Ā wǔ nuò

27. Nuò zhù dú

28. Dú zhù wǔ

29. Wǔ lǎo cuō

30. Cuō zhū dú

According to the preface by the translator, Luo Wenbi, "From the time of the human ancestor Xī mǔ zhē to the era of Cuō zhū dú, there were a total of thirty generations. During this period, there were no written records, only oral transmission. Up to the twenty-ninth generation, Wǔ lǎo cuō, it was thanks to the divine intervention of a priest named Fù Ā Dié, who came to establish the sacrificial rites, create writing, set up laws and regulations, and initiate the culture. It was the beginning of civilization and the establishment of rituals. However, there should have been a great flood mentioned during this time, but since there is no text available, I cannot provide a detailed account." The so-called "flood" refers to a phase, and looking back further, it connects to the mythological origin of humanity, starting

181

with their ancestor Xī mǔ zhē. The thirtieth generation, Cuō zhū dú, is linked by name to the ancestral mother of the Shuǐxī'ān clan, Dù mǔ wú.

B. The "Post-Tian Dù mǔ" genealogy in *Cuan Wen Cong Ke: The Chronicle of the Emperors*, which is the genealogy of the Shuixi Luoluo's An clan of Guizhou, covers a total of eighty-four generations, from the ancestor Dù mǔ wú of the Ān clan to Yī fēn míng zōng.

1.Dù mǔ wú	20.Bì yī méi
2.Mǔ qí qí	21.Méi ā liàng
3.Qí yà hóng	22.Liàng ā zōng
4.Hóng yà dé	23.Zōng yà bǔ
5.Dé gǔ shā	24.Bǔ yà sháo
6.Shā gǔ mǔ	25.Sháo yà tǎo
7.Gǔ mǔ gōng	26.Tǎo ā cháng
8.Gōng yà lǒng	27.Ā cháng bì
9.Lǒng yà gào	28.Bì yì mèng
10.Gào yà shǒu	29.Mèng wú shǒu
11.Shǒu yà měi	30.Shǒu ā diǎn
12.Měi ā dé	31.Diǎn yà fǎ
13.Dé yà shī	32.Fǎ yī yí
14.Shī měi wǔ	33.Yī yí chǐ
15.Měi wǔ mèng	34.Chǐ yà zhǔ
16.Mèng dié duō	35.Zhǔ ā diǎn
17.Duō yà zhì	36.Diǎn ā jí
18.Zhì wú sháo	37.Jí yà dēng
19.Wú sháo bì	38.Dēng yà dǔ

39.Dǔ ā dá

40.Ā dá duō

41.Duō ā tā

42.Tā ā qī

43.Qī ā fǒu

44.Fǒu nà zhī

45.Nà zhī Dù

According to Luo Wenbi, "After thoroughly examining the genealogy of our ancestral grandmother Qíqí, it spans a total of eighty-four generations, extending until the time when our ruler Ān Kūn was captured by Wú Sānguì. During this period, there were fluctuations between peace and chaos, but they cannot be fully detailed." From the time Wú Sānguì destroyed the Shuǐxī Ān clan until Luo Wénbǐ, there were six more generations. If counted from their ancestor Xī mǔ zhē, it amounts to a total of 120 generations, all consistently following the father-son linkage naming system.

C. The Ancient History of the Wǔdìng Yí Tribe:

This part of the material was obtained by Ma Xueliang from the Wuding Feng Tusi family. One version includes six consecutive generations:

"Zhú" (竹), "Chè" (彻), "Kè" (客) – First

dʏ˩ ʈʰɛ˩ kʰʏ˥ ɲi˩ tʰa˩

"Chè" (彻), "Kè" (客), "Shì" (士) – Second

ʈʰɛ˩ kʰʏ˥ ʂ̩˥ ɲi˩ ɲi˥

"Shì" (士), "Ā" (阿), "Shā" (沙) – Third

ʂ̩˥ ʏa˨ ʂa˨ ɲi˨ so˨

"Shā" (沙), "Lǔ" (鲁), "Zhuó" (濯) – Fourth

183

ʂa˧ lʮ˧ tʂwo˥ ni˩ ɬi˧

"Lǔ" (鲁), "Zhuó" (濯), "Chǔ" (楚) – **Fifth**

lʮ˧ tʂwo˥ t'ɣ˧ ni˩ ŋɣ˧

"Chǔ" (楚), "Shū" (舒), "Zú" (族) – **Sixth**

t'ɣ˧ ʂɿ˧ tsʻɣ˧ ni˩ tʂʻʊ˥

Another version includes ten consecutive generations:

"Mǔ" (母), "Ā" (阿), "Qí" (齐) – **First**

mɣ˧ ɣa˧ tsʻi˧ ni˩ t'a˩

"Qí" (齐), "Ā" (阿), "Hóng" (宏) – **Second**

tsʻi˧ ɣa˧ hũ˧ ni˩ ni˥

"Hóng" (宏), "Ā" (阿), "Dé" (德) – **Third**

hũ˧ ɣa˧ dɣ̃˥ ni˩ so˧

"Dé" (德), "Wō" (窝), "Suǒ" (所) – **Fourth**

dɣ̃˥ ɣuʔ˥ swo˧ ni˩ ɬi˧

"Suǒ" (所), "Wù" (务), "Mǔ" (母) – **Fifth**

swo˧ ˈɣ˧ mɣ˧ ni˩ ŋɣ˧

"Mǔ" (母), "Chóu" (筹) – **Sixth**

ɣ˧ mɣ˧ ʂʻwo˥ ni˩ tʂʻʊ˥

"Chóu" (筹), "Ā" (阿), "Nù" (怒) – **Seventh**

ʂʻwo˥ ɣa˧ nũ˧ ni˩ ɕi˥

184

"Nù" (怒), "Ā" (阿), "Lǔ" (鲁) – **Eighth**

ɳu˦ ɣa˦ lɣ˦ ɳi˩ hɪ˥

"Lǔ" (鲁), "Ā" (阿), "Shì" (士) – **Ninth**

lɣ˦ ɣa˦ ʂ˥ ɳi˩ kɣ˦

"Shì" (士), "Ā" (阿), "Mò" (末) – **Tenth**

ʂ˥ ɣa˦ mo˦ ɳi˩ tsʻɛ˩

The first three generations of the second sequence are identical to the second to fourth generations of the Shuixi An clan. Additional Notes: This genealogical information comes from multiple sources. The material provided includes a variety of such genealogies, with different versions and details, but only two examples are given here.

D. The Father-Son Linkage Naming System of the Minning Luoluo Clan: This section of materials was collected by Fu Maojie from the report of Hei Luoluo in Mianning Xiaoxianggongling . He wrote an article titled *The Genesis in Luoluo Legends* which was published in *Border Services* in Chengdu, and he first sent me a copy of these materials. The transcription he provided is as follows:

ɣ˥ dʐɯ˥ ʂɿ˩ ɿ˩ tsɿ˥ (self)

ʂɿ˩ ɿ˩ ɣɯ˥ tʻɯ˥ tsʻɿ˩ (one generation)

ɣɯ˥ tʻɯ˥ vo˩ lɯ˥ ɳie˩ (second)

vo˩ lɯ˥ tɕʻy˥ pu˩ sua˩ (third)

185

tʂʻy ˥ pu ˩ dʑy ˥ m̩ ˩ ʅ ˦ (fourth)

dʑy ˥ m̩ ˩ zɯ ˦ ʂo ˦ ɡo ˦ (third son)

dʑy ˥ m̩ ˩ dʑy ˥ tʻɯ ˩ ɡɛ ˥ (broken root)

dʑy ˥ m̩ ˩ dʑy ˥ ʅ ˩ ɡɛ ˥ (broken root)

dʑy ˥ m̩ ˩ ʏ ˥ ʏ ˥ dzu ˦ (descendants)

ʏ ˥ ʏ ˩ zɯ ˦ ʂo ˦ ɡo ˦ (third son)

ʏ ˥ ʏ ˩ la ˥ iɛ ˩ iɛ ˦ lɛ ˦ hɛ ˩ ŋɡa ˥ (Han people)

ʏ ˥ ʏ ˩ ʂʅ ˩ ʂa ˩ lɛ ˦ o ˅ dzu ˩ (Heiyi)

ʏ ˥ ʏ ˩ ʂʅ ˩ ʂa ˩ lɛ ˦ o ˅ dzu ˩ (Xifan)

In this example, besides the names, there are also significant terms indicating meaning, with a curved line drawn under the characters. Although the genealogical system only includes six generations, the consecutive naming system is clearly evident. Additionally, the relationships between the Yi (夷), Han (汉), and other ethnic groups (番) are represented as perceived by the Yi people themselves.

E. The Genealogy of the Ahe and Luohong Families in Western Sichuan:

186

This is part of the material collected by Fu Maoji during his investigation in the Sichuan-Kang region. Both the Ahe and Luohong families are prominent branches of the local Luoluo people. The Ahe family genealogy has twelve generations, while the Luohong family has fourteen generations, both fully adopting the father-son linkage naming system:

1.Ahe Family Genealogy (see Appendix 1)

2.Luohong Family Genealogy (see Appendix 2)

The two genealogies above were recorded by Fu Maoji based on oral recitations from descendants of the Ahe and Luohong families. The information was initially recorded in Luoluo script and later translated into Chinese characters. This valuable material, now added from the Western Sichuan region, shows that this system is widely spread.

Additionally, according to Ling Chunsheng, "In 1935, while in Yunnan, I met a Luoluo (罗罗)[283] youth from the Daliangshan area of Sichuan named Qu Cangming, who told me that his father could recite the family genealogy, with the names of successive generations passed down accurately, spanning dozens of generations without error." This supports the records made by Fu Maoji and confirms that this naming system is widely practiced among the Yi people in the Sichuan and Kang regions.

---

[283] Luoluo, that is, the Lolo ethnic group.

5. Woni[284] Woni, also known as Heni, is the term used by the Han people to refer to various tribes speaking the Luoluo dialect in the southern part of Yunnan. The Woni people live in regions that do not extend beyond the northern latitude of 24°. According to Mao Qiling's *Man Si He Zhi (Records of the Native Chiefs)*, Volume 8, it is noted that: "The people of Zhu Dian, including the Luoluo and Heni tribes, frequently fought with one another, and when a death occurred, compensation was made with wealth. They did not have surnames; those with names might inherit the final character of their father's name, but they had no surnames." During the Hongzhi period (1488–1505 A.D.), Governor Chen Sheng added a character from the *Hundred Family Surnames* to the beginning of each name, which was adopted by all regions except Nalou. This shows that the Woni people also used the father-son linkage naming system. In 1943 and 1944, Gao Huanye and Yuan Jiahua went to Xinping and Eshan counties in southern Yunnan to investigate the Woni language. Unfortunately, they did not focus on this aspect, preventing me from verifying Mao Qiling's statements, much like I could with the Luoluo.

6. A-ka The A-ka people, also called the Ka people, are numerous and live in the eastern part of Jingdong[285], southern Yunnan, and Laos. In 1935, Tao Yunhui investigated the southern part of Yunnan and recorded two genealogies from two elderly A-ka people while passing

---

[284] Woni, the name for the Hani ethnic group in historical records. Also known as Woni or Woni.

[285] Kengtung, a place name in present-day Myanmar, also known as "Kengtung", located in the eastern part of Myanmar, with Yunnan in China and Laos to the east and Thailand to the south.

through a village called Jiufang on the route from Menglian to Mengzhe:

A. The lineage of Ka Luosai, spanning fifty-six generations (recorded based on Tao Yunhui's original system):

1.Su-mi-o	23.Ji-la-bi
2.O-tzou-lö	24.Bi-mŏ-tzwo
3.Tzou-lö-tzung	25.Tzwo-hwā
4.Tzung-mö-yieh	26.Hwā-jiä
5.Mö-yieh-ch'ia	27.Jiä-tzä
6.Ch'ia-di-hsi	28.Tzä-jiō
7.Di-hsi-li	29.Jiō-blung
8.Li-ho-bä	30.Blung-läi
9.Ho-bä-wu	31.Lui-mi
10.Wu-nio-za	32.Mi-hsia
11.Nio-za-tzwo	33.Hsia-yi
12.Tzwo-mö-er	34.Yi-ch'iä
13.Mö-er-chü	35.Ch'iä-kung
14.Chü-two-p'uo	36.Kung-kang
15.Two-p'uo-muo	37.Hsia-tzwo
16.Muo-kŭo-twŏ	38.Tzwo-ji
17.Kŭo-twŏ-ji	39.Ji-z'a
18.Ji-le-nio	40.Z'a-bang
19.Nio-ch'i-la	41.Bang-lai
20.La-tang-buŏ	42.Lai-ni
21.Buŏ-muo-buo	43.Ni-buo
22.Muo-buo-ji	44.Buo-pö

45.Ma-buo (female)

46.Buo-gong

47.P'u-da

48.Da-tzung

49.Tzung-ch' iwo

50.Ch'iwo-ji

51.Ji-z'a

52.Z'a-nio

53.Nio-chwo

54.Chwo-zä

55.Zä-bluo

56.Bluo-sä (individual)

Genealogy of Oulai: 47 Generations

1.Su-mi-o

2.O-tzou-lö

3.Tzou-lö-tzung

4.Tzung-mö-yieh

5.Mö-yieh-ch'ia

6.Ch'ia-di-hsi

7.Di-hsi-li

8.Li-ho-bä

9.Ho-bä-wu

10.Wu-nio-za

11.Nio-za-tzwo

12.Tzwo-mö-er

13.Mö-er-chu

14.Chü-twǒ-p'uo

15.Two-p'uo-muo

16.Muo-kǔo-two

17.Kuǒ-two-ji

18.Ji-le-niǒ

19.Niǒ-ch'i-la

20.La-tang-buo

21.Tang-buo-sö

22.Buo-sö-lai

23.Lai-lung-buo

24.Buo-yi-nŏ

25.Nŏ-muo-buo

26.Muo-buo-di

27.Di-hsia-biu

28.Biu-muŏ-tzö

29.Tzö-wo-yi

30.Wo-yi-jia

31.Jia-tzä

32.Tzä-jia

33.Jia-blung

34.Blung-läi

35.Läi-hsia

36.Hsia-yi

37.Yi-chiä

38.Chiä-kung

39.Kung-kong

40.Hsia-tzwo*

41.Tzwo-ji

42.Ji-za

43.Za-bang

44.O-de*

45.De-gong

46.Gong-tzwŏ

47.Ou-lä* (himself)

(* indicates non-connection)

The first twenty generations of these two family lines are identical. From the 27th to the 40th generation of Line A, excluding the 31st and 32nd generations, it is also the same as the 31st to 43rd generations of Line B. However, from the 21st to the 26th generation and the 41st to the 56th generation of Line A, and from the 21st to the 30th generation and the 14th to the 47th generation of Line B, these form separate branches. Therefore, we can conclude that the two family lines are very closely related. As for why the 37th generation and the 47th generation of Line A, and the 40th, 44th, and 47th generations of Line B, do not connect with the previous generations, it might be due to transcription errors or other unknown reasons, which cannot be determined at this point.

What has been discussed above is based on the materials I have currently found. Of course, other tribes within the Tibetan and Burmese ethnic groups, or nearby tribes, may also have this cultural feature, and there may be more to be added in the future. This article is merely raising a question using the "magnet attracting iron" method, hoping to attract attention from various parties. As more materials accumulate, the issue can eventually be resolved.

What is the purpose of this system? In my opinion, the first purpose is to aid memory. Except for the Luoluo and Mexie people, all the branches mentioned above do not have written characters, and even if they do, they are not used in daily life. With this "stringing beads" style of generational naming system, it becomes much easier to memorize. Secondly, because it is easy to remember, each person can commit to memory the names of their ancestors from the founding ancestor to themselves. This way, they can recognize that anyone who can trace their lineage to the same founding ancestor belongs to the same clan. Additionally, from this continuous chain of ancestors, one can distinguish the generations, similar to the character generations in Han Chinese family trees, which is crucial for identifying tribal groups.

Another function of this system is that it can help us solve some historical issues related to ethnicity.

Regarding the ancient history of Yunnan, although Chinese historical texts such as Sima Qian's *Records of the Grand Historian*, Ban Gu's *Book of Han*, Chang Qiu's *Chronicles of Huayang*, and Fan Chuo's *Book of the Barbarians* have records, they are often vague and unclear. It wasn't until the Yuan and Ming Dynasties when the Chinese discovered the indigenous *Ancient Chronicles of the Bai* written in vernacular, that more knowledge about the ancient history of Yunnan became available. Therefore, in the Yuan Dynasty, Zhang Daozong wrote *Records of Ancient Dian*, and in the Ming Dynasty, Yuan Yuansheng wrote *Unofficial History of Nanzhao* and Yang Shen wrote *Records of Dian*, all of which include records about the genealogies of the ancestors of Nanzhao. However, the story of the Ailao Yi people in the *Book of Later Han* and the story of King Ashoka after the introduction of Buddhism often get mixed up. In 1941, Dong Zuobin, in his work *New Evidence of the Cuan People's Genealogy*[286], compared the nine sons of Di Mengzhu recorded in *Ancient Records*

---

[286] The second issue of the *Ethnological Research Collection* of the Zhongshan Cultural and Educational Institute, pages 181 - 200.

of Bai with the twelve sons of Lu Zhu (edited as Lu Wuzhu) in *The Chronicle of the Emperors*, offering some insightful opinions, but this will not be discussed in detail here. We will now focus solely on the genealogy of Nanzhao.

Some historians and Western scholars of Oriental studies (Sinology) or studies of the Baiyi (Shan) ethnic group, such as Hervey de Saint-Devis, Parker, Rocher, Cochrane, and others, believe that Nanzhao and Baiyi are closely related and should belong to the Tai Family and that Nanzhao was a kingdom established by the Baiyi. According to the translation by Wang Youshen of the original work *Ancient History of Siam* by Damaluan Lachanupa, it says:

According to records from China, the five independent regions of the Tai people combined to form a single kingdom during the Tang Dynasty, known as the Nanzhao Kingdom. The capital of Nanzhao was Angsai, which is today Dali Prefecture in Yunnan Province. The Tai people of Nanzhao were known for their strength and courage, and they frequently invaded Tang territory and Tibet. However, in the year 1420 of the Buddhist Era (877 A.D.), they reconciled with the Tang Dynasty. The king of Nanzhao even married a princess from the Tang Dynasty. From then on, the royal family began to intermingle with Han Chinese blood, and the Tai people gradually abandoned their traditional customs and assimilated into Chinese society. Nevertheless, the Tai people managed to maintain a degree of independence. It was not until the reign of Kublai Khan, the Emperor of the Yuan Dynasty, who ascended the throne in China, that in the year 1797 of the Buddhist Era (1254 A.D.), a large military campaign was launched against the Tai kingdom, extending as far as the border of Myanmar. From that time onwards, the land once occupied by the Tai people gradually became incorporated into China.

As for this viewpoint, we will not argue against it on other grounds, but just focusing on the genealogical aspect, is already sufficient to prove that it is incorrect.

According to the *Unofficial History of Nanzhao* compiled by Yang Shen, which cites the *Ancient Records of Bai*, the ancestral lineage of Nanzhao is as follows:

Biao Jü Di — Di Meng Jü — Meng Jü Du...

From here, the lineage continued for thirty-six generations to

Xi Nu Luo — Luo Sheng — Sheng Luo Pi — Pi Luo Ge — Ge Luo Feng — Feng Jia Yi — Yi Bian Xun — Xun Ge Quan — Quan Long Sheng, Quan Li Sheng — Sheng Feng You — Yi Shi Long — Long Shun — Shun Hua Zhen

If we accept that the father-son linkage naming system is a cultural trait of the Tibetan-Burmese peoples, and as Tao Yun Kui reported that no such phenomenon was found in the genealogy of the Baiyi (Puyi) from the Chuli Xuanwei Office, then after reviewing the genealogy of the Nanzhao Meng family, the above-mentioned opinion should be easily refuted.

As for the genealogies of the other five kingdoms outside Nanzhao, most of them also employed the father-son linkage naming system. For example:

Mengxi Kingdom (4 generations):

Xi Fushou – Qieyang Zhao (brother) – Zhao Yuan – Yuan Luo

Yuexi Kingdom (2 generations):

Bo Chong – Yu Zeng (brother's son)

Langqiong Kingdom (6 generations):

Feng Shi – Luo Duo – Duo Luo Wang – Wang Pian – Pian Luo Yi – Yi Luo Jun

Tengdan Kingdom (5 generations):

Feng Mie – Mie Luo Pi – Pi Luo Deng – Deng Luo Dian – Dian Wen Tuo

Shilang Kingdom (4 generations):

Wang Mu – Wang Qian (younger brother) – Qian Bang – Bang Luo Dian[287]

Later, the Duan family of Dali became more deeply assimilated into Han Chinese culture, and this cultural trait became less prominent. However, the son of Duan Zhixiang was named Xiangxing, and his grandson was named Xingzhi, which unintentionally revealed a remnant of the father-son linkage naming system. As for the Gao family, which founded "Great China," they also continued to maintain this custom. Their lineage is as follows:

Gao Zhisheng — Gao Shengtai — Gao Taiming — Gao Mingqing

Descendants of the Gao clan served as local officials in Yao'an Prefecture during the early Qing period, continuing to use the father-son linkage naming system. According to the *Yunnan Tongzhi*

---

[287] The genealogy of the Six Zhaos was determined by referring to Fan Chuo's *Book of the Barbarians*, the *New Book of Tang: Biographies of the Southern Barbarians* and Yang Shen's *Unofficial History of Nanzhao*.

(General Annals of Yunnan), Volume 13, Page 17, compiled in the 20th year of Guangxu, citing the "Old Chronicles," it says:

At the beginning of the Shunzhi era, Gao Wengying submitted his loyalty and was still granted a hereditary position. Upon Gao Wengying's death, his son Yinghou inherited it; after Yinghou's death, his son Houde succeeded him. In the third year of the Yongzheng reign, Gao Houde was dismissed for illegal actions and was exiled to Jiangnan.

According to the *Biography of the Baiyi* in volume 19 of *Yunlong Ji Wang (Records of Yunlong in the Past)*, there is a record stating:

At first, the Yi people had no surnames. A Miao man had four sons, who began using the father's name as their surname: the eldest was Miao Nan, the second was Miao Dan, the third was Miao Wei, and the fourth was Miao Zhi. Miao Dan had five sons: Dan Jia, Dan Ti, Dan Niao, Dan Deng, and Dan Jiang. Among the five sons, only Dan Jia had a son named Jia Deng.[288]

Their genealogies should be arranged as follows:

◆ Miáo Nán (苗难)

◆ Miáo Dān (苗丹)

　◆ Dān Xià (丹夏) — Xià Dēng（夏登）, Dān Tī (丹梯), Dān Niǎo (丹鸟), Dān Dèng (丹邓), Dān Jiǎng (丹讲), Ā Miáo (阿苗)

◆ Miáo Wěi (苗委)

---

[288] Volume Nineteen of *Yunnan Preparatory Records for Collection*. I'm especially grateful to Zhang Zhengdong for copying and sending this item from Weixi in the summer of 1944

◆ Miáo Zhí (苗跖)

This is clearly also a case of the father-son linkage naming system. However, the original text refers to "摆夷" (Baiyi), which should likely be an error for "僰夷" (Boyi) or "白夷" (Baiyi), meaning "Bai people" or "commoners." As I mentioned earlier, the Tai ethnic group does not have this cultural trait, and from the current distribution of ethnic groups, Yunlong has only the Bai people, not the Baiyi. Hence, I corrected the above. If my correction is accurate, then comparing this material with the genealogies of the Dali Duan family, the "Great China" Gao family, and the Yao'an Gao family could offer us a clearer understanding of the ethnic affiliation issue. However, the evidence does not stop there.

In July 1944, a group of thirty-three of us, at the invitation of Ma Jin San (Chong Liu), Yan Dan Fu (Xu), Chen Xun Zhong (Fu Guang), and Wang Mei Wu (Shu), went to Dali to gather county historical materials. The analysis was meticulous, and the number of participants was considerable, making it quite a prominent event. Wu Qian focused specifically on the historical facts about Du Wenxiu[289]. But because his interests were wide-ranging and his diligence great, the results were rich in secondary findings. For instance, issues like double surnames and marriages within the same surname were topics he took note of and recorded wherever he went. Unexpectedly, he

---

[289] Du Wenxiu (1828—1872), the leader of the Hui ethnic group's uprising in Yunnan in the late Qing Dynasty. His courtesy name was Yunhuan, and his literary name was Baixiang. In the sixth year of Xianfeng (1856), he united the people of the Hui, Yi and Bai ethnic groups to launch an uprising in Menghua (now Weishan), captured Dali, occupied 53 prefectures and counties in Yunnan successively, persisted for 15 years, and was defeated and killed in 1872.

returned to Kunming ten days later than I did but managed to find some historical materials regarding the father-son linkage naming system in Dali's Xiaguan. This discovery really delighted me!

He came across two sets of materials: One was the *Inscription and Epitaph of the Virtuous Yang Sheng*, from the third year of Chenghua in the Ming Dynasty (1467), written by the monk Yang Wenxin, with the original inscription located at the slope of the Xiayang Peak in Dali, Xiguang; The other was the *Genealogy of the Zhao Clan of Taihe and Longguan*, written in the sixth year of Tianshun (1462), with the preface written by Xu Tingduan, an official of the Nanjing Imperial Academy, dated to February of that year.[290] In the first material, we find:

Yang Xian-Yang Xianqing-Yang Qingding

Three generations of grandfather, father, and grandson used the same name in succession, but from the time of Qingding onward, this practice no longer existed. According to the annotation by Qianjiu: "Qingding was a person from the Hongwu period in the Ming Dynasty. Around the 15th year of Hongwu, General Lan Yu and Mu Ying led an army to conquer Dali and established a military government. Qingding was appointed as the Duli Chief. This shows that during the Yuan Dynasty, the Duan clan in Dali and the Yang clan still followed the father-son linkage naming tradition. However, as more Han people migrated to the region, the local indigenous people gradually became

---

[290] The original texts of the two materials and Mr. Wu's postscript are included in the combined 1st and 2nd issues of Volume 2 of *Frontier Humanities* of Nankai University, the appendix of my work *On the Patronymic System of the Tibeto-Burman Ethnic Groups for the Third Time*.

sinicized, and the Yang clan abandoned their old practice of father-son linkage naming system. This is one of the reasons why the custom was abandoned." In another source, we find:

Zhao Fuxiang → Zhao Xiangshun → Zhao Shunhai

Three generations of grandfather, father, and grandson also followed the father-son name succession. However, from Zhao Ci onward, this cultural practice disappeared. According to Qianjiu's annotation: "The Zhao clan, from Zhao Fuxiang to Zhao Xiangshun and Zhao Shunhai, followed the father-son linkage naming system for three generations. The same system likely existed for several generations before them, starting with their ancestor Yongya, but their names have been lost and cannot be traced. After Zhao Shunhai's son, Zhao Ci, the father-son linkage naming system was discontinued. Zhao Ci, from the late Yuan to early Ming period, practiced Esoteric Buddhism and once visited the monastery of Gantong in the Hongwu period. This is comparable to the Yang clan of Longguan, who, starting with Yang Sheng in the Hongwu period, also stopped using the father-son linkage naming system. Therefore, it is clear that the indigenous people of Dali followed the father-son linkage naming system until the Yuan period, but after the Ming Hongwu period when Lan Yu, Mu Ying, and others conquered Dali, the number of Han settlers increased, and the local people began to gradually assimilate into Han culture, abandoning their ancient customs. This is undeniable."

By cross-referencing these examples with the Duan family of Dali, the Gao family of "Great China," and the Yao'an Gao family, I propose three new conclusions:

1.From this cultural trace, we can infer that a portion of the indigenous people in Dali and the surrounding counties in western Yunnan had a historical connection with the Tibetan-Burmese peoples.

2.The location of the *Inscription and Epitaph of the Virtuous Yang Sheng* is at "Mexie Ping" at the foot of Xiayang Peak in Dali, Xiaguang. When comparing this geographic name with the surname systems described by Yu Qingyuan in *Notes from Weixi* and the 34 generations of father-son linakge names in the *Mu Clan Genealogy* from Lijiang, I believe this is no coincidence. At the very least, it can be said that the ancestors of Yang Sheng had a blood relationship with the broader Tibetan-Burmese ethnic group. Furthermore, according to the legend in the *Yulong Mountain Lingjiao Yangbena*, the third son of the seventh generation ancestor "Caoxianliweiwei" was the ancestor of the Minjia ("Lä-bbu" in the Minjia language), which further confirms the evidence.

3.Based on previous speculations by Terrien de Lacouperie, H. R. Davies, Ding Wenjiang, and Ling Chunsheng regarding the Minjia's ethnic origins, this cultural feature warrants a reevaluation. As of now, only Li Fanggui's hypothesis that the Minjia language is closely related to the Luoluo language seems to remain the most consistent with the facts.

In Chinese ancient history, there was also a system where the grandfather's title or name was used as the surname. Zheng Qiao's

Tongzhi: Shizu Lüexu (Preface to Treatise on Clans and Surnames) states:

Section Seven: Using the grandfather's title as a surname: All sons of the nobles were called 'gongzi' (prince), and the sons of a 'gongzi' were called 'gongsun' (grandson). When the title of 'gongsun' was no longer used, the family adopted the grandfather's title as their surname. For example:

The son of Duke Mu of Zheng was called "Gongzi Fei" (公子), whose courtesy name was "Zisi" (子驷). His son was named "Gongsun Xia" (公孙夏). And his grandsons were named "Sidai" (驷带) and "Siqi" (驷乞).

The son of Duke Huan of Song was named "Gongzi Muyi" (公子目夷), with the courtesy name of "Ziyu" (子鱼). His son was named "Gongsun You" (公孙友). His grandsons were named "Yu Ju" (鱼莒) and "Yu Shi" (鱼石).

This is what is meant by taking the character of the grandfather's courtesy name as the surname.

Section Eight: Using the given name as a surname: For those without a courtesy name, the given name was used. For example:

The son of Duke Xiao of Lu was called "Gongzi Zhan" (公子展). His son was named "Gongsun Yibo" (公孙夷伯). His grandsons were named "Zhan Wuai" (展无骇) and "Zhan Qin" (展禽).

The son of Duke Mu of Zheng was named "Gongzi Feng" (公子丰). His son was named "Gongsun Duan" (公孙段). His grandsons were named "Feng Juan" (丰卷) and "Feng Shi" (丰施). These are the sons of feudal lords. The same was true for the sons of the Son of Heaven. For example, the descendants of Prince Hu (王子狐) took "Hu" as their surname, and the descendants of Prince Chao (王子朝) took "Chao" as their surname. Those without a courtesy name took their given name as their surname. However, some took their given name instead of their courtesy name as their surname. For example, Fan Pi's courtesy name was Zhongwen (仲文), but his descendants took "Pi" as their surname. Wu Yun's courtesy name was Zixu (子胥), and his descendants took "Xu" as their surname. All of these were because they were more commonly known by their given names.

Treatise on Clan and Surname volume two also states:

Some didn't take the character of their grandfather's courtesy name as their surname but took the character of their father's courtesy name as their surname. For example:

The son of Gongzi Sui (公子遂) was named Gongsun Guifu (公孙归父), with the courtesy name of Zijia (子家). His descendants took "Jia" (家) as their surname.

Gongsun Zhi (公孙枝) had the courtesy name of Zisang (子桑). His descendants took "Zisang" as their surname.

Some didn't take the grandfather's given name as their surname but took the father's given name as their surname. For example:

The son of Gongzi Ya (公子牙) was named Gongsun Zi (公孙兹), with the courtesy name of Daibo (戴伯). His descendants took

"Zi"(兹) as their surname. Ji Gong (季公) had the courtesy name of Zimi (子弥). His descendants took "Gong" (公) as their surname.

There were numerous cases of taking the given name as the surname. Zuo's Commentary only recorded the character of the grandfather's courtesy name.

This system of surnaming might appear similar to the father-son or grandfather-grandson name succession, but once the surname was established, the names of the father and son were no longer linked in a chain. Therefore, this practice differs from the father-son linkage naming system of the Tibetan-Burmese peoples.

Lastly, I am reminded of a statement made by Hu Shi in his *Canghuishi Zhaji (Diary During Study in the U.S.)* on July 20, 1914, where he mentioned that in India, there is no system of family surnames:

"When I spoke to a man from India, he told me that India has no family surname system. People have only personal names and no family names. The order of inheritance is as follows: if a father's name is John Joseph Matthew, then his son would be named Joseph Matthew Lique, with Lique being the new name, and the first two names being those of the father. His grandson would be named Lique Philip Charles, and his great-grandson would be named Philip Charles William, and so on."

The names "John," "Lique," and so on in the original text are merely used as examples, borrowing from Western names to explain the Indian system. It is not meant to imply that Indians actually use these names. I find this observation quite interesting, but unfortunately,

I know too little about India, so I would have to rely on the assistance of Indian friends to further explore this matter, hoping that I may have the opportunity to supplement and correct this article in the future. As for the name systems of Persia, the Arab world, and Russia, although they do exhibit some characteristics of showing generational order, they are not the same as the father-son linkage naming system discussed here, so I will not go into them in this article.

The first draft of this article was completed on December 10, 1943, and revised on February 25 of the following year. On March 20, 1949, two additional essays, "Further Discussion" and "The Third Discussion," were added to complete the full text.

At the time this article was being written, I had received two genealogies of the A-ka people from Mr. Tao Yunkui, along with some invaluable suggestions for revision. On December 21, I read this paper at a lecture at the Southwest United University's Literature and History Conference, and Mr. Tao personally attended, offering suggestions. He also requested a manuscript for *Frontier Humanities*. Unfortunately, I had not finished revising the article when Mr. Tao was suddenly struck by illness. By the time he was bedridden, he was still deeply concerned about the matter, and asked his wife, Ms. Lin Tingyu, to search for the manuscript in his belongings. I sent a note asking for the article to be submitted after he had recovered. I could only find peace of mind after receiving confirmation of his recovery. Now, although the article has been hastily completed, Mr. Tao will no longer be able to read it! With the sword suspended in the empty field, how can one not feel regret? Mr. Tao's *"Chicken Bone Divination of the Southwestern Tribes"* had just been published in *Frontier Humanities*, Volume 2, and his comprehensive studies are of great value. Had he been given more time, there is no doubt that his contributions to this field would have been immeasurable. Now, he has passed so suddenly, and it is not just a private sorrow for his friends. He passed away on January 26, 1944, at 5 PM at the Yunnan University Affiliated Hospital in Kunming. On February 16, various academic groups held a memorial meeting for him. I wrote a elegiac couplet for his memorial:

"Raving in fevered illness, never forgetting the father-son linkage naming system;

Heartbroken, in the chest of his trunk, tirelessly working on the bone divination."

This is a true record. Alas, Yunkui! If you still possess awareness, would you find comfort in the fulfillment of your friends' promises and peacefully close your eyes? Or will you forever hold endless sorrow as you depart this world with unfulfilled aspirations?

Annexed Table 1: The Genealogy of the Ahe Family (Twelve Generations)

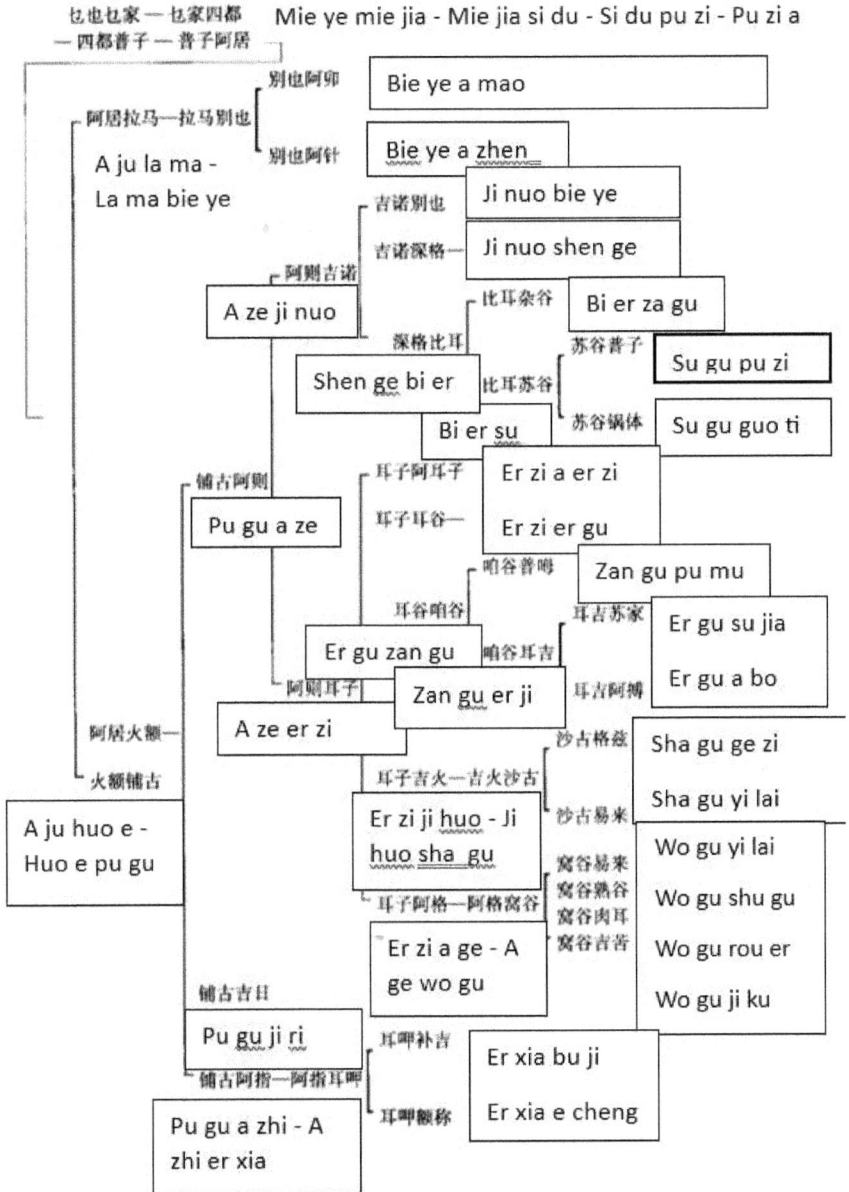

包也包家—包家四都—四都普子—普子阿居
Mie ye mie jia - Mie jia si du - Si du pu zi - Pu zi a

别也阿卯 — Bie ye a mao

阿居拉马—拉马别也
A ju la ma - La ma bie ye

别也阿针 — Bie ye a zhen

吉诺别也 — Ji nuo bie ye

吉诺深格 — Ji nuo shen ge

阿则吉诺
A ze ji nuo

比耳杂谷 — Bi er za gu

深格比耳
Shen ge bi er

苏谷普子 — Su gu pu zi

比耳苏谷
Bi er su

苏谷锅体 — Su gu guo ti

耳子阿耳子 — Er zi a er zi

耳子耳谷 — Er zi er gu

铺古阿则
Pu gu a ze

咱谷普姆 — Zan gu pu mu

耳谷咱谷
Er gu zan gu

耳吉苏家 — Er gu su jia

咱谷耳吉
Zan gu er ji

耳吉阿搏 — Er gu a bo

阿则耳子
A ze er zi

沙古格兹 — Sha gu ge zi

沙古易来 — Sha gu yi lai

耳子吉火—吉火沙古
Er zi ji huo - Ji huo sha gu

窝谷易来 — Wo gu yi lai

窝谷熟谷 — Wo gu shu gu

窝谷肉耳 — Wo gu rou er

窝谷吉苦 — Wo gu ji ku

阿居火额—
火额铺古

A ju huo e - Huo e pu gu

耳子阿格—阿格窝谷
Er zi a ge - A ge wo gu

铺古吉日
Pu gu ji ri

耳呷补吉 — Er xia bu ji

铺古阿指—阿指耳呷
Pu gu a zhi - A zhi er xia

耳呷额称 — Er xia e cheng

207

Annexed Table 2: The Genealogy of the Luohong Family (Fourteen Generations)

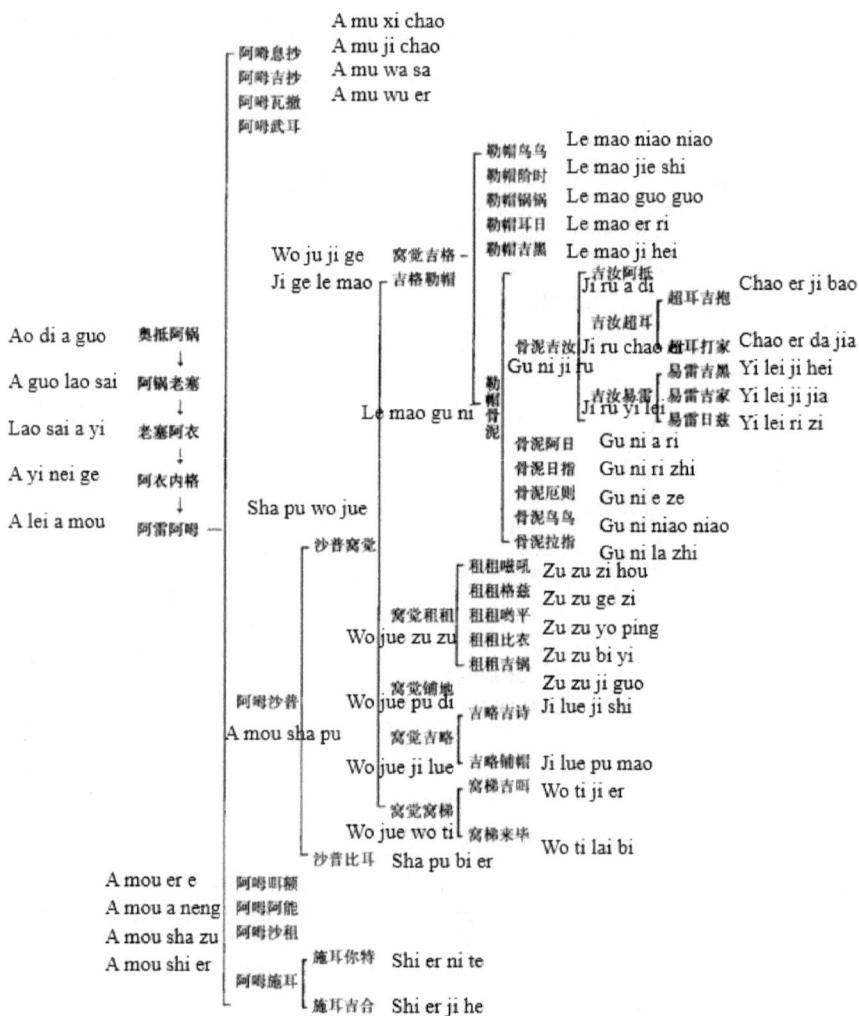

Appendix: Two Documents Related to the "Father-Son Linkage Naming System" Recorded by Wu Qian
Inscription and Epitaph of the Virtuous Yang Sheng

Composed by the monk Yang Wenxin of Longguan, a practitioner of esoteric Buddhism.

I believe that when a filial son performs the funeral rites for his deceased relatives, the first thing to be considered is the construction of the Ming Hall. This distinguished member of the Yang family was a virtuous figure in the Longguan area of Dali. His great-great-grandfather, Yang Xian, held an official position during the Yuan Dynasty, issuing wise edicts that brought peace and prosperity to the people. His great-grandfather, Yang Xianqing, succeeded the position of warehouse manager and commanded great authority. His grandfather, Yang Qingding, contributed to the establishment of counties and prefectures in the Cang'er region during the Hongwu era and was appointed as the head of the local administrative unit. He had three sons: the eldest named Chang, the second named Ping, and the third named Sheng. Yang Sheng married a member of the Yang family and had three sons: the eldest was named Shan, the second was named Lu, and the third was named Hui. Later, he married a woman of the He family, and they had a son named Lan, who in turn had a son named Haineng. Additionally, there were several grandchildren, both male and female, including Wen, Gui, Jian, and Min, as well as the granddaughters Chou, Zhu, and Shan, who were married to Yang Gui, Zhao Si, and Su He, respectively. All these descendants were intelligent and capable, with generations of virtuous and upright offspring, continuing the family line without end.

In the second lunar month of the third year of Chenghua, Yang Sheng passed away at the age of over sixty. His family selected an auspicious day for his burial in a place where the setting sun shines. His eldest son, Yang Shan, with deep filial piety, visited the scholar (the writer of this epitaph) and asked him to praise the virtue of his father and ancestors and to spread the story of his great-grandfather's deeds to bring prosperity to future generations. The epitaph mentions the Yang family's traditional virtues and charitable acts, such as distributing land and grain to help the poor. Therefore, the Yang family's sons were diligent in learning and achieved mastery in both civil and military matters, while the daughters upheld the proper conduct of women, being gentle and virtuous.

What a great family! The inscription reads:

The Yang family, originating from Hongnong, whose given name was Sheng, was born at the time of the morning moon, having both fame and virtue. The virtuous sons and grandsons followed the way of their teachers, learning benevolence and love. Their descendants are forever grateful, and this stone stele is erected in their honor.

The filial sons Yang Shan, Yang Sanshilu, Yang Hui, and Yang Haining

Erected on an auspicious day in the first month of spring in the third year of the Chenghua period of the Ming Dynasty, with the help of the stonemason He Song.

Wu Qian's Note: The original stele is located at the Mexie Ping of the Xieyang Peak in the Lower Guan area of Dali. The tombs in this area date back to the Yuan and Ming dynasties. Prior to the Yuan Dynasty, burials were conducted by cremation, with the ashes placed in a clay urn and buried underground, upon which a stone slab was placed and a stone pillar was erected. The stone pillar, about three feet high, was inscribed with Tibetan mantras, as was customary among these people. During the Ming Dynasty, burials changed to mounded stone graves, with a stone stele placed in front of the tomb. The inscriptions were written from right to left. The main inscription was in Chinese, and the back of the stele was engraved with Tibetan characters in horizontal script, neatly and beautifully written. This was the standard practice for Ming-era steles, and this stele is no exception.

There are several notable points in this epitaph:

1. From Yang Xian to Yang Xianqing and then to Yang Qingding, the three generations of grandfather, father, and son all followed the father-son linkage naming system. However, after Qingding, this tradition was no longer continued. Qingding, who lived during the Hongwu period of the Ming Dynasty, was appointed town chief around the fifteenth year of Hongwu when Vice-General Lan Yu and Mu Ying led the army to capture Dali, establishing local government and military garrisons. This suggests that during the Yuan Dynasty under the Duan family's rule, the Yang family still adhered to the father-son linkage naming system. However, with the large-scale migration of Han people to the area, (as recorded in *The History of Ming*, Volume 2, "Yunnan Tusi Dali", which mentions that in the

211

sixteenth year of Hongwu, military commanders Wang Zhi, Marquis of Liu'an, Qiu Cheng, Marquis of Anqing, and Zhang Long, Marquis of Fengxiang were sent to Yunnan to repair the city walls, build military outposts, and pacify the people. In the twentieth year of Hongwu, an imperial edict was issued to Cao Zhen, Marquis of Jingchuan, and the military command of Sichuan to select 25,000 elite soldiers, provide them with military weapons and farming tools, and have them engage in farming and garrisoning in Pindian in Yunnan, waiting for orders to go on expeditions. Thus, the large-scale migration of the Han people to engage in farming and garrisoning in the areas under the jurisdiction of Dali Prefecture took place in the twentieth year of Hongwu.) the local indigenous people gradually underwent sinicization. The abandonment of the father-son linkage naming system by the Yang family is one such sign of this process. The original inscription states, "Great-great-grandfather Yang Xian held an official position during the Yuan Dynasty...," although it only traces the family line back to Yang Shan's great-grandfather, who resided in Longwei Guan during the Yuan Dynasty, it does not mention the origin of the family's earliest ancestors. However, on the southern side of the stele, there is another inscription by the Confucian scholar Yang Yong of Dali Prefecture, titled *Epitaph of the Deceased Scholar Yang Gong*, which states: "According to the record: The deceased was named Jiao, of the Yang family. He came from a prominent family in Longwei. The origin of his ancestors is no longer traceable.... On a fine day in the third month of spring in the year of Bingxu in the second year of the Chenghua period, his filial wife Mrs.

212

Shi, and filial sons Yang De, Yang Ming, and others erected this stele together." This inscription was also erected in the Chenghua period, one year earlier than the *Yang Sheng Epitaph*. Yang Sheng was probably of the same clan as Yang Jiao, and "the origin of his family can no longer be traced", but he "came from a prominent family in Longwei." This confirms that the Yang family was indigenous to the Dali region.

2. Yang Sheng's marriage to a woman from the Yang family, and his daughter Yang Chou's marriage to Yang Gui, indicate that the practice of marriage between people of the same surname was not taboo—this was likely a local custom among the Dali natives. This phenomenon of marriages between people of the same surname in Dali has a long history.

3. Regarding the literary style, the character "于" appears four times in the text. The "于" in "Yuan Dynasty in governance" likely functions as a synonym for "以" (to), while the "于" in "born to three sons" and "born to Hai Neng" seems redundant and could be omitted. These phrases share the same structure, yet the presence of "于" in all of them raises the question—was this a redundant particle in the local dialect?

4. According to Confucian customs, women are usually referred to by their clan and not by their personal names. However, in this inscription, Yang Sheng's second wife is named He Lan, and his daughters-in-law are referred to by their given names, such as Hao, Cai, Chun, and Yinjie. (According to what is written below the

original stele: "The successive grandsons are named Wen, Gui, Jian, and Min." The term "successive grandsons" doesn't make sense in this context. If it means that Yang Sheng had these four grandsons, it is stated later: "The four sons and three daughters each gave birth to intelligent and handsome descendants." Here, the numbers of sons and daughters are both totaled, but not the grandsons. So it is quite clear from the context that it doesn't mean Yang Sheng had these four grandsons. Yang Sheng had four sons and four daughters-in-law, and the four "successive grandsons" are closely followed after the names of the four daughters-in-law. Therefore, the so-called "successive grandsons" are probably a misprint for "second wife" [in Chinese, the two phrases have similar pronunciations]. It means that Yang Sheng's four sons each married a wife first and then took another four wives later. The "successive grandsons" of Yang Shan and others are probably just like their fathers' "second wives". If this speculation is credible, then all eight daughters-in-law of Yang Sheng are named in full while their surnames are omitted.) It is rather strange that their given names are all mentioned while their surnames are omitted instead. Perhaps the Naxi people had relatively primitive clan names and did not have the surnames derived from family names that emerged later. Family names were not commonly used. (For example, the Manchu family name Aisin Gioro was also not often put before their given names. Because the whole clan had the same family name, there was no need for such a redundant way of addressing.) They used to put their father's name before their own name to indicate that someone was the son of so-and-so, which was equivalent to what the

Han people called surnames. Since Yang Sheng's generation, the Yang family began to abandon the patronymic naming system. The early Ming Dynasty was not far from their old customs, so the surnames that emerged later (probably established after being influenced by the Han people's customs) were often overlooked by people at that time. Now, the daughters-in-law of Yang Sheng's sons are named while their surnames are omitted in the inscription on the stele. Could it be for this reason?

5. In the inscription, it says: "This is the Qing Yang (庆杨) clan of Longguan in Dali." The use of "庆" in "庆杨" (Qing Yang) is difficult to interpret. If it is intended as an adjective, it does not seem to make sense. Since Yang Sheng abandoned the father-son linkage naming tradition, he likely adopted the final character from his grandfather's name, Yang Qingding, following the practice from the Spring and Autumn period, where descendants would adopt the character from their grandfather's name as their surname. Therefore, "庆" may well be used as a proper name, meaning that the Yang family could be referred to as "庆杨."

There are additional peculiarities such as the missing character in Yang Sheng's wife's name, "Zunjian Cui," and the use of "Thirty Lu" in the name of Yang Lu. (It should be noted that "thirty" here was probably not part of the character "Lu". Yang Shan, Yang Hui, and Yang Haineng did not have their courtesy names connected with their given names when written down. Moreover, among the names on the stele, many people only had given names and no courtesy names, indicating that people at that time had not yet formed the habit of using courtesy names.) These anomalies might require further investigation to understand their significance.

Genealogy of the Zhao Clan of Taihe and Longguan

In the universe, there exists something infinite, immeasurable, boundless both in its vastness and its minuteness. That is the Buddha, the Dharma, and the Sangha. There are various sects in Buddhism, and among them, the Esoteric Sect is the most superior among the Three Jewels. The teachings of this sect originated from Dipankara Buddha, who passed them on to Shakyamuni Buddha. Shakyamuni Buddha then imparted them to the Honorable Vajrapani at the Nirvana Assembly. The Honorable Vajrapani further transmitted them to the kings of the various kingdoms in the Five Indies and the Brahmins who practiced the Vajrayana, thus forming the causal connection of the Five Patriarchs of the Esoteric Sect. Today, the Azhali Sect belongs to the Esoteric Sect of Central India. During the reign of Meng Shengluo, an Indian named Mokajada spread the Yoga teachings and passed them on to the people of the Azhali Sect in Dali, and the Zhao family was also involved. Since then, this sect has spread southward. Among the ancestors of the Zhao family, there was a man named Zhao Yongya, who was blessed with great fortune and had numerous miraculous deeds that are too many to be recounted in detail. After several generations of inheritance, it came down to Zhao Fuxiang, Zhao Xiangshun, and Zhao Shunhai, who lived for generations in the White Python Village at Longwei Pass in Taihe, Dali. During the Mongol Yuan period, there was a white python in Longwei Pass that

216

often devoured passers-by and caused great harm. Coincidentally, there was a righteous man named Qi Chicheng, who held a sharp long knife and sacrificed himself by entering the python's belly, and thus the disaster caused by the python was eliminated. The local residents were grateful for his heroic deeds and buried Qi Chicheng in the Lingta Temple. They also built a pagoda to suppress the place and cremated the python's bones, so this place was named the White Python Village. Now people mistakenly call it the White Horse Village, which is incorrect. Zhao Shunhai was born with a clever and sharp mind. He was deeply devoted to the Taoist teachings and practiced diligently. He could command ghosts and spirits, summon wind and rain, and use magic to dispel epidemics and relieve disasters. It can be said that he won the admiration of the people with his virtues. Zhao Shunhai's grandfather and father both had extraordinary insight and wisdom. They could control wind and thunder and subdue dragons and tigers. When there was a drought and they prayed for rain, it would surely fall. When there was excessive rain and they prayed for it to stop, it would stop. They both served as national preceptors during the Mongol Yuan period. Zhao Shunhai had a son named Zhao Ci, and Zhao Ci had three sons named Zhao Shou, Zhao Jun, and Zhao Hu. They also practiced the Taoist career of their ancestors and were all famous for their virtues. In the fifteenth year of the Hongwu period, the imperial army recovered Yunnan and captured Dali. Zhao Ci went to the capital to pay tribute, and Zhao Jun requested to follow him. At that time, there were evil spirits (the character "Chong" here should be "Sui", a wrong character) causing chaos in the imperial palace.

Zhao Jun went deep into the inner court of the imperial palace, sat quietly, and practiced magic. In less than ten days, the evil spirits were eliminated. The emperor was overjoyed and bestowed a sheepskin imperial edict, exempting his family from corvée labor for generations. He also granted precious items such as a human skull, a water basin, a ritual drum, imperial embroidery, and a cassock, as well as eighteen chapters of poems written by the emperor himself. Then Zhao Jun was sent back by post-horse. Zhao Hu went to Yunnan to meet Zhao Jun, and the people in Yunnan asked Zhao Hu to stay and deal with the evil dragon causing trouble. So Zhao Hu settled down at the estuary of Dianchi Lake. The situation of his descendants is now hard to trace. After Zhao Jun returned home, he worked with the monk Wuji to engrave (the character "Qin" here should be "Le", a wrong character) the poems written by the emperor himself and hung them in the Gantong Temple. Then he built a temple at the left foot of the mountain. This temple was repeatedly flooded, so it was later relocated to the top of the Dangshan Mountain and named the Baodu Temple. Zhao Jun was born in the year of Wuzhi in the Zhizheng period of the Yuan Dynasty and lived to be seventy-two years old. In the eighteenth year of the Yongle period, he passed away while sitting in meditation without any illness. At that time, white gas rose from the tiles and didn't dissipate until after a meal's time. On the day of his cremation, his relics were crystal clear. He was buried at the foot of the Xieyang Mountain. On the day of the funeral, people came in large numbers, as lively as going to a market. Everyone saw auspicious cranes hovering in the sky and beautiful rosy clouds presenting a wonderful scene. Everyone was amazed. In the sixth year of the Tianshun period, it happened that Zhao Shou, the eldest son, was summoned by the imperial court for the second time according to the imperial edict. He was worried that the deeds of his ancestors would be lost, so he came to me with the family genealogy and earnestly asked me to write a preface at the beginning. This can really be said to be a good deed that can glorify the ancestors and benefit the descendants. Although I'm not very talented, I'll briefly describe these circumstances so that these deeds can be passed down and remain immortal and also record the time.

It was on an auspicious day in February of the sixth year of Tianshun

The article was written by Xu Tingduan, a Jinshi (a successful candidate in the highest imperial examinations), the supervisor of the Imperial College in Nanjing, and a hermit named Yangxuan Shanren. He wrote this article about the origin of the Zhao family in Taihe with a respectful bow. This article is from the book "Caomuzi".

Zhao Yongya

Lord Zhao Yongya lived in the late Tang and early Song periods, and traveled with six companions including Dong Xishi, Yang Huishi, and Wang Xuanxing, roaming among the local chieftains.

The holy monks of the Western Regions descended from the lineage of Yongya Gong, responding to every request, their merits boundless. The bloodline of this illustrious figure continues through the river of Tianshui, and even today, the aura of mist and clouds still clings to his robe.

Presented by Gao Ji of Dun Suzi, a native of Tianmu Mountain also known as Dun Suzi.

Zhao Fuxiang

Lord Zhao Fuxiang was born during the reigns of the Mongol and Dali Kingdoms and was the great-grandson of Yongya Gong.

Though there were no Buddhist seeds in the Western lands, he was revered as a master during the Mengzhao period.

He could summon winds and rain, subdue demons, and slay dragons.

Alas, who could compare with him in pursuit and legacy?

Presented by Wang Yue from Yinxi, an editor of the Hanlin Academy.

Zhao Xiangshun

Lord Zhao Xiangshun was born in the Yuan Dynasty, was the son of Zhao Fuxiang, and was known for his filial piety.

He could spit out white hairs, and within them could be seen the image of the Buddha.

When he prayed for rain, it would come; when he prayed for clear skies, the sun would shine.

Ghosts and spirits were in awe of his divine powers, and even the sun and moon lost their shine.

His deeds surpassed the ancients and the present, standing far beyond reach.

Presented by Yang Xuan, a supervisory censor from Xicong.

Zhao Shunhai.

Lord Zhao Shunhai was born in the Yuan Dynasty and was the son of Xiangshun Gong. He lived to the age of 82 and married a woman of the Yang family.

In the human world, demons may cause mischief, but the holy master can drive them away. How dare they act wantonly?

No matter how the winds and rains call, the balance of heaven and earth has its design.

Inscribed by Zhang Peng, a patrol censor from Cuifeng.

Zhao Ci

Lord Zhao Ci was born during the Yuan Dynasty, and was the son of Zhao Shunhai. In the fifteenth year of the Hongwu reign, after the Ming military forces pacified Yunnan, Mu Ying, the Western Pacification Duke, was appointed to govern. At this time, a monk named Wuji from the Gantong Temple led his disciples to the capital to pay homage. Zhao Ci, accompanied by his son Zhao Jun, also made the journey, bringing with them a white steed and a book of white mountain tea. Emperor Gao accepted their offerings, and miraculously, the tea suddenly bloomed. The Emperor was overjoyed and commanded Hanlin Academy Chancellor Li Chong to compose a poem in return. Zhao Ci was granted eighteen poems written by the Emperor himself, along with a formal imperial decree, and was sent back on a relay horse. On their way to Dianchi Lake, Zhao Ci's son Zhao Hu was met by the local people who requested his help in governing the Sea Dragon of Kunming. Zhao Hu then settled there. Zhao Ci lived to the age of 72.

The secret wheel of the Zhu Huang Mi, who practiced in Lingque Mountain for three months.

Upon his return, his virtuous deeds were perfected, and the essence of the Western land was expounded, far beyond a mere thousandth. The doctrines of the capital city, are solitary and lonely.

Presented by Yang Shen, an editor of the Chequan.

(The following omitted.)

Wu Qian's Note: A careful inspection reveals that the Zhao clan genealogy from the Taihe and Longguan lineage is recorded on a scroll of yellow paper with several large red seals, reading "The Emperor's Sacred Virtue, Worshipping the Mystic Pearl." The paper is damaged in places and has been backed with cotton paper, with the scroll now divided into two sections. The size of the paper is uniform, but the color varies between reddish-yellow and pale yellow, indicating old and new sections. One side of the scroll contains the "Great Prajna Paramita Sutra, Volume 41," written in regular script, with a note at the end saying, "This edition of the Great Prajna Sutra was respectfully created by Zhao Taisheng in the Kingdom of Dali for the consecration ceremony. The inscription reads: 'At the time of the 19th year of Tiankai, during the Mid-Autumn Festival, Master You Qingqi wrote this with an insightful mind.'" The handwriting is neat and tidy, and it was all written by the same person. The other side of the scroll contains the "Zhao Clan Genealogy," written in various hands, some neat, others rough, indicating additions over time. The genealogy was likely written after the completion of the sutra.

In addition to the selected entries on the family lineages, there are later additions, including *Postscript to the Zhao Clan Genealogy* by Duan Zicheng, who was the magistrate of De'an Prefecture[291] in Huguang [292] and the Jieyuan (the top scorer in the provincial examination) of Yunnan and Guizhou during the Chenghua period; a postscript by Zhao Rulian, a member of the family, in the 30th year of Jiajing (it should be noted that the original postscript did not mention the specific date, but it stated in the text that in the year of Jiajia Xinhai, he retired from his position as the Censor-in-Chief and stayed at home. "Having feelings about this genealogy, I once again entrusted the famous writer of the Zhongxi Library to write a postscript to complete it as expected." So Zhao Zuo's work should have been done after the thirtieth year of the Jiajing period); *Brief Postscript to the Zhao Clan Genealogy* by Li Yuanyang during the Longqing era; and *Preface to the Zhao Clan Genealogy in Kunyang* by Zhang Yangjie of Kunming in the 24th year of Wanli. These postscript entries all discuss the origins of the Zhao clan, and they are largely consistent with Xu Tingduan's *Genealogy of the Zhao Clan of Taihe and Longguan*.

Now, we note that from Zhao Fuxiang to Zhao Xiangshun and Zhao Shunhai, the three generations of grandfather, father, and son all followed the father-son linkage naming system. Their ancestral figure, Zhao Yongya, lived in the late Tang Dynasty, and this naming tradition

---

[291] De'an Prefecture, established in the first year of Xuanhe in the Northern Song Dynasty, with its administrative seat located in present-day Anlu, Hubei. It was abolished in 1912.

[292] Huguang, the name of a provincial administrative region established in the Yuan Dynasty, with a relatively large scope. In the Ming Dynasty, it governed the areas of present-day Hubei and Hunan provinces.

likely continued for several generations until Fuxiang Gong. However, these early names have been lost to history and cannot be verified. It was only with Zhao Shunhai's son, Zhao Ci, that the tradition of father-son linkage naming system was abandoned. Zhao Ci, who lived at the end of the Yuan Dynasty and the beginning of the Ming Dynasty, studied Esoteric Buddhism and visited the court during the Hongwu period with Wuji, a monk from Gantong Temple. This is consistent with the practice of the Longguan Yang family, where, starting with Yang Sheng during the Hongwu reign, they no longer used their father's name as part of their own name. Therefore, it is reasonable to conclude that the native people of Dali followed the tradition of adding the father's name to the son's name until the end of the Yuan Dynasty. After the Ming armies pacified Dali in the fifteenth year of Hongwu, with the increasing presence of Han Chinese immigrants, the locals began to gradually adopt Han customs and abandon their ancient practices. This conclusion is unquestionable.

Appendix 2: Chashan Songs[293]

In January 1943, I was invited to Dali to give lectures at the Western Yunnan Wartime Cadre Training Corps. After the lectures, I brought back two friends from Chashan: Dong Changshao from Pianma and Kong Kelang from Shijia. Both had received secondary education in Myitkyina. After learning their language to a basic level, I began recording the songs they sang starting on March 15th. Although this was an intriguing and enjoyable task, they had grown weary of our repeated, interrogative approach to recording and seemed to lose interest in singing. Therefore, the recording process didn't go smoothly.

Noticing their mood, I realized that continuing with a purely oral recording method would likely yield poor results. I put aside my pen and paper for a while and chatted with them. I then expressed my wish to learn their songs and asked if they could teach me. Upon seeing that I had no paper or pen, they were much happier, and the tension in the air seemed to dissipate.

The first to sing was Dong Changshao. After a bit of modesty on his part, and some praise from me, he began to sing from a set of lyrics he had written in advance. Having grown accustomed to our months of sound recording training, he was used to stopping frequently after singing a couple of beats to look at me. This left me in a dilemma. How could I apply the sound recording method to song recording? The song was breaking apart, like broken pieces of glazed pottery.

---

[293] The first draft of this article was originally published in the combined issue of the 5th and 6th issues of Volume 1 of *Frontier Humanities* of Nankai University (in July 1944, Kunming).

Realizing I had to let him relax, I propped my chin up with both hands, pretending to be deeply impressed, and said, "Wonderful! Wonderful!" This made him feel at ease, and he started again, singing the entire first half of the song in one breath. However, when he reached the sixth line, the halfway point of the song, he stopped again. When I asked why, he explained that the next part was just like the previous one. His answer made me ponder. Despite knowing things were not that simple, I figured it was best not to press the issue. So, I acted as though he had finished and asked him to teach me the song, line by line.

When he sang the first line again, I was surprised to find that it was different from the previous rendition.

I paid close attention to the rhythm, elongated notes, tempo, pitch, and sliding tones, recording all these elements on the music score I had prepared. After I sang it back to him, he confirmed that I had sung it correctly. With that, I quickly finished writing down the first half of the song. I noticed that at the end of the sixth line, he had two different ways of singing the last three beats, sometimes one way, sometimes another, without a fixed pattern.

He said the second half of the song was the same as the first. However, when I asked him to sing it again, he grew impatient. The second half he sang was completely different from the first. The final line, too, had two versions. To my surprise, he raised the pitch of the entire second half by a third. I followed along, but then he lowered it again. It dawned on me that he wasn't "modulating," but simply adjusting his voice because he wasn't feeling well.

I recorded the second half as a new song. Seeing me struggle to rewrite and re-record, and carefully hiding the lyrics and music from the first half, he couldn't help but laugh. Since he couldn't see the first half of the lyrics and music, he naturally sang it differently, just as I had predicted. I stuck to my principle of making him sing it again, and then I sang along with him, and only when he agreed that I had sung it exactly the same as he did (down to the smallest details), did he fully praise my speed and accuracy.

At this point, I asked him to remove the lyrics and sing the entire song naturally, as if in his hometown. He became awkward and insisted that he could not sing without the lyrics. I found this quite surprising. Nevertheless, I yielded and let him continue. With the lyrics in hand, he sang less naturally than I had hoped, and I made the final corrections to my notes, noticing that his singing lacked flexibility.

Next, Kong Kelang came up. He immediately pulled out a song called "Kachin Song" (Jing p'aw mak'awn), with both lyrics and music prepared. Realizing that the situation was not ideal, I quickly offered him tea to shift his attention. Yet, he held on to the score with one hand while drinking with the other. As I conversed with him to distract him, I secretly borrowed the score and copied the lyrics onto a fresh sheet of paper, asking him to sing from what I had written (which only contained the lyrics and not the music). He insisted that he could not change the way he sang, and sang the same song four times in a row, exactly the same each time. Finally, he softened a bit

227

after seeing my constant politeness and told me, "The first line should be sung quietly, the second loudly." After some further conversation, he also revealed that the first line was a solo and the second was a unison. Had I not pressed further, I might have mixed up the piano (quiet) with the solo (high-pitched solo) and the forte (strong and loud) with the unison (all voices together).

I was surprised by his firm attitude but had no choice but to accept it and change the topic to ask if he knew the long song sung by Dong Changshao. He replied that he didn't. It seemed they had an unspoken agreement—each would sing a song and leave the others unshared. Normally, given that they were both from the same area, they should be quite familiar with each other's songs, yet here they were each knowing only one song while remaining oblivious to the others. This made me wonder whether their roles in this social context were truly divided.

Shortly after the song recording, they returned to western Yunnan. I had originally wanted to compare the tone rises and falls of the lyrics with those of the song, and to contrast the emotional content of the lyrics with that of the song. However, due to the insufficient material, I hesitated, fearing that I might not draw any significant conclusions.

In the summer, I accidentally overheard someone humming the line "Kachin Song" from behind a wall in the countryside. The first line was identical to what Kong Kelang had sung before, but the ending of the second line was changed to "sol." There was also a third line that resembled the first. According to the way the person was singing, there should have been a fourth line, but at that point, they suddenly stopped. What followed was a burst of laughter and playfulness. I waited for quite a while, but there was no further development, so I reluctantly left, feeling disappointed. On one hand, I was a bit melancholic, but on the other hand, I was more convinced that the second song must have other variations in its performance.

This situation left me quite frustrated. I had put in a lot of effort—being as meticulous and patient as when recording speech, and as alert and tense as listening to a symphony—yet I had gained nothing, like trying to catch a rabbit and ending up empty-handed. So, I put the matter aside in a drawer and didn't think about it for an entire year.

Recently, I came across Mr. Xu Menglin's *History of Rural Folk Opera in Yunnan,* in which he included an appendix on the *Chashan Tune* from the Huadeng opera. It turned out to be completely different from the two songs I had recorded earlier. Mr. Zhang Qingchang believes that, since the Huadeng opera includes instrumental accompaniment, interludes, and lyrics in Chinese, it has deviated far from the original Chashan songs, and thus does not need to be cited.

When I spoke to Mr. Zhang about the two Chashan people I had recorded singing, he explained that my effort had not been a failure at all, but actually yielded some important findings. He clarified the reasons behind the difficulties I encountered:

1. In culturally less developed areas, professional singers are rare, and while almost everyone may sing, few sing very well. Given that the overall standard is similar, even if the people I recorded were not great, I would have encountered the same level of singing if I had gone to Chashan itself.

2. Folk songs inherently do not have fixed, accurate ways of being sung—they vary from person to person and from place to place. Even the same person will alter the way they sing depending on their mood, enthusiasm, or slight changes in the lyrics. So, when the first singer began and then changed the way they sang, it was still irregular, but that's precisely the unpolished, natural style found in the fields. The second singer, although they had written out the melody in advance, did so just for convenience. When they were out in the fields or mountains, they would naturally start adding flourishes to their singing.

Mr. Zhang felt that the melodies I had recorded were closely aligned with the style of folk songs from China's mainland (he had already published two short articles on this subject: one in 1941 titled *The Issue of Using Folk Song Styles in Anti-Japanese War Songs*, and another in the third issue of *Frontier Humanities* from Nankai University titled *From Inland Folk Songs to Borderland Ballad Investigations*). Music is the most genuine expression of a nation's spirit, and this shows that the Han people from China's mainland and the Chashan people are essentially the same. The Chashan people should not be easily swayed by the divisive tactics of outsiders.

Hearing Mr. Zhang's perspective made me very happy. Not only had I learned about the language, grammar, and vocabulary of the Chashan people, but I also discovered that their songs shared the same style as folk songs from China's mainland—an unexpected but delightful surprise.

Now, I've copied out the scores of the songs I had recorded earlier below:

The first song, sung by Dong Changshao, is one commonly sung during intimate moments between men and women. Because he used falsetto, his compass was quite wide.

Andante(♩ =70-90)

nyu   e   nyan   nu   xang   su

(The beginning) (Literal translation of lyrics) We people

(Liberal translation of lyrics) We, the people

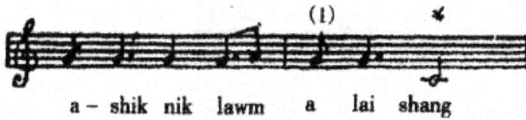

a – shik nik lawm   a   lai shang

"Not giving up heart" / "Unyielding heart"

"We don't change, our hearts don't love."

chang yam we nyik we chek shang

"Love from afar"

"The farther the lover is, the deeper the love grows."

ban sauk we xu   we nam shang

"Chestnut flowers, the farther you smell, the stronger the fragrance."

"The farther the chestnut flowers are, the richer the fragrance."

231

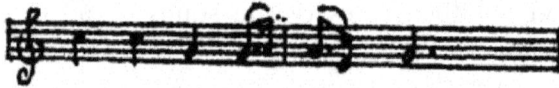

nyang nu nyik law kyaw ri

"We are in the gathering of men and women."

"When we are in the gathering of men and women."

nyik law layung kyaw ri

"In the gathering of men and women."

"When men and women gather together."

Allegro (♩=160) (2)

gawng gyaw ley yaw a wang shang

"In the middle of the body, wind and rain do not enter."

"In the center of the body, wind and rain do not enter."

(3)

waw szu gyik yaw a dek shang

"Bamboo skin does not get wet when exposed to water."

"Bamboo skin does not become wet even when it touches water."

Tempo I

tung p'uk ming maw tung p'uk

"The Púmán region is inhabited by Púmán."

"Púmán and Han people."

ta – he –   ming   maw

"The place where Han people live."

"The place where Han people live."

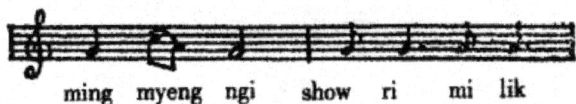

ming myeng ngi show ri mi lik

"Money is found in every place, in Mi Le."

"Find money everywhere, in Mi Le."

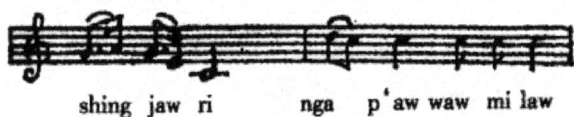

shing jaw ri   nga p'aw waw mi law

"I go to my father's village to search for gold."

"I hurry towards my father's village to find gold."

hga   xang   zaw   a – shik waw mi

"The son of the person, not dead, heads towards the village."

"Go — heading towards the son, not dead."

law   hga   nga mi?   by – ap mi

"I go to my mother's tree, to the village."

"I go to my mother's tree and head to the village where my mother is."

law hga   ngaw? zaw

"The son of the bird has gone."

"Climb the tree and head towards."

a – shik by – ap   mi law hga

"The unyielding tree has gone."

"The chick goes up to the unyielding tree."

hkyaw saw yawm t'ang yuk law hga

"The road goes to the edge of the house roof."

"The road has reached the edge of the house."

gyit gu sheng t'ang k'ap law hga

"The water has flowed past the lake's edge."

"The water has reached the edge of the lake."

* Indicates a gliding note (appoggiando).

(1) Or sing as.

(2)Or sing as.

(3)Or sing as.

(4) Or sing as.

 或

The second song, the Kachin Song sung by Kong Kelang, is relatively simple. It is sung during the completion of a new house, with both men and women singing together. It is sung four times, with two lines each time. It is said that the first line is sung solo by one person, and the second line is sung by everyone together:

Jing p'aw mak'awn

Andante solo Jingpo song

1.chyi law ga wa nau law?ai:

"The voice rises, and many words come (particle)."

2.chyi law ga wa nau lai ai:

"The voice rises, and many words come (particle)."

3.ma ling p'ungaw preng ai law:

235

"The big trees are tall and straight (particle)."

4.a jan gum din tsaw ai aw:

"The sun is round and high (particle)."

Unison

1.kʻa shi kʻa gi ma gaw ai

"The stream and the river both wind."

2.nam na num ru ma nai ai

"In the small forest, creeping vines wind around."

3.ma sha sai mung kʻyeng ai law

"The human blood is red."

4.a shu shan mung law?ai law

"The wild beasts are many."

Translation

First, when speaking, there are indeed many words, like the winding streams and rivers.

(Note: The winding water metaphorically refers to an unreliable or deceitful heart.)

Second, when speaking, the words are especially numerous, like creeping vines winding around the small forest.

(Note: The creeping vines also metaphorically represent a deceitful or unstable heart.)

Third, in the forest, the tall and straight trees stand, and human blood is red.

(Note: The tall trees and red blood symbolize good qualities.)

Fourth, the sun is round and high, and the wild beasts are many. The sun can be seen but not reached, and though there are many wild beasts, they cannot be caught.

Appendix 3: The Hakka-Gan Dialect Connection Traced through Hakka Migration History[294]

(1) Similarities Between Hakka and Jiangxi Dialects

When I studied the Linchuan[295] dialect of Jiangxi, I found that this dialect shares many similarities with Hakka. If we compare the Linchuan dialect with the Meixian dialect, which is representative of Hakka, we can point out the following common features:

1. Ancient voiced stop consonants uniformly change to aspirated voiceless stops. In the Mandarin dialects, the ancient voiced stops and the related initials have undergone changes: the level tones (ping sheng) have evolved into aspirated voiceless stops, while the oblique tones (ze sheng) have become unaspirated voiceless stops.. However, both the Linchuan and Meixian dialects uniformly change these voiced stop consonants to aspirated voiceless stops, regardless of tone. For example: The ancient voiced stops **b'** as in "蒲" (pú) and "部" (bù) are both pronounced as **p'**. Similarly, the ancient voiced stops **d'** as in "徒" (tú) and "度" (dù) are both pronounced as **t'**.

---

[294] The first draft of this article was originally published in the combined 3rd and 4th issues of Volume 1 of *Frontier Humanities* of Nankai University (March 1944). Later, the follow-up work *On the Patronymic System of the Tibeto-Burman Ethnic Groups Again* was published in the 9th issue of Volume 3 of *Frontier Administration Review* (September 1944), and *On the Patronymic System of the Tibeto-Burman Ethnic Groups for the Third Time* was published in the combined 1st and 2nd issues of Volume 2 of *Frontier Humanities* (December 1944). This appendix is a comprehensive revision and compilation of the above three articles.

[295] Linchuan was an old county name in the southeastern part of Jiangxi Province. Linru County was established in the Han Dynasty, and it was renamed Linchuan County in the Sui Dynasty. During the Ming and Qing Dynasties, it was the administrative seat of Fuzhou Prefecture. In 1949, Fuzhou City was established. In 1987, Linchuan County and Fuzhou City were merged and renamed Linchuan City.

2. The labialized initials of the ancient Xiao (晓) and Xia (匣) groups change into "f." For example, characters such as "呼" (hū), "火" (huǒ), "化" (huà), and "忽" (hū) belong to the ancient Xiao (x) initial group, and characters such as "胡" (hú), "户" (hù), and "活" (huó) belong to the ancient Xia (h) initial group. While these characters may be pronounced with either "x" or "h" in other dialects, they are both pronounced with an "f" initial in these two dialects.

3. Retention of closed final consonants -m and -p. For instance, the characters "贪" (tān), "南" (nán), and "三" (sān) have the final -m, and "答" (dá), "杂" (zá), and "纳" (nà) have the final -p, which is a phenomenon shared with Cantonese and Hoklo dialects.

4. Residual distinctions between the first and second ranks of rhymes of the "xian (咸)," "shan (山)," and "xie (蟹)" groups after the "Jian (见)" initials (velar initials).

According to the reconstructed pronunciation in the *Guangyun* phonological dictionary, the main vowels of the first-rank rhymes such as "覃" (tán), "谈" (tán), "寒" (hán), "桓" (huán), "咍" (hāi), and "泰" (tài) are broad "ɑ," while the main vowels of the second-rank rhymes such as "蟹" (xiè), "衔" (xián), "山" (shān), "删" (shān), "皆" (jiē), and "佳" (jiā) are narrow "a." This distinction, which has largely merged in most dialects, is still retained in Linchuan and Meixian dialects[296] but is only evident after certain velar initials. For example,

---

[296] For the part about the Linchuan dialect, please refer to Luo Changpei's *The Phonetic System of Linchuan*, No. 16 of the single publications of Type A of the former Institute of

239

in these dialects, the main vowel of words like "感" (gǎn), "甘" (gān), "鸽" (gē), "盍" (hé), "干" (gān), "喝" (hè), "括" (kuò or guā), "该" (gāi), and "盖" (gài or gě) is pronounced as **o**, while the vowel of words like "减" (jiǎn), "监" (jiān), "夹" (jiá), "匣" (xiá), "奸" (jiān), "瞎" (xiā), "关" (guān), "刮" (guā), "皆" (jiē), and "佳" (jiā) is pronounced as **a**. Although this is only preserved after the initials of the Jian (见) group, the distinction between the ancient broad [ɑ] and narrow [a] is still reflected to some extent after all.

5. The rhyme groups of "yu" (鱼) and "yu" (虞) are merged into "i" when combined with the initials of the jing (精) group, jian (见) series, and lai (来) series. For example, "居" (jū), "鱼" (yú), "句" (jù), "驱" (qū) and "饥" (jī), "尼" (ní), "冀" (jì), and "欺" (qī) are pronounced identically, as well as "徐" (xú) and "齐" (qí), "驴" (lú) and "缕" (lǚ), "黎" (lí) and "旨" (zhǐ).

6. The "hou" (侯) rhyme is pronounced as "ɛu." For instance, "头" (tóu), "猴" (hóu), "口" (kǒu), and "走" (zǒu) have the vowel ɛu, which gives these dialects a distinctive accent.

7. The "geng" (庚), "geng" (耕), "qing" (清), and "qing" (青) rhymes are pronounced as "ang" or "iang." For example, words like "棚" (péng), "冷" (lěng), and "生" (shēng) are pronounced with

---

History and Philology, Academia Sinica, printed and published by The Commercial Press in 1940. For the part about the Meixian dialect, it was based on Zhao Yuanren's records of the dialect survey in Guangdong and Guangxi.

the **ang** rhyme, and words like "饼" (bǐng), "井" (jǐng), "晴" (qíng) are pronounced with the **iang** rhyme.

These are some of the similarities between the Linchuan and Meixian dialects. However, in the Linchuan dialect, the characters with the initials of "章" (zhāng) and "昌" (chāng) change into "t" and "t'" in the same way as those with the initials of "知" (zhī) and "彻" (chè), and the initial "来" (lái) changes into "t" when it is before the present i-vowel initial syllables. These features are not found in the Meixian dialect. In the Meixian dialect, the departing tone is not differentiated into yin and yang, the initials "n" and "l" are not confused, the finals of the characters with the initials of the Jing (精) group in the "模" (mú) rhyme and the initials of the Zhuang (庄) group in the "鱼" (yú) and "虞" (yú) rhymes change into "z", and the entering tones of the three divisions of "宕" (dàng), "江" (jiāng), and "通" (tōng) preserve the final "-k". These are also obviously different from the Linchuan phonetic system. Nevertheless, overall, the two dialects show broad similarities with some distinct differences. Therefore, I suspect that these two dialects belong to the same family but are distinct branches.

Of course, relying solely on phonological similarities is insufficient to determine the relationship between two dialects. We must also consider vocabulary and grammar. But at this moment, I am eager to find a clue from the historical migration of the Hakka people.

(2) The Causes of Hakka Migration

According to historical records and Hakka clan genealogies, there were three main waves of Hakka migration before the Southern Song Dynasty: the first occurred after the Yongjia Rebellion during the Jin Dynasty and the crossing of the Yangtze River by Emperor Yuan; the second was during the end of the Tang Dynasty, with the Huang Chao Uprising; and the third took place in the late Southern Song Dynasty when the Mongols invaded the south. Regarding the background and process of these three migrations, Luo Xianglin has provided a detailed account in the chapter on the origins of the Hakka in his *Introduction to Hakka Studies*.[297] His conclusion is as follows:

The Hakka ancestors' homeland before the Eastern Jin was located in the northern part of Bingzhou, extending west to Sizhou, east to Yangzhou, and south to Yuzhou. In other words, their territory covered the area east of the Ru River, west of the Ying River, north of the Huai River, and extending to the Yellow River and Shangdang. Shangdang is located in present-day Changzhi County, Shanxi; Hongnong is located 40 li south of Lingbao County, Henan; Huainan is in present-day Shou County, Anhui; Xincai is present-day Xincai County, Henan; and Anfeng is near present-day Huangchuan and Gushi counties, Henan. While the Hakka ancestors may not have all originated from these exact locations, they were generally the core areas of their habitation. To study the origins of the Hakka, it is crucial to consider these areas.

---

[297] Please refer to *An Introduction to Hakka Studies*, pages 40-58 [1933; Shanghai Literature and Art Publishing House, 1992].

The first wave of migration from the Hakka ancestors likely began in present-day Changzhi, Shanxi, crossed the Yellow River, followed the Ying River, and gradually moved southward, passing through the Ru-Ying Plain and reaching both sides of the Yangtze River. Alternatively, they may have traveled from present-day Lingbao, Henan, followed the Luo River, crossed the Shaoshi Mountain, and passed through Linru to the same region. In essence, the first migration period of the Hakka ancestors mostly followed the river basins of the Ying, Ru, and Huai Rivers southward, which can be inferred from the region's natural geography.

As for the second wave of migration, the farthest ancestors came from present-day Guangshan, Huangchuan, Gushi, Shou County, and Fuyang, crossing the Yangtze River into Jiangxi, and later migrating south to Fujian. Closer migrations, however, went directly from northern or central Jiangxi to southern Jiangxi, southern Fujian, or the northern border of Guangdong.

The third wave of migration primarily came from southern Jiangxi or southern Fujian to eastern and northern Guangdong.[298]

Additionally, the early Qing Dynasty saw population expansion, and the migration during the Xianfeng and Tongzhi reigns, marked by the conflict between the "local" and Hakka people, is not relevant to this discussion, and thus will not be addressed here.

---

[298] Please refer to *An Introduction to Hakka Studies*, pages 63-64.

(3) The Three Waves of Hakka Migration and Their Connection to Jiangxi

Now, let's briefly revise and supplement the materials related to the immigrants from Jiangxi in Mr. Luo's book and describe them separately as follows.

Regarding the record of the first migration, according to the *Wen Clan Genealogy from Xingning*:

Our Wen family originated from Shanxi and Henan, with numerous descendants. During the Eastern Jin Dynasty, when the Five Barbarians disturbed the Han, Emperor Huai and Emperor Huaimin were captured by Liu Yuan. At that time, our ancestor, Wen Qiao, served as the secretary to Liu Kun. When Emperor Yuan of Jin crossed the Yangtze River to the south, Wen Qiao, following Liu Kun's orders, sent a memorial urging Emperor Yuan to ascend the throne.

Additionally, in *Chongzheng Tongren Genealogy*, the "Wen Clan" entry states:

Later, Wen Qiao was appointed to guard Hongdu[299] (present-day Nanchang), and his descendants settled there.

The same book's "Lai Clan" entry further records:

Currently, the Lai Clan's ancestral seat is also referred to as Songyang. Lai Kuang, the son of Lai Yu, was prominent during the Yixi period of the Eastern Jin. Later, seeing the decline of the Jin royal family, he resigned from his official post and returned to his homeland.

---

[299] Hongdu refers to present-day Nanchang City.

His son, Lai Shuo, courtesy name Zhongfang, experienced the turmoil of the late Jin Dynasty and, to avoid the chaos, migrated to Nankang.

Now, let us examine the "Zhong Clan" entry from the same book:

The Zhong family originally resided in the Central Plains (present-day Henan). In the late Eastern Jin period, a man named Zhong Jian, who had lived in Yingzhou for generations, had three sons: the eldest, named Shan, the second, named Sheng, and the third, named Xian. In the second year of Yuanxi, to avoid the chaos of the invading forces, they migrated south... Zhong Xian settled in Ganzhou, Jiangxi.

Compared with the official historical texts, the *Book of Jin: Treatise on Geography* under the "Sizhou" entry mentions:

Emperor Yuan of Jin (317-322 A.D.) crossed the Yangtze River... later, due to the war, the people of Hongnong[300] were displaced and resettled in Xunyang (present-day Jiujiang, Jiangxi).

The "Yangzhou" entry also states:

When the Hu people invaded, the people of Huainan crossed the Yangtze River. In the early years of Emperor Cheng (325-342 A.D.), when Su Jun and Zu Yue caused turmoil in the Jianghuai area and the Hu people launched another large-scale invasion, more and more people migrated south across the Yangtze River. Thus, in... Xunyang,

---

[300] Hongnong was the name of a prefecture established in the Western Han Dynasty, governing the areas south of the Yellow River in Henan and west of Luoyang. When the Western Jin Dynasty had its capital in Luoyang, the territory of Hongnong Prefecture shrank, but its name remained unchanged. After the Eastern Jin Dynasty moved southward, the people from the original Hongnong area who migrated southward were scattered around Xunyang (present-day Jiujiang, Jiangxi), so Hongnong Prefecture was established as a refugee prefecture in Xunyang.

the Songzi Prefecture [301] was established and came under the jurisdiction of Yangzhou.

During the reign of Emperor An, He Wuji suggested that both the Hongnong region of Sizhou and the Songzi region of Yangzhou, where displaced people from these areas lived, should be managed together. His proposal was accepted. Later, Songzi and Hongnong were converted into two counties, both under Xunyang. In the *Book of Song: Records of States and Prefectures*, under the "Jiangzhou Xunyang Taishou" entry, it records:

During the Eastern Jin period, refugees resided in Xunyang, and the Songzi and Anfeng prefectures were established under the jurisdiction of Yangzhou. In the reign of Emperor An, these two prefectures were later merged into Songzi County. In the 18th year of Emperor Wen of the Southern Dynasty, Hongnong County's refugees were also merged into Songzi County.

In Xu Wenfan's *Table of Administrative Regions and Counties of the Northern and Southern Dynasties*, Volume 11, under "Eastern Jin Xunyang prefecture," integrates the accounts from the Jin and Song histories:

Emperor Yuan established the Hongnong prefecture; Emperor Cheng established the Songzi and Anfeng prefectures, all under

---

[301] The old city site of Songzi in the Jin Dynasty was 15 li east of present-day Huoqiu County, Anhui. (Songzi Prefecture was originally located in the southwestern part of present-day Anhui Province. During the Eastern Jin Dynasty, it was established as a refugee prefecture in the area of present-day Songzi City, south of Jingzhou, Hubei. Songzi Prefecture originally belonged to Yangzhou. Although it was not within the territory of Yangzhou at that time, its administrative relationship still belonged to Yangzhou, so it was said to be "remotely affiliated".)

Yangzhou.[302] By the end of Emperor An's reign, the Songzi and Hongnong prefectures were consolidated into counties, and soon afterward, the Anfeng prefecture was also turned into a county, all under the Xunyang prefecture.

According to the *Book of Jin: Treatise on Geography* under the "Yuzhou" entry:

(During the Eastern Jin, Emperor Xiaowu) Due to the refugees from Xincai County, the Southern Xincai Prefecture was established in the old city of Yingbu, the Prince of Jiujiang of the Han Dynasty.

The *Book of Song: Records of States and Prefectures* records that the magistrate of Nanxincai was placed under Jiangzhou. During the Eastern Jin period, the Nanxincai prefecture governed three counties: Baoxin, Shen, and Song[303]. In Xu Wenfan's *Table of Administrative Regions and Counties of the Northern and Southern Dynasties*, according to the *Book of Song*, Southern Xincai prefecture was also included under the jurisdiction of Xunyang prefecture in Eastern Jin. At that time, to settle the refugees from Henan and Anhui, many prefectures and counties were established in the area under Xunyang, reflecting the large number of displaced people who fled to Jiangxi. Additionally, in the *Jiangxi Tongzhi (General Annals of Jiangxi): Geographic Outline* by Liu Duo, under the section discussing the customs of Guangxin, it is noted:

---

[302] The original text of the "Yangzhou" entry in the *History of Jin: Treatise on Geography*.
[303] Baoxin, Shen, and Song counties: Baoxin was originally located south of present-day Xincai County, Henan. Shen County was originally located north of present-day Feidong County, Anhui. Song County was originally located in present-day Shangqiu City, Henan.

Since the Yongjia Rebellion, many scholars fled here to seek refuge, and the culture of Guangxin gradually became more refined.

The entry of "Ji'an Prefecture" in the same work also cites the *Tongdian (Comprehensive Institutions)* as saying:

Many scholars gathered here, and both the arts and Confucianism flourished. Even ordinary people, while working, would often chant and recite.

Thus, we can conclude that after the Yongjia Rebellion of Eastern Jin, the refugees from the Central Plains fled to Jiangxi, from the northern part of Jiujiang to the eastern part of Shangrao, and through Ji'an to Ganzhou and Nankang, leaving their marks across the region. This is the connection between the first Hakka migration and Jiangxi.

In the second year of Emperor Xizong of the Tang Dynasty (875 A.D.), Wang Xianzhi of Puzhou[304] launched a rebellion in Changyuan with over three thousand followers. They captured Caizhou[305] and Puzhou, and their forces grew to over ten thousand. The momentum was massive. Huang Chao, a person from Caizhou, and his eight companions recruited thousands of followers in support of Wang Xianzhi. These two forces combined and began attacking fifteen states along the Henan route. Soon, they gathered tens of thousands of people, splitting into separate groups to attack the Shenzhou, Guangzhou, Anzhou, Shuzhou, Luzhou, Shouzou, Hezhou,

---

[304] Puzhou was an ancient place name, governing areas such as present-day Juancheng in Shandong and Puyang in Henan. It was renamed Pu County in 1913 and belonged to Shandong Province. It was abolished in 1956 and incorporated into Fan County. In 1964, Fan County was placed under the jurisdiction of Henan Province.
[305] Caozhou refers to present-day Cao County in the southwestern part of Shandong Province.

Huangzhou, and Qizhou[306] along the Huainan route, as well as Dengzhou, Yingzhou, Fuzhou, Suizhou, Langzhou[307], and other states along the Shannan route, and Jiangnan states such as Jiangzhou, Hongzhou, Yuezhou, Tanzhou, Xuanzhou, and Runzhou[308].

By the fifth year of the reign of Emperor Xizong (878 A.D.), after Wang Xianzhi's death, Shang Rang led the defeated army to join Huang Chao, who was proclaimed the "General of Heaven's Charge." Huang Chao then led the people of Henan and Shannan, totaling over a hundred thousand, to attack Huainan. They were blocked by the imperial army but then moved into Zhejiang East, crossed the Yangtze River to the west, and captured the states of Qianzhou, Jizhou,

---

[306] Huainan Circuit had its administrative seat in Yangzhou and governed the areas north of the Yangtze River, south of the Huai River, stretching westward to the line of Guangshui and Wuhan in present-day Hubei, and eastward to the Yellow Sea area. Shenzhou refers to present-day Xinyang City, Henan. Anzhou had its administrative seat in present-day Anlu County, Hubei. Shuzhou had its administrative seat in the territory of present-day Lujiang County, Anhui. Luzhou had its administrative seat in present-day Hefei City. Shouzhou had its administrative seat in present-day Shouxian County, Anhui. Hezhou was established in the Northern Qi Dynasty, with its administrative seat in present-day He County, Anhui. It was changed into a county in 1912. Huangzhou had its administrative seat in present-day Huanggang City, Hubei. Qizhou had its administrative seat in present-day Qichun, Hubei.
[307] Shannan Circuit governed the areas east of the Jialing River, south of the Qinling Mountains, west of the Yunshui River in Hubei, southwest of the Funiu Mountains in Henan, and extended to the northwestern part of Hunan. Yingzhou had its administrative seat in present-day Zhongxiang City, Hubei. Fuzhou had its administrative seat in present-day Xiantao City, Hubei. Suizhou (i.e., Sui Prefecture) had its administrative seat in present-day Suizhou City, Hubei. Langzhou had its administrative seat in present-day Changde City, Hunan.
[308] Jiangnan Circuit governed the areas of present-day Zhejiang, Fujian, Jiangxi, Hunan provinces and the areas south of the Yangtze River in Jiangsu and Anhui provinces. Jiangzhou had its administrative seat in present-day Jiujiang City, Jiangxi. Hongzhou had its administrative seat in present-day Nanchang City. Yuezhou had its administrative seat in present-day Yueyang City, Hunan. Tanzhou had its administrative seat in present-day Changsha City. Xuanzhou had its administrative seat in present-day Xuanzhou City, Anhui. After the Sui and Tang Dynasties, it became Xuancheng County and was renamed Xuanzhou City in 1987. Runzhou had its administrative seat in present-day Zhenjiang City, Jiangsu.

Raozhou, Xinzou, etc.[309] They cleared mountains and built roads, opening up a 700-mile-long path that led straight to Jianzhou in the western Fujian region.[310]

In the sixth year of Emperor Xizong's reign (879 A.D.), Huang Chao encircled Fuzhou from another route. Soon after, they moved into Hunan and Hubei, capturing Guiguan[311], and then advanced to Guangzhou. Unfortunately, they were struck by a great plague, leading to the death of many of his forces. Forced to retreat, they built large wooden rafts in Guizhou[312], floated down the Xiang River, passed through Hengyang and Yongzhou[313], captured Tanzhou, and advanced on Jiangling, occupying Jingnan by October. They claimed an army of five hundred thousand. In Jingmen, they were defeated by Cao Quansheng and Liu Jurong, and Huang Chao fled eastward, with many of his men captured.

They reorganized and attacked Ezhou[314], then turned their attention to Jiangxi, re-entering Raozhou, Xinzou, and Hangzhou, and

---

[309] "Shanxi" here should be a misprint for "Jiangxi". Qianzhou (with its administrative seat in present-day Ganzhou City, Jiangxi), Jizhou (with its administrative seat in present-day Ji'an City, Jiangxi), Raozhou (with its administrative seat in present-day Poyang County, Jiangxi), and Xinzhou (with its administrative seat in present-day Shangrao City, Jiangxi) all belonged to Jiangxi Province.

[310] Jianzhou had its administrative seat in present-day Jian'ou City, Fujian.

[311] Guiguan belonged to the Lingnan West Circuit Military Commissioner. In the Tang Dynasty, special administrative regions were established in the Lingnan region. The Lingnan Military Commissioner was divided into five circuits (also known as Jinglüe Armies): Guang (zhou) Circuit, Gui (zhou, present-day Guilin City, Guangxi) Circuit, Yong (zhou, present-day Nanning City, Guangxi) Circuit, Rong (zhou, present-day Rong County, Guangxi) Circuit, and Annan Circuit. Guiguan governed thirteen states including Gui, Wu, He, Liu, Fu, Zhao, Huan, Rong, Gu, Si, Tang, Gong, and Xiang, all in the northeastern part of present-day Guangxi Zhuang Autonomous Region.

[312] Guizhou had its administrative seat in present-day Guilin, Guangxi.

[313] Heng and Yong: Hengzhou had its administrative seat in present-day Hengyang City, Hunan; Yongzhou had its administrative seat in present-day Yongzhou City, Hunan.

[314] Ezhou had its administrative seat in present-day Wuchang.

even attacking Lin'an but were repelled by the defending general Dong Chang. They then turned back and repeatedly attacked Xuanzhou, Shezhou, and fifteen other states, facing numerous setbacks. Eventually, they retreated to Raozhou, where they managed to capture Muzhou, Wuzhou[315], and Xuanzhou, and allied with Liu Hanhong's remnants, crossing the Caishi Rock and invading Yangzhou. As they passed through, the local population fled, and the officials surrendered at the sight of them. In September of the first year of Guangming (880 A.D.), the entire army crossed the Huai River, attacking Shenzhou, Guangzhou, Yingzhou, Songzhou, Xuzhou, Yanzhou, Ruzhou[316], and other states, eventually capturing Luoyang by November and then moving on to Shaanzhou and Guanzhou[317]. After breaking through Tongguan, they entered Chang'an, where Huang Chao declared himself the Emperor of Qi.[318] From the beginning of the rebellion until he proclaimed himself emperor, Huang Chao's forces waged war in nearly ten provinces, with the most intense battles occurring in present-day southwestern Henan, southeastern Hubei, both southern and northern parts of Hunan, northeastern Guangxi, central Guangdong, central and northern Jiangxi, northwestern and northern Fujian, southwestern

---

[315] Muzhou had its administrative seat in present-day Jiande City, Zhejiang. Wuzhou had its administrative seat in present-day Jinhua City, Zhejiang.

[316] Shen, Guang, Ying, Song, Xu, Yan, and Ru are the names of prefectures. Yingzhou had its administrative seat in present-day Fuyang City, Anhui. Xuzhou governed the areas around present-day Xuzhou. Yanzhou had its administrative seat in present-day Yanzhou City, Shandong. Ruzhou had its administrative seat in present-day Ruzhou City, Henan.

[317] Shanzhou had its administrative seat in the territory of present-day Shan County, Henan. Guozhou had its administrative seat in present-day Lushan County, Henan.

[318] Please refer to Volume 200, Part 2 of the *Old Book of Tang* and Volume 225 of the *New Book of Tang*: *Biography of Huang Chao*.

Anhui, and northwestern Zhejiang. These areas were precisely where the Hakka people, who had migrated after the first wave, had settled. To avoid the ravages of war, they had to flee again. During this time, the whole country was in turmoil, and there were no peaceful places for the people to live. Only the southeastern part of Jiangxi (south of Shangrao, east of the Gan River), the southwestern part of Fujian (the old eight prefectures of Tingzhou)[319], and the eastern and northern parts of Guangdong (including Huizhou, Chaozhou, Jiaying, Heping, Qingyuan, Nanxiong, Shaoguan, Lianzhou) remained largely untouched by the war.

Thus, after the Yongjia Rebellion in Eastern Jin, the Hakka who had migrated to southwestern Henan, central and northern Jiangxi, and southern Anhui, by this time, a large portion of them moved to these safer regions mentioned above. Some, such as those migrating from Jiangxi to other areas, are recorded in the *Revised Genealogy of the Rao Clan of Pingyangtang* from Shixing:

Our first ancestor, named Yuanliang, originally from Poyang in Raozhou, held an official post during the reign of Emperor Dezong of the Tang Dynasty. In his later years, he resided in Nancheng (Jianchang Prefecture). He had five sons... Later, due to the wars, the family was forced to move and could not record all the details.

The *Lu Clan Genealogy from Fanyang* from Shixing says:

---

[319] The eight counties affiliated with Tingzhou refer to Changting, Shanghang, Yongding, Wuping, Ninghua, Qingliu, Guihua, and Liancheng counties under the jurisdiction of Tingzhou Prefecture.

In the Tang Dynasty, a man named Lu Fu, from the Nanjing branch, later moved to Qianhua[320] County in the Jiangyou region of southern Jiangxi. He had a son named Lu Guang, grandson named Lu Zhuo, and great-grandson named Lu Guangchou. In the second year of Emperor Xizong's reign, when Wang Xianzhi and Huang Chao conspired, looting and ravaging states, Lu Guangchou was the only one to submit a request to the imperial court, willing to open up the roads for tribute deliveries... Lu Guangchou had three sons: the eldest, Lu Xiyi, the second, Lu Yanchang, and the third, Lu Mengjian... Lu Yanchang's eighth-generation grandson, Lu Yi, and Lu Mengjian's eighth-generation grandson, Lu Xianyin, consulted divination and decided to migrate to Fujian, initially to Putian County for official duty. Afterward, they moved to Yongding County, residing in Shanghang Dantangao Wazi Village.

The *Luo Clan Genealogy from Jiangxi* says:

At the end of Emperor Xizong's reign in the Tang Dynasty (873-888 A.D.), when Huang Chao rebelled, our ancestor Luo Yizhen resigned from his post and retired to Ji'an, where he settled. His eldest son, Luo Jingxin, departed from Ningdu in Ganzhou, and after several decades, migrated to Shibi Village in Ninghua County, Tingzhou, Fujian, where he established his family.

According to the *Chongzheng Tongren Genealogy*, under the "Luo Clan" entry:

---

[320] Qianhua refers to present-day Ningdu County, Jiangxi.

Through generations, our Luo family has flourished in the Central Plains. Since the Eastern Jin period, after migrating south, some of our clan members moved south and settled between Jiangsu and Zhejiang. According to the *Luo Clan Genealogy*, in the late Tang Dynasty, there was a man named Luo Tieshi. His son, Luo Jingxin, escaped the chaos of the Huang Chao rebellion and was separated from his father in Qianzhou. He later migrated to Yuzhang, and eventually to Shibi Cave, Ziyuan Li, Ge Teng Village, Ninghua County, Tingzhou, Fujian.

According to the *Zhong Clan Genealogy from Songkou* :

Zhong Xiang once served as the Governor of Jiangyang (which may be a geographic name, but the original text is unclear). At that time, due to the wars, he fled from Yingchuan and took refuge in Zhuzi Ba, Chiji Township, Yudu[321] County, Jiangxi. Later, he wandered to Baihu Village, Ninghua County, Fujian, where he settled down and lived peacefully.

In the *Chongzheng Tongren Genealogy*, under the entry for the "Wen Clan," it is said:

Wen Jiulang (who originally lived in Nanchang, Jiangxi) migrated to Shanghang in Fujian's Tingzhou to escape the Huang Chao Rebellion.

The same genealogy, under the entry for the "Gu Clan", also mentions :

---

[321] Yudu, after replacing the rare and uncommon characters in the place name, is now written as Yudu.

During the Five Dynasties period, Gu Fan (originally from Hongzhou) was born in the fourth year of Tang Qianfu (877 A.D.). He once served as the capital commandant of Douzhou[322]. He had six sons. At that time, due to the chaos in Central China, they migrated to Lingbiao (present-day Guangdong). The first son, Quanjiao, settled in Guyun; the second son, Quangui, settled in Jiangxia; the third son, Quanze, settled in Baisha; the fourth son, Quanwang, settled in Zengcheng; the fifth son, Quanrang, settled in Huizhou; and the sixth son, Quanshang, settled in Gaozhou.

In Hu Xi's *"A Brief Examination of the Lives of Song Dynasty's Local Scholar Luo"*, he references the *Luo Clan Genealogy of Xingguo State*, which states:

Chang Ru (whose family had been living in Yuzhang) was a scholar during the reign of Emperor Zhaozong of the Tang Dynasty and served as the Governor of Xunzhou[323]. Due to the chaos caused by the Huang Chao Rebellion and the blockade of roads, he became stranded and could not return home.

There were also migrations from other regions to the southern or eastern parts of Jiangxi. For example, the *Chongzheng Tongren Genealogy* states under the "Xiao Clan" entry:

The thirtieth-generation descendant Xiao Jue, who served as an official during the Tang Dynasty, fled due to the war. His entire clan fled to regions such as Huguang and various counties in Jiangxi, including Taihe and Luling.

---

[322] Douzhou was located in the territory of present-day Cangwu County, Guangxi.
[323] Xunzhou was located east of present-day Huizhou City, Guangdong.

The *Wu Clan Genealogy* from Xingning quotes an old record, the *Historical Record of Wenfu*, which says:

Our ancestor, Wu Xuan followed his official position and lived in Langzhou, Shu. ... Our ancestors had a far-reaching plan and, together with the entire family, returned to their hometown. In the first year of the reign of Emperor Gaozu of the Later Jin Dynasty (930A.D.), when I was four years old, my grandfather, at the age of 63, together with my grandmother, my father, Lord Lun, my uncles, Lord Jing and Lord Shao, our whole family crossed the river and migrated to Shijing, Lincun County, Fuzhou Prefecture, Jiangxi. We left my second uncle, Lord Jing, to live there. Then, along with my father, Lord Lun, and my third uncle, Lord Shao, we moved to Nanfeng County in Jianchang Prefecture, Jiangxi... It was in September of the year of Wu Shen in the first year of Qianyou during the reign of Emperor Gaozu of the Later Han Dynasty.

These major Hakka families migrated in various directions, some from northern Jiangxi to southern Jiangxi (like the Pao Clan), some from southern Jiangxi to Tingzhou (like the Liao, Lu, Luo, Zhong, and others), some from central Jiangxi to Guangdong (like the Gu Clan and Xingguo Luo Clan), and others from other provinces to southern or eastern Jiangxi (like the Xiao and Wu clans). This constitutes the second wave of Hakka migration and its connection to Jiangxi.

After the second Hakka migration, about 400 years later, when the Yuan army began its massive conquest of the Song Dynasty, the capital Lin'an fell in the second year of Deyou during Emperor Duanzong's reign (1276 A.D.). The emperor and his officials swore

256

allegiance at the Xiangxi Hall and ordered the counties to surrender to the Yuan Dynasty. In May, Chen Yizhong and others in Fuzhou declared the Yi King Emperor and changed the era name to Jingyan. In September, the Yuan forces advanced from Mingzhou[324] and Jiangxi, and the General of the Eastern Provinces joined forces with the military at Fuzhou, pushing towards Meiling. By the second year of Jingyan (1277 A.D.), the Yuan forces broke through the Ting Pass. At that time, Song ministers like Wen Tianxiang, Zhang Shijie, Chen Yizhong, and Lu Xiufu continued to resist; loyal citizens from Fujian, Guangdong, and Jiangxi rose to support the emperor. As a result, the border regions of Fujian, Guangdong, and Jiangxi became the battleground. The Hakka people, who originally lived in these regions, fled in different directions, with some seeking refuge in eastern and northern Guangdong, while others, infuriated by the war, fought to protect the emperor and died in Fengzhou or Yamen.[325][326] This marked the third wave of Hakka migration. Some of the migration records from this period can still be found in Hakka genealogies. For example, the *Wei Clan Genealogy from Wuhua* says:

The thirty-ninth-generation descendant Wei Shuyu (originally from Shicheng County, Jiangxi) had four sons: Yuan, Heng, Li, and Zhen. At the time of the late Song Dynasty, the world was in chaos. With Wen Tianxiang, Lu Xiufu, and Zhang Shijie trying to help the Song emperor in Ganzhou and cutting off the waterways, Yuan Zhu

---

[324] Mingzhou had its administrative seat in present-day Ningbo City, Zhejiang.
[325] Please refer to Volume 47 of the *History of Song: Biography of Duke of Ying*.
[326] Naozhou, that is, Naozhou Island, is now written as Naozhou. It is an island outside Leizhou Bay, Guangdong. Yamen is located on the southwest side of the Pearl River Delta.

led an army of 200,000 men from Jianchang[327]. They massacred the people, and our ancestors, with four brothers, wept in fear. After deliberating, they decided to migrate for survival. After passing through Ninghua, they reluctantly separated and migrated to different counties. Wei Yuan moved to Longle, Huizhou (modern-day Wuhua), becoming the founding ancestor of their line.... Wei Heng migrated to Shanghang, Tingzhou in Fujian, and later moved to Longchuan County in Huizhou...

The *Huangpi Zeng Clan Genealogy* from Xingning says:

Zeng Dun was conferred the title of Duke of the State of Lu. In the year of Ren Chen during the Zhenghe period of the Song Dynasty (1112 A.D.) he moved from Nanfeng to live under the Stone Wall in Ninghua County, Fujian. He had a son named Zhonghui. Zhonghui's sons were Zhengsun and Yousun. Due to the disturbances caused by wars in the Song and Yuan Dynasties, they couldn't live in peace. So they moved from Ninghua to Changle County, Guangdong, and settled down there. The people surnamed Zeng who now live in counties such as Xingning, Meixian, Pingyuan, Zhenping[328], Wuhua, Longchuan, Huizhou, Heyuan, Heping, Guangzhou, and Xinning are all descendants of this ancestor.

The *Xu Clan Genealogy* from Heping says:

---

[327] Jianchang was an old county name, which is present-day Nancheng County, Jiangxi.
[328] Zhenping is located in present-day Nanyang City, Henan. However, most of the contexts here are the names of present-day counties in Guangdong. Xinning County is located in present-day Shaoyang City, Hunan. It is suspected that this does not refer to the Zhenping in present-day Henan. There are also Lianping County, Raoping County, and Kaiping City in Guangdong, and it may be one of them.

Our ancestor, Delong, was the sixth-generation grandson of Shiji. His grandfather, Xuan, was the governor of the Song Dynasty under Emperor Ningzong, but after being sidelined by political factions, he moved to Jishui, Yuzhang. Delong had two sons: Daolong and Delong, both of whom served as judicial officers during the reign of Emperor Duozong of the Song Dynasty. After their retirement, the Yuan forces invaded the south. Daolong rose to defend the Song emperor and died in battle, while Delong followed the Song emperor to the south. After the fall of the Song Dynasty, Delong, unwilling to serve the Yuan, chose to settle in Wulong Town, Longchuan, Heiping County (now known as Heiping County).

The *Chongzheng Tongren Genealogy* further documents another migration of the Xu Clan, stating:

In the late Song Dynasty, Xu Yilang, originally from Ningdu, Jiangxi, migrated to Shanghang in Fujian. His younger brother, Erlang, migrated to Liancheng. Five generations later, one of their descendants, Zhenren, moved to Longle (modern-day Wuhua).

The "Xie Clan" entry in the same book also mentions:

In the Jingyan period in the Song Dynasty (1276-1278A.D.), Xie Xin from Ningdu, Ganzhou, and Jiangxi, followed Wen Tianxiang to protect the emperor. He recaptured Meizhou and was appointed as the Prefect of Meizhou. His eldest son, Tianyou, settled in Hongfu Township, Meizhou.

The "Rao Clan" entry in the same book says:

In the late Song Dynasty, a man named Silang from the Pao family, whose father had served as the judge in Tingzhou, Fujian,

259

sought refuge during the turmoil and settled in the Eight Corner Tower of Tingzhou. Later, Silang moved to Shenquan Township in Chaozhou, now part of Dabu County.

These five families, who migrated from central or southern Jiangxi to southwestern Fujian or eastern Guangdong, represent the third wave of Hakka migration and its relationship with Jiangxi. As for the later migrations after the Kangxi period in the Qing Dynasty, due to overpopulation, many Hakka people from Jiaxing, Tingzhou, and Ganzhou moved to the western regions of Jiangxi, such as Suichuan, Wanzai, Pingxiang, and Xiushui. These are not yet included in this account.

From these records, we can trace the connection between the Hakka migration and Jiangxi. Additionally, by examining the phonological system, we can hypothesize that some of the Jiangxi dialects might represent the language left behind by the second wave of Hakka migration.

(4) Conclusion

Although this hypothesis is merely the starting point of a question, it is worth further exploration. I propose that if someone were to thoroughly study the Hakka issue, we would gain a much clearer understanding of the migration routes and language evolution of certain Chinese ethnic groups. This work could be approached in two ways: one could trace the migration paths of the people based on the linguistic systems, while also using the history of the ethnic migrations to connect the relationships between languages. This study is a preliminary attempt in this regard.

According to investigations by Mr. Luo Xianglin, there are still ten counties in Jiangxi Province that are predominantly inhabited by Hakka people, including Xunwu, Anyuan, Dingnan, Longnan, Qiannan[329], Xinfeng, Nankang, Dayu, Chongyi, and Shangyou. In these counties, some Hakka people have lived there since the Tang and Song dynasties, while others arrived during the Ming and Qing dynasties from Fujian and Guangdong. As for the non-pure Hakka counties already identified, they include Ganxian, Xingguo, Yudu, Huichang, Ningdu, Shicheng, Ruijin, Guangchang, Yongfeng, Wan'an, Suichuan, Ji'an, Wanzai, Pingxiang, Xiushui, Jishui, and Taihe. The Hakka people living in these counties coexist with people of the Hunan and Jiangxi and have much interaction, yet their language and customs have remained distinctly separate to this day.[330] I believe that not only should we conduct a thorough investigation of the "pure Hakka counties" and "non-pure Hakka counties" mentioned by Mr. Luo, but we must also carefully compare other Jiangxi dialects that are similar to the Hakka language system. This will help identify the linguistic changes over different periods of Hakka, and then further compare these with the Hakka dialects spoken in Guangdong, Guangxi, Fujian, Hunan, Sichuan, Taiwan, and other regions. At the same time, we should strive to gather more Hakka genealogies to assist in tracing migration routes. By doing so, both the horizontal and vertical aspects of the entire Hakka language group might become

---

[329] Qiannan, after replacing the rare and uncommon characters in the place name, is now written as Quannan.
[330] Please refer to Chapter 3 of *An Introduction to Hakka Studies*, page 94.

clearer. Only then will my hypothesis have a chance of being confirmed.

Appendix 4: Linguistics in Yunnan[331]

The Englishman H. R. Davies said: "In the areas bordering Assam and eastern Yunnan, as well as many countries to the south in Indochina, I have heard that there are almost no languages or dialects as divergent as those found in this region." (*Yunnan* p. 332) Indeed, this statement is not an exaggeration, and anyone who has visited this area can attest to its truth. If several trained linguists were to spend half of their lives in this region, they would have an inexhaustible wealth of material to work with.

Since the spring of 1938, when the Institute of History and Linguistics of the National Central Research Institute and the Institute of Humanities at Peking University moved to Kunming, some linguists have been trying to uncover the linguistic riches of this region. However, lacking adequate books and instruments, and faced with challenges in other areas, they intended to make use of the current environment for some pioneering work. Over the past five years, under the leadership of two or three middle-aged individuals and a group of young researchers, despite obstacles like limited transportation, high living costs, tight funding, and printing difficulties, they managed to carry out some work. This article is a simple report of these years of effort, both as a source of self-encouragement and to share with the public.

Our work over the past few years can be summarized into five main categories and forty-one subtopics:

[331] The first draft of this article was originally published in the combined issue of the 9th and 10th issues of *Frontier Administration Review* (in 1943, Chongqing).

(I) Chinese Language Research

The Chinese spoken in Yunnan belongs to a branch of Southwestern Mandarin, with a simple phonetic system, similar to northern Mandarin. The tones consist of four categories: Yinping (level), Yangping (rising), Shangsheng (falling-rising), and Qusheng (falling). The entering tone has largely become the Yangping tone, but a few dialects have developed their own distinct categories. When we first arrived in Kunming, the similarity of this dialect to Mandarin did not inspire a systematic study. Thus, in 1938 and 1939, our research was limited and lacked a large-scale survey. Later, I realized that when studying dialects, we should not just focus on the phonological proximity to archaic forms or the uniqueness of vocabulary. Instead, we should also enrich the dialectal map and define the "isoglosses." If any part of the country has not been thoroughly surveyed, that section of the dialect map will remain incomplete. Therefore, I suggested that the Institute of History and Linguistics take advantage of the current situation to conduct a full provincial dialect survey in Yunnan. In 1939, we printed the "281" survey form, and by the following year, the plan had been fully realized. Below, I have listed the work I remember from these years:

1)A Study on the Differences Between Kunming Dialect and Mandarin, by Luo Changpei, 1938, published in *Eastern Miscellany*, Vol. 38, No. 3.

This article was based on the phonetic recordings of a fifteen-year-old student named Zhu Jiong. The content raised the following points regarding consonants: (1) There is no distinction between the apical and palatal initials; (2) The pronunciations of the initials "ㄓ" (zh), "ㄔ" (ch), and "ㄕ" (sh); (3) The pronunciation of the initial "ㄖ" (r); (4) The initials "ㄋ" (n) and "ㄌ" (l) are not confused. Regarding vowels: (1) The rounded-lip vowls change into the i-medial vowels; (2) The diphthongs are monophthongized; (3) The finals "ㄢ" (an) and "ㄤ" (ang) are lost; (4) The finals "ㄣ" (en) and "ㄥ" (eng) are lost; (5) In Mandarin, "ㄧㄣ" (in) and "ㄧㄥ" (ing) become the same rhyme due to the loss of finals; (6) In Mandarin, "ㄧㄢ" (ian) and "ㄩㄢ" (üan) become the same rhyme; (7) The degree of lip rounding of the final "ㄛ" (o) is slightly reduced; (8) After the labial initials, the degree of lip rounding of the main vowel of the final "ㄥ" (eng) is strengthened. There are eight points in total. For the tones, a comparison table of the similarities and differences in the curves of the four types of tones, namely yin (阴), yang (阳), shang (上), and qu (去), is also listed.

2)A Study of Baoshan Dialect, by Dong Tonghe, 1938, unpublished.

Before coming to Yunnan, I was intrigued by a story in *Yunnan Waishi* that described Du Wenxiu's Beijing accent, which piqued my interest in the Baoshan dialect. After arriving in Kunming, some said the Baoshan dialect resembled the Nanjing dialect, while others said it was similar to the Beiping dialect, further sparking our curiosity. To clarify this, Dong Tonghe invited Mr. Zhang from Baoshan to record the dialect, and we also made audio recordings. The results showed that while the Baoshan dialect was somewhat similar to Nanjing and Beiping, it was not identical.

3)A Study of the Dialects of the Four Counties along the Erhai Lake, by Chen Shilin, 1939, Bachelor's thesis at Peking University, unpublished.

This paper covers the dialects of four areas: Dali, Fengyi[332], Binchuan, and Dengchuan[333], documenting their phonological systems, homophonic vocabulary, and comparisons of historical and contemporary pronunciations. The major discovery was that the entering tone in Dengchuan, although close to the Yangping tone, formed its own distinct phonetic unit.

4)Homophonic Vocabulary in Mengzi, by Zhan Tie, 1939, Bachelor's thesis at Peking University, unpublished.

Based on the 1929 survey form issued by the Institute of History and Linguistics, this paper records homophonic vocabulary and offers detailed accounts of the phonological system and historical versus contemporary variations.

5)Provincial Dialect Survey of Yunnan, by Ding Shengshu, Dong Tonghe, and Yang Shifeng, 1940, final report unpublished.[334]

This was the first large-scale dialect survey conducted by the Institute of History and Linguistics during the War of Resistance,

---

[332] Fengyi was an old county name in Yunnan Province. It was merged into Dali County in 1960. In 1983, Dali County and Xiaguan City were merged into Dali City.

[333] Dengchuan was an old county name in Yunnan Province. It was incorporated into Eryuan County in 1960.

[334] The *Report on the Investigation of Yunnan Dialects (Chinese Part)* by Yang Shifeng et al. was published in Taipei in 1969 as No. 56 of the special publications of the Institute of History and Philology.

comparable to later surveys in Sichuan. In addition to phonetic recordings, many audio files were also made. The areas surveyed included: Kunming (City), Songming (City, Benak Village), Jinning (Qinghe Township), Kunyang*[335] (City), Fumin (City), Yuxi (Bei Lake Village, Xinmin Village, Zhu Mao Ying), Chenggong (Jiangwei Village), Jijiang (Dai Village), Yimen (Xincheng), Tonghai (City), Hexi* (Hanyi), Luxi (City), Kaiyuan (City), Mengzi (Datun), Eshan (City), Lunan (Xineng Village, City), Mile (City), Luoping (Leyao Village, Fuluo Street, City), Yiliang (City, Wenxing Township), Luliang (Jingning Street), Jianshui (City), Shiping (City, Baoxiu Town), Gejiu (City), Pingbian (City), Wenshan (City, Pingba Street,

---

[335] Kunyang was an old county name in Yunnan Province. It was incorporated into Jinning County in 1958.

Hexi was an old county name in Yunnan Province. It was merged with Tonghai County into Qilu County in 1956 and renamed Tonghai County in 1960.

Ninger is now the location of Ninger Town, the seat of the government of Pu'er Hani and Yi Autonomous County in Yunnan Province. In the Yuan Dynasty, Yuanjiang Road was established. In the Ming Dynasty, it belonged to the Cheli Military and Civilian Pacification Office. In the Qing Dynasty, Ninger County was established and it was the administrative seat of Pu'er Prefecture. It was renamed Pu'er County in 1951 and was renamed Pu'er Hani and Yi Autonomous County in 1956.

Mianning was an old county name in Yunnan Province. It was renamed Lincang County in 1954.

Shunning was an old county name in Yunnan Province. It was renamed Fengqing County in 1954.

Zhennan was an old county name in Yunnan Province. It was renamed Nanhua County in 1954.

Menghua was an old county name in Yunnan Province. It was renamed Weishan County in 1954. In 1956, it was divided into Weishan Yi Autonomous County and Yongjian Hui Autonomous County. In 1960, they were merged into Weishan Yi and Hui Autonomous County.

Yanxing was an old county name in Yunnan Province. It was incorporated into Guangtong County in 1958. In 1960, Guangtong County was incorporated into Lufeng County.

Luozi was an old county name in Yunnan Province. It was incorporated into Lufeng County in 1960.

Pingyi was an old county name in Yunnan Province. It was renamed Fuyuan County in 1954. Guangtong was an old county name in Yunnan Province. It was incorporated into Lufeng County in 1960.

Yanshan Township), Yongping (City), Ning'er* (Fengyang Town), Mianning* (City), Simao (City), Yuanjiang (Yisa), Mojiang (Bixi Town), Jingdong (City), Zhenkang (Minglang Street), Shunning* (Yonghe Village), Gengma, Maguan (Xinhua Town), Wuding (City), Yuanmou (City, Shangleiwowo Village), Yunxian (Xincheng, Dazhai Village), Anning (City), Lufeng (City), Zennan (City), Chuxiong (City), Midu (City, Ruanjia Camp), Menghua* (City), Dayao, Yao'an (City), Xiangyun (Zuosuo), Fengyi (Shangjinchang), Binchuan (Wase), Dali (City), Dengchuan (Zhongshuo, Xiayangwei), Eryuan (Longmen Village), Heqing (City), Jianchuan (City), Yangbi (City), Lanping (Zhonghe Village), Huaping (City), Yanjin (Puerdu), Yanxing* (Heijing), Yunlong (Shimenjing, Nuodengjing), Lijiang (Yulongguan), Weixi (Qiaotou Village, Yezhi Village), Baoshan (City), Tengchong (City, Jiubao Town), Longling (City, Zhen'an Station), Zhenyuan (Anbanjing), Lusi (Mengjia), Lancang (Munai), Luoci* (City), Qujing (City), Zhanyi (Wenhua Township), Luquan (City, Wanxigu Village), Xundian (Yizhuang), Malong (Zhangjiatun), Xuanwei, Pingyi* (City), Yongsheng (City, Majun Township), Qiaojia (City), Huize (City), Zhaotong (City), Daguan (City), Suijiang (City, Guankou Town), Jiangchuan (Longjie), Shizong (Sheye Village), Shuangbai (City), Funing (Bai'ai), Huaning (City), Changning (Dabing Town), Mouding (City, Shidalu), Xichou (Chouyangxinjie), Zhenxiong (Renhe Township), Yongshan (Jingshe), Xinping (City), Qiubei (Taiping Town), Yongren (Datian, Renhe Town), Guangnan (City, Zhulin Township), Guangtong* (Xicun, Huxi Township). In total, 98 counties, and 123 units were surveyed, with almost every major area represented except a few remote and sparsely populated counties. In addition, in 1939, Fang Shiduo was assisted by the British-Chinese War Relief Fund Board to investigate the areas of Cheli and Fohai, and his report covered several counties, complementing the previous surveys.

(II) Research on Tai Languages

When it comes to the study of Tai languages, we must first acknowledge Li Fanggui. In 1931, he spent eight months in Siam and later conducted surveys in the Longzhou and Wuming areas of Guangxi. [336] In 1942, he returned to Guizhou and Guangxi to investigate the Zhongjia, Dong, Mo[337], and Yanghuang languages. The materials he collected are now sufficient for comparative studies. Before the war, Li had planned to come to Yunnan, but due to unforeseen circumstances, he was unable to complete this trip. However, he did manage to record materials from a speaker of the Zhengdong[338] Baiyi dialect in Nanjing. In 1940, before the Institute of History and Linguistics relocated to Lizhuang, he again visited

---

[336] Li Fanggui's *Longzhou Vernacular* was published by The Commercial Press in Shanghai in 1940 as No. 16 of the single publications of Type A of the Institute of History and Philology. *Wuming Zhuang Language* was printed by the Institute of Linguistics of the Chinese Academy of Sciences as internal reference materials at The Commercial Press in Shanghai in 1953 and was published in Taipei in 1956 as No. 19 of the single publications of Type A of the Institute of History and Philology. *A Brief Record of Mo Language* was first published in 1941 as the twentieth single publication of the Institute of History and Philology and was included in the nineteenth volume of the *Journal of the Institute of History and Philology* in 1948.

[337] Mo language is the language spoken by a part of the Bouyei people living in Libo County, Qiandongnan Bouyei and Miao Autonomous Prefecture, Guizhou Province. People who speak this language all have the surname Mo. According to statistics in 1985, there were about 15,000 people in total. Mo language is also called Mo dialect and belongs to the Dong-Shui branch of the Tai-Kadai language family.

[338] Zhengdong is a town name, located southwest of Jiangcheng City, Pu'er City today.

Kunming to study the local dialect of Bo'ai. Had the Institute not moved, Li's research on Tai languages in Yunnan would have yielded a wealth of data. Below are Li's and other researchers' works:

6)A Study of the Baiyi Language in Zhengdong, by Li Fanggui, 1936, unpublished.

In 1935, Tao Yunkui helped Li find a Baiyi speaker, Zhao Yingpin, from the Zhengdong area of Jiangcheng County in southern Yunnan. Li then recorded stories and vocabulary from him and made audio recordings. Tao also collected a wealth of materials regarding the history and culture of the Baiyi people.

7)A Study of the Bo'ai Dialect, by Li Fanggui, 1940, unpublished.[339]

Bo'ai is a small village in Funing County, Yunnan, near the Guangxi border. The local dialect belongs to the Tai language family. In the fall of 1940, Ma Xueliang helped Li find a middle school student who spoke the dialect. Li spent two months in Longquan Town recording the student's speeches and also made audio recordings.

8)Vocabulary of the Baiyi Language in Yingjiang, by Zhang Kun, 1939, unpublished.

Zhang Kun, with the assistance of the British-Chinese War Relief Fund Board, found a Baiyi student from Yingjiang at the Dali branch of the Central Political School. He spent two months recording his

---

[339] *Bo'ai Vernacular* was published in the 28th and 29th volumes of the *Journal of the Institute of History and Philology* in Taipei in 1951. Longzhou Vernacular, Wuming Zhuang Language and Bo'ai Vernacular are all dialects of the Zhuang language.

language. This report consists of over 1,000 words, arranged in the order of Baiyi phonemes.

9)Preliminary Study of the Baiyi Language in Lianshan[340], by Luo Changpei, February 1942, unpublished.[341]

The author first traveled to Dali, where he met a Lianshan Baiyi student named Li Yueheng at the National Dali Normal School, among the borderland students. Lianshan is now part of Tengchong County, which was once under the jurisdiction of the Zanda Tusi. Li was proficient in the Baiyi script. I first recorded the phonetic values of the so-called "local alphabet," then documented over a thousand vocabulary items and more than twenty conversation segments. Each word and sentence was transcribed in both Baiyi script and IPA (International Phonetic Alphabet). Unfortunately, Li could not narrate long stories, so the materials collected were limited to these vocabulary items and conversations.

10)Tai Language in Luoping County of Yunnan, by Xing Qinglan, 1942, unpublished.

Luoping is located on the southern bank of the Panjiang River, bordering Pengzha in Guangxi.[342] Within the county, there exists an ethnic group that speaks Tai language, referred to locally as Shuihu (Water People) or Laoshui (Old Water). This group can be further divided into two subgroups: one is the Zhongjia language, spoken in

---

[340] Lianshan was an old county name in Yunnan Province, located in the Dehong region. It was incorporated into Yingjiang County in 1960.
[341] This book was published by the Publishing Department of Peking University in 1950.
[342] Pengzha now belongs to Xingyi City, Guizhou Province. Its language belongs to the first vernacular of the Bouyei language (according to the "Report on the Investigation of the Bouyei Language" by Yu Shichang et al., published by Science Press in 1959).

the Xijiu Creek and Kuai Ze River basins. The local records in the *Luoping County Annals* refer to them as "Sharen" (Sand People). The other is the Nong language[343], spoken in the Bahe and Duoyi River basins. In the Zhongjia region, where the mountains are high and springs are plentiful, and the climate is pleasant, there has been a significant settlement of Han Chinese, and thus the Zhongjia people have undergone substantial Hanification. Except for the elderly, almost no one speaks this language anymore. The Yi language region, however, is characterized by high mountains, dense forests, damp weather, and poisonous water, and Han Chinese do not dare to settle there, so the language remains widely spoken. Xing's materials include over 3,000 vocabulary items, two full-length dialogues titled *Life Conversations*, three sections on *Customs Conversations*, one on kinship systems, and three stories and legends.

11)Mosha Dialect Survey, by Xing Qinglan, February 1943, unpublished.[344]

Mosha is a settlement in the upper reaches of the Honghe River, inhabited by the Huayao Baiyi (a subgroup of the Baiyi people, located in Xinpian County, Yunnan). In February of that year, Xing was commissioned by the Humanities Research Center of Nankai University to conduct a survey there. The materials collected included over twenty folk stories and myths, ten or more translations of stories and casual talks about customs, and several folk songs.

---

[343] Nong language is the language used by the Zhuang people who call themselves Bunu.
[344] This investigation draft was rechecked and revised in 1980 and was published by the Language and Literature Press in 1989 with the title *Taiya Language in the Upper Reaches of the Red River*.

12)Shui Baiyi [345] Language Survey in Yuanjiang, by Xing Qinglan, May 1943.

After completing the Huayao Baiyi language survey in late April, Xing continued his research in Yuanjiang, which is the center of the Shui Baiyi. The results of this investigation are still pending further reporting.

(III) Tibeto-Burman Language Research

The Tibeto-Burman language family in Yunnan consists of five branches: Luoluo, Xifan, Tibetan, Burmese, and Kachin. Over the past few years, we have conducted one or two surveys of all these branches except the Tibetan one. The surveys are listed below:

13)A Study of a Luoluo Dialect Near Mengzi, by Fu Maoji, 1939.

This is Fu's thesis from the Department of Chinese Literature, Peking University, published in the *Anthropological Journal of the Central Research Institute of History and Linguistics*, Volume 1, Issue 2.

Mr. Fu organized this study based on the language of a Mengzi middle school student, Zhang. The work is divided into phonology, grammar, and vocabulary, and was included in the *Anthropological Journal of the Central Research Institute of History and Linguistics*, edited by Wu Dingliang.

14)Libo Language Research, by Fu Maoji, 1940, submitted to *Harvard Journal of Asiatic Studies*, unpublished.

---

[345] Shui (Water) Baiyi is the name given by the Han people to some of the Dai people. They got this name because they lived near water and lived in bamboo houses.

Libo is a subgroup of the Luoluo branch. Mr. Fu conducted this research while teaching at the Department of Chinese Literature, Huazhong University, with funding from the Harvard-Yenching Institute. The original manuscript was written in English.

15)A Survey of a Samin Language Near Kunming, by Fu Maoji, 1941, submitted to *Harvard Journal of Asiatic Studies*, unpublished.

The term "Sanmin" is a subgroup of the Luoluo ethnic group, also referred to as Sani. This article is also one of the research works by Mr. Fu during his time at Huazhong University, and the original manuscript was written in English.

16)Grammar of the Sani Luoluo Language, by Ma Xueliang, 1941, thesis at the Department of Literature, Peking University.[346]

Sani is a subgroup of the Luoluo ethnic group, and the region where they reside includes the counties of Lunan, Yiliang, Luxi, and Luliang in Yunnan, as well as several villages on the outskirts of Kunming. The materials for this paper were obtained from Heini Village in Lunan County, located thirty miles southeast of Lunan County town, where all the residents are Sani. The informant, Zhang Yuanchang, assisted in the study. The research was conducted over four months, during which Ma not only supplemented Paul Vial's *Luoluo Dictionary* with many new vocabulary items but also recorded over fifty stories, several folklore, and riddles. This grammar covers

---

[346] It was later renamed *Research on Sani Yi Language* and was published by The Commercial Press in 1951 as a special publication on linguistics of the Institute of Linguistics of the Chinese Academy of Sciences.

only half of the total work, with the vocabulary and stories still needing further organization.

17)Survey of Heiyi Language in Xundian and Luquan Counties, by Ma Xueliang, 1941, unpublished.

In the winter of 1941, the Institute of History and Linguistics, Academia Sinica, commissioned Ma to investigate the Heiyi language in Yunnan. He spent a year surveying Xundian and Luquan counties. The materials collected included dialects from Xundian's Jigaoxiao and Ximaining villages, as well as Luquan's Anduokang village. Besides documenting their phonology, Ma also recorded some ancient poems and long stories. In terms of writing, he initially studied the Luoluo script with a local Bimo (shaman) in Xundian, learning over 900 characters. Later, he spent more than half a year in Luquan with an experienced Bimo, who helped him translate ten Yi ethnic classics into Chinese and compile a nearly 2,000-character *Yi Language Dictionary*. Additionally, Ma compiled a catalog of over 1,000 Yi ethnic classics, with summaries of each classic's content and instructions on how shamans use them. He also conducted surveys on rituals and collected numerous artifacts related to customs.

18)Research on the Heiyi Language in Kunming, by Gao Huanians, 1942, thesis at the Department of Literature, Peking University, part of the grammar was mimeographed by the Humanities Research Center, Nankai University.[347]

---

[347] It was later renamed *Research on the Grammar of Yi Language* with an appendix of *Research on Chinese Loanwords in Nasu Language* and was published by Science Press in November 1958.

In the fall of 1941, Mr. Gao located a Heiyi informant named Yang Fushun in the village of Hetaodi in Kunming's eighth district. Over four months, Gao recorded over thirty stories and more than 2,000 vocabulary items. He later wrote this paper based on the materials. The content is divided into phonology, borrowing, grammar, and vocabulary, with the chapter on loanwords being the most noteworthy.

19)Survey of the Nasu Language[348] in Yangwu Ba, Xinpian County, by Gao Huanians, 1942, unpublished.

In the summer of 1941, Gao was commissioned by the Humanities Research Center, Nankai University, to survey the Nasu language in Yangwu Ba, Xinpian County. The Nasu are a subgroup of the Heiyi, and this language is the self-referred ethnic name of the Heiyi. However, the language has some dialectal differences from the Heiyi spoken near Kunming. The area where it is spoken extends widely, from Yuxi to the Luoluo region of Xinpian. Gao documented the phonology and grammar points of the language and also studied many characters. Notably, the Nasu script shared similarities and differences with those found in Lunan, Xundian, and Luquan.

20)Woni Language Near Yangwu Ba in Xinping County, by Gao Huanians, 1942, unpublished.[349]

Woni is also a subgroup of Luoluo, distributed in areas including Yuanjiang, Mojiang, Eshan, Xinpian, Jiangcheng, Ning'er, and the

---

[348] Nasu, also known as Nuosu, is the self-address of the Yi people.
[349] It was later changed into *A Preliminary Study of Hani Language in Yangwu* and was published in the second issue of the *Journal of Sun Yat-sen University* in 1955.

mountainous areas along the Baobian River. This material was collected by Gao during the summer of 1942 in Yangwu Ba. The Woni language lacks the full-voiced stops in its consonant system but features a tongue-root nasal coda. The grammar and phonology are similar to those of the Heiyi and Nasu languages, but it has some notable differences, especially in the pronouns' nominative and accusative forms.

21)Preliminary Study of the Woni Language in Eshan, by Yuan Jiahua, 1943.

In August 1943, Yuan surveyed Eshan, where he found two Woni informants in Jiaoluo Village and Abaozhu Village. One was Li Yongkai, a 47-year-old man skilled in storytelling, and the other was Lin Enchen, a 60-year-old former scholar who had undergone significant sinicization. The materials gathered included over 1,400 words and seventeen stories, carefully compiled from both informants. Yuan identified several characteristics of the language: (1) there are no fully voiced consonants; (2) there is a rich variety of diphthongs, differing from Heiyi; (3) there are six tones and tone changes can affect grammar; (4) the phenomenon of allomorphy in conjunctions. The paper was published in *Frontier Humanities* Volume 4 by Nankai University. Additionally, an article on the Woni phonology appeared in *Xueyuan* Volume 1, Issue 12.

22)Notes on the Lisu Phonology and the so-called Lisu Script, by Rui Yifu, 1939.

The Lisu also belong to the Luoluo subgroup, distributed in the northwestern Yunnan plateau bordering Tibetan areas, as well as in the

Yunling Snow Mountains, Biluo Snow Mountains, and Gaoligong Mountains. This paper was published in the *Anthropological Journal* of the Central Research Institute of History and Linguistics Volume 1, Issue 2. Rui collected materials from the winter of 1935 to the spring of 1936 while participating in the Sino-British border demarcation work in the southern section of the Yunnan-Burma border. He located two Lisu informants about twenty miles from the Gengma Tusi city, at a place called Dapingshitou. From these informants, he recorded over 300 words, and several simple phrases, and gathered a Lisu phonetic system compiled by Western missionaries, which included 28 consonants, 10 vowels, 5 diphthongs, and six tones. Rui also identified four distinctive features of the Lisu language: (1) monosyllabic words; (2) tonal language; (3) no final consonant; and (4) nasalized vowels derived from borrowed Chinese characters. Finally, he compared the Lisu script created by J.O. Frazer and two other versions of the so-called Lisu script, offering critical remarks.

23)Preliminary Study of the Lisu Languagein Fugong, by Luo Changpei, February 1942, unpublished.

In the spring of 1942, the author traveled to Dali for the first time, where he found a Lisu student named Sun Jianting from Fugu at the Dali Normal School among the borderland students. He was a Lisu speaker and could also write in the Lisu script created by J.O. Fraser. I asked him to be an informant and recorded over 1,000 vocabulary items and several lengthy conversations. The manuscript has been fully organized.

The above nine studies all belong to the Luoluo subgroup.

24)Investigation of the Mexie Language in Lijiang, by Luo Changpei, 1940, unpublished.

In the spring of 1940, the author found a student from Yunnan University, Zhou Rumian from Lijiang, in Kunming to be a speaker. Several stories and songs were recorded, but the work was interrupted when Zhou returned home. The collected materials have now been compiled into an article and are ready for printing.

25)Study of the Mexie Language in Weixi, by Fu Maoji, 1942, published in *The Journal of the Cultural Research Institute of West China University*, Vol. 1, Issue 4 (1940), and Vol. 2 (1941).

In the spring of 1941, while teaching at Huazhong University, Mr. Fu found a student from Weixi County who spoke Mexie Language. This article was based on the materials recorded at that time. The article is divided into two parts: the first part covers phonology, which was printed in Shanghai and has not been seen in inland areas; the second part, which deals with grammar, was printed in Chengdu using the Roman alphabet instead of the International Phonetic Alphabet. Some of the grammatical points in this work are more advanced than those proposed by the scholar Bacot.

26)Preliminary Study of the Trung (Dulong) Language in Gongshan, by Luo Changpei, August 1942, University of Beijing, Department of Arts Research Institute, mimeographed edition.[350]

---

[350] It was later published in the third issue of the seventh volume of the *Quarterly Journal of Chinese Studies* of Peking University in 1952. Trung language is now called Dulong language and may belong to the northern language group of the Tibeto-Burman language family.

In February 1942, the author traveled to Dali, where he found a Trung language speaker, Kong Zhiqing, among the students at the Dali Teacher's College. After spending over fifty hours recording more than 700 words and several long conversations, the material was compiled into an article upon his return to Kunming. The article covers (1) an Introduction; (2) an Overview of phonology; (3) Grammar overview; (4) Classification of the Trung language; (5) Daily conversation; and (6) Chinese-Trung vocabulary.

27)Gongshan Nu Language Vocabulary[351], by Luo Changpei, 1942, unpublished.

This material was collected from a Nuzi [352] student, Yang Zhenchang, from Dali Teacher's College. His father was from Heqing, and his mother was a Nuzi. Due to his youth, Yang could not tell stories, so only around 1,000 common words were recorded, with no other materials.

The four works above belong to the Xifan branch.

28)Chashan Language Investigation, by Luo Changpei, 1943, unpublished.

In 1943, during the author's second trip to Dali, he met two speakers of the Chashan language (A-chit), Dong Changshao from Pianma and Kong Kelang from Shijia. They spoke Chashan, Langsu, and Kachin dialects, were familiar with Burmese, and had some knowledge of English. The author kept them in Kunming for two and

---

[351] After in-depth investigation and research on Gongshan Nu language after the 1950s, it was determined to be the Nujiang dialect of Dulong language. This material is included in the fourth volume of *The Collected Works of Luo Changpei*.
[352] Nuzi refers to the Nu people.

a half months, recording more than twenty stories, twelve lessons of conversation, and over two thousand words, and also gathering materials on Langsu and Kachin.

29)Langsu Language Investigation, by Luo Changpei, 1943, unpublished.

Langsu (Maru) and Chashan are sister languages. Their phonology is slightly different, but there is not much difference in the language itself. This material consists of five stories, twelve conversation lessons, and over a thousand vocabularies. It was also obtained indirectly from Dong Changshao and Kong Kelang.

The above two tasks belong to the Burmese branch.

30)Investigation on Kachin Language, by Luo Changpei, in 1943, unpublished.

The Shantou people were formerly called "Wild People" and also known as "Kachin"[353]. In the area of Pianma, they are also called "Puman". I'm afraid that it would be confused with the Puman of the Mengjimie ethnic group[354], so I still call them Kachin people. They are distributed between the Nu River and the Great Jinsha River, that is, in the border area between Yunnan and Myanmar in the northwest

---

[353] Kachin, now known as the Jingpo people, call themselves Jingpo. They are a Burmese ethnic group and there are also some in India. They have the same origin as the Jingpo people in China.

[354] Puman, also known as Puziman, was the name of the Pu people in ancient books and was the ancestors of the Blang people.

Mengjimi should be the old translation of Mon-Khmer. The current Blang language belongs to the Va-De'ang branch of the Mon-Khmer language family. Here, the Mengjimi ethnic group should refer to the current Blang people. They were called Pu in the Han and Jin Dynasties, Puziman in the Tang and Song Dynasties, Puman or Puman in the Yuan to Qing Dynasties. In the Ming Dynasty, the part that later became the Wa people was called Hala, and in the Qing Dynasty, they were called Benglong (which should be related to "Wa Benglong" below). The rest of the parts were still called Puman.

of Yunnan. This language is more commonly used than Chashan and Maru languages, and there are alphabets created by an American named O. Hanson which can be used to print books and newspapers. Both Dong Changshao and Kong Kelang are proficient in the Kachin language. I recorded ten stories, twelve conversation lessons, and over a thousand vocabularies from them, and also slightly revised and supplemented Hanson's phonetic system.

This kind of work belongs to the Kachin branch.

(IV) Minjia Language Study

Regarding the classification of the Minjia language, some say it belongs to the Mengjimie ethnic group, others say it is related to the Baiyi, Luoluo, or Kalun groups. In my opinion, it is a mixed language between the Yi and Han, with the majority of the borrowed components being Tibeto-Burman languages, though about seventy percent of it has already been Sinicized. I traveled to Dali primarily to investigate the Minjia language.

During my two-week stay in Xizhou at Huazhong University, I obtained quite a bit of material. Unfortunately, due to being occupied with other matters over the years, I have not yet managed to compile it. For now, I will list the items as follows:

31)Lanping Lama Language[355] Investigation, by Luo Changpei, 1942, unpublished.

In the chapter on the "Yi People" in Yu Qingyuan's *Notes from Weixi*, it is said, "The Nama people were originally from the Minjia,

---

[355] Lama, that is, Nama, is the name given by the Naxi people to the Bai people in the areas of Lanping and Weixi in Yunnan Province.

that is, the Bo people. They can be found in both the Langcang and Gonglong areas. Their territory borders Lanzhou. The Minjia people flowed in, but it's impossible to examine the specific period, and many of them can't even remember their own surnames. The Mo people call them Nama, and thus they are named as such. Their language is actually no different from that of the Minjia people." According to this statement, the Lamo people are the Minjia people. In February 1942, I found a Lama student, Yang Genyu, at Dali Teacher's College. He recorded many words and answered questions on grammatical points. Although he considered himself a Lama when speaking Chinese when using his native language, he identified as a "Baizi" person. Therefore, I believe the Lama language is an un-Sinicized form of Baizi, while Minjia represents the Sinicized version, both originating from the same source.

32)Investigation of the Minjia Language in Dali, by Luo Changpei, 1942, unpublished.

For the Minjia language in Dali, I recorded three sources: (1) Xizhou, speakers Dong Xuelong, Yang Guodong, and Zhang Shizu; (2) Shangdian Zhong, speaker Hong Hanqing; (3) Shangma Jiao Yi, speaker Zhao Yanshou. The materials from Xizhou were the most extensive, including vocabulary, numerous folk songs, and stories.

33)Investigation of the Minjia Language in Binchuan, by Luo Changpei, 1942, unpublished.

The speaker for this material was Yang Wenbin, a student from Wutai Middle School. Although his hometown was Binchuan, he lived in Kanglang Township across from Xizhou, so his dialect was quite similar to Xizhou.

34)Investigation of the Minjia Language in Dengchuan, by Luo Changpei, 1942, unpublished.

The speaker for this material was Yang Jinyong, also a student from Wutai Middle School.

35)Investigation of the Minjia Language in Eryuan, by Luo Changpei, 1942, unpublished.

The speaker for this material was Li Yuechao, a student from Wutai Middle School. Both Eyuan and Dengchuan feature voiced stop consonants, which distinguishes them from Dali and Binchuan.

36)Investigation of the Minjia Language in Heqing, by Luo Changpei, 1942, unpublished.

The speaker for this material was Chen Zengpei, a student from Wutai Middle School.

37)Investigation of the Minjia Language in Jianchuan, by Luo Changpei, 1942, unpublished.

Before traveling to Dali, I found two speakers of the Jianchuan Minjia language, Yang Jiyan, a student from Yunnan University, and Wang Guanglv, a student from the Sino-French University. After arriving in Dali, I had another student from Dali Teacher's College, Zhao Yanshun, who was the grandson of Zhao Shiming, the author of *Baiwen Kao (Research on Bai-language Writings)*, assist me with recording additional materials.

38)Jianchuan Minjia Story Transcription, by Yuan Jiahua, 1942, unpublished.

When I first investigated the Jianchuan dialect in Kunming, Mr. Yuan was also very interested and participated in the transcription. Later, when I went to Dali, he asked Mr. Wang Guanglv to continue with the transcription. Together, they recorded more than ten stories, and later a student from Yunnan University, Zhang Jiyu, was asked to verify the results. Mr. Yuan's academic attitude is very rigorous, and the results he obtained were certainly very precise.

39)Minjia Dialect in Yunlong, by Luo Changpei, 1942, unpublished.

The informant was Yang Shaohou, a student from Dali Normal School, who later studied at Yunnan University.

40)Investigation of the Minjia Dialect in Lushui, by Luo Changpei, 1942, unpublished.

The informant was Duan Junzhong, a student from Dali Normal School.

(V) Miao Language Research

People who speak the Miao language in Yunnan are scattered across the mountains, making it difficult to find informants. In recent years, we have only done one survey:

41)Qingmiao Dialect Survey[356] in Eshan, by Gao Huonian, 1943.

In August 1943, Mr. Gao, commissioned by the Humanities Research Department of Nankai University's Frontier Studies, found an informant from the Qingmiao people in Moyou Village, Huanian

---

[356] It was later written as *The Phonology of Qing-miao* and was published in the fourth issue of the *Journal of Sun Yat-sen University* in 1982. There is a Chinese summary at the beginning of the article

Township, Eshan. They recorded over 2,000 words, twenty stories, and twenty mountain songs. He identified several key features of this language: (1) Two sets of stop sounds—one produced with the root of the tongue and the other with the uvula; (2) nasal and stop consonants combined into one sound; (3) the presence of consonant clusters; (4) aspirated nasal, lateral, and fricative consonants; (5) eight tones, with two short tones merging into the long tones.

The above five categories and forty-one items provide an overview of our work in Yunnan language research in recent years. The direct and indirect participants have been closely connected to Mr. Li Fanggui and myself. In the future, we hope that each researcher will specialize in one branch and then integrate the findings for a more comprehensive study. Unfortunately, due to the inability to delve deeper into the "Hulu Wang District" and the lack of suitable informants, work on languages belonging to the Mengjimie tribe, such as the Puman and Wabenglong languages[357], has not yet commenced. This is truly a great regret. Additionally, in 1939, Zhang Kun also collected some materials on Minjia and Trung languages during his time in Dali. However, the original manuscripts are currently stored with the Sino-British Board of Directors for the management of Gengzi Reparations and cannot be accessed, so they have not been included here. I've also heard that during his time at Yunnan

---

[357] Wabenglong language. After the ethnic investigation in the 1950s, it was determined that Wa and Benglong were two ethnic groups. The Wa people were named the Wa ethnic group. The Benglong ethnic group was renamed the De'ang ethnic group with the approval of the State Council in 1985. The ancestors of the Wa ethnic group, the De'ang ethnic group and the Blang ethnic group all belonged to a branch of the ancient Pu people.

University, Wen Zaiyou collected materials on Minjia, Bahei, Moxie, and Baiyi languages, but unfortunately, his full text has not been published yet, so I will not include it in this article.

Lastly, I would like to conclude with a story. In his article *On Functionalist Culture*, Mr. Fei Xiaotong wrote about his teacher, B. Malinowski, who worked on Trobriand Island during the First European War. Since he was of Polish nationality and was a friend among the enemies of the Allied Powers, although he couldn't leave the island freely, he could still continue his fieldwork among the local people. This wartime situation inadvertently allowed him to pursue his research, and Trobriand Island became the birthplace of functionalist anthropology. Naturally, our current situation differs from Professor Malinowski's in many ways, but since the War of Resistance against Japanese Aggression, I have been in Yunnan for six years. Due to moral, personal, and logistical constraints, I have been unable or unwilling to "freely leave," and this is true. So, why not emulate the spirit of Professor Malinowski on Trobriand Island, fully utilizing the current conditions to collect all the language materials from this land? This would lay a foundation for comparative research within the Sino-Tibetan language family, and wouldn't it add a new chapter to the history of Chinese linguistics?

May 21, 1943, in Qingyuan, Kunming.

www.ingramcontent.com/pod-product-compliance
Lightning Source LLC
Chambersburg PA
CBHW051414090426
42737CB00014B/2662